Osmond Ancestry and Genealogies

Originated by and Dedicated to:

George Virl Osmond (1917-2007)
Olive May Davis Osmond (1925-2004)

With Contributions from:

Alan Ralph Osmond and Donald (Donny) Clark Osmond

And Support of:

George Virl Osmond Jr., Thomas Rulon Osmond, Alan Ralph Osmond
Melvin Wayne Osmond, Merrill Davis Osmond, Jay Wesley Osmond
Donald Clark Osmond, Olive Marie Osmond, James Arthur Osmond

Compiled by:

R. Clayton Brough and Ethel Mickelson Brough

Published by:

Osmond Genealogy Research Committee, 2010

Table of Contents

A Thousand Years of Osmond History

The Name of Osmond

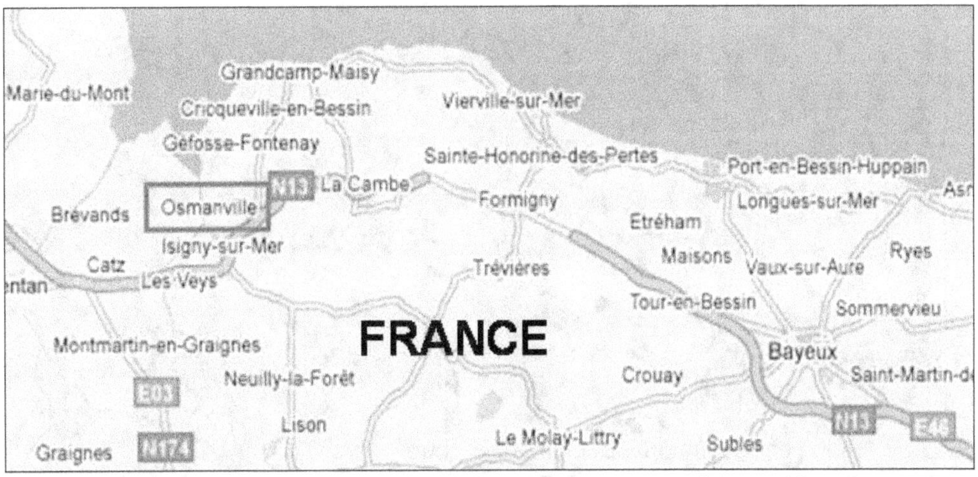

Osmanville, Normandy, France, has existed for hundreds of years (Google map)

The name "Osmund" apparently developed from a pre-seventh century Olde English personal name that combined "os"--or "god", with "mund"--or "protection", thereby meaning "god protector". During the 700's to the 1000's, the Osmund surname appeared in parts of western and northern Europe. Following the Norman conquest of England in 1066 AD, the Osmund name spread across England during 1100 to 1600. Over hundreds of years, the Osmund name took on several variants--including Osemund and Osman--but by the late 1700's the name was widely known and spelled as "Osmond" throughout the British Isles.

The Beginning of the Osmonds

Dominions of William the Conqueror

William the Conqueror (Lichfield Cathedral)

St. Osmund was a Norman priest and chaplain to William the Conqueror (St. Mary's, Winkfield, Berkshire)

The story of the Osmonds begins with the Norman invasion of England. In the Fall of 1066 AD, William the Duke of Normandy (1027-1087), crossed the English Channel with about 600 ships and 12,000 men. At the Battle of Hastings, William--who was also known as William the Conqueror--defeated King Harold of England and his Anglo-Saxon forces. On Christmas Day, 1066, William was crowed King of England, and he eventually rewarded his Norman supporters with large grants of land and important positions.

St. Osmund, Bishop of Salisbury, England

Statue of St. Osmund, Bishop of Salisbury, in Salisbury Cathedral, Wilshire, England

Statue of St. Osmund on an outside wall of St. Osmund's Catholic Church, Salisbury, England

Osmund of Normandy was a Norman priest and chaplain to William the Conqueror. Osmund was reportedly the son of Henry, Count of Seez, and Isabella, daughter of Robert, Duke of Normandy, who was the father of William the Conqueror. Osmund accompanied his uncle, William the Conqueror, during the Norman conquest of England, and was eventually appointed Chancellor of England (1072-1078) and Bishop of Salisbury (1078-1099). Osmund died on December 3, 1099. On January 1, 1457, Osmund was canonized as "St. Osmund" by Pope Callixtus III, and his feast day is December 4th.

Past Displays of Osmond Coat of Arms

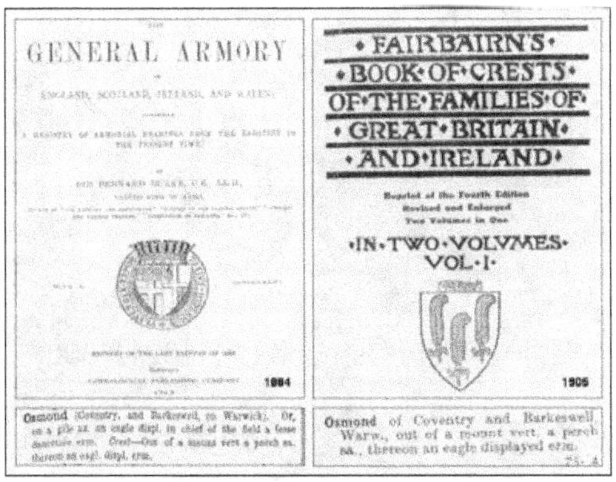

Left: Osmond Coat of Arms: Burke (1884) "Or [gold], on a pile [wedge-shaped figure pointing downward] az [azure or blue]. an eagle displ. [an eagle displayed as shown by Fairbairn] in chief [upper part] of the field [surface of a shield] a fesse [space between two horizontal lines drawn across the field, occupying from a third to a fifth part of the shield] dancettee [a zigzag line large and wide] erm [representation of fur—consisting of a white field with black spots]."

Right: Osmond Coat of Arms: Burke's (1884) and Fairbairn's (1905) "Crest – out of a mount [small hill, on which crests are represented] vert [green], a perch [horizontal pole provided as a roost for birds] sa. [sable or black], thereon an eagle displayed erm [representation of fur—consisting of a white field with black spots]."

Fairbairn's famous 1905 "Book of Crests" contained a description of the Osmond crest that included the above picture of the Eagle.

www.houseofnames.com

www.zazzle.co.uk

www.4crests.com

www.heraldry.ws

Osmond Coat of Arms and Shield

In July 2009, the Osmond Family Organization (OFO) of Utah asked two professionals to accurately recreate the Osmond "Coat of Arms" and "Shield". John M. Kitzmiller, a well-respected professional Heraldist and Medieval Genealogist, drew the Osmond "Coat of Arms" (left). Then using Mr. Kitzmiller's drawing, Juan Maestas, a professional graphic artist, computerized the "Shield" part of the Osmond Coat of Arms (above right).

Osmonds of Salisbury Cathedral, England

Salisbury Cathedral in Wiltshire

Salisbury Cathedral was built in 1220-1258 AD. It has Britain's tallest spire--of 404 feet, and largest Cathedral Close--covering 80 acres. It also contains Europe's oldest working clock--made in 1386, and displays the best preserved of only four surviving original Magna Carta (1215 AD). Throughout the centuries many Osmond families have lived and worshiped in Salisbury--including the two William Osmond's whose memorials are displayed (right) in Salisbury Cathedral.

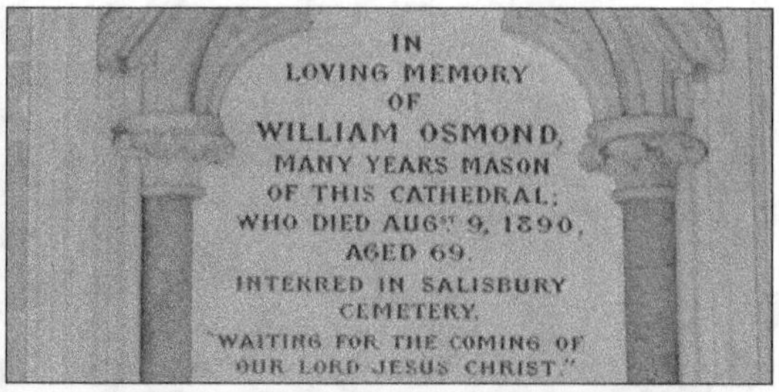
IN
LOVING MEMORY
OF
WILLIAM OSMOND,
MANY YEARS MASON
OF THIS CATHEDRAL;
WHO DIED AUGST 9, 1890,
AGED 69.
INTERRED IN SALISBURY
CEMETERY.
"WAITING FOR THE COMING OF
OUR LORD JESUS CHRIST."

William Osmond (Jr., 1821-1890)

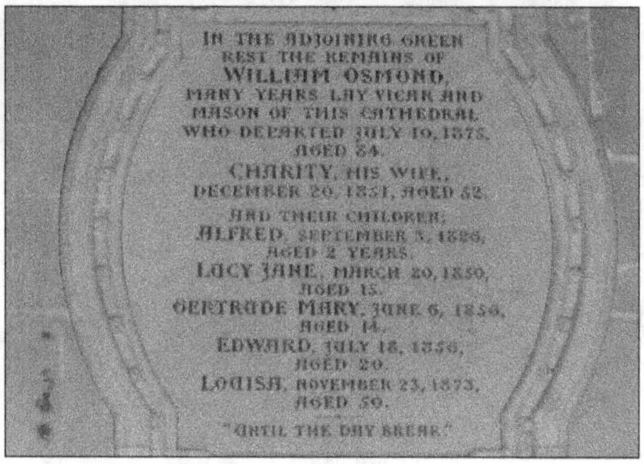
IN THE ADJOINING GREEN
REST THE REMAINS OF
WILLIAM OSMOND,
MANY YEARS LAY VICAR AND
MASON OF THIS CATHEDRAL
WHO DEPARTED JULY 10, 1875,
AGED 84.
CHARITY, HIS WIFE,
DECEMBER 20, 1851, AGED 52.
AND THEIR CHILDREN:
ALFRED, SEPTEMBER 3, 1826,
AGED 2 YEARS.
LUCY JANE, MARCH 20, 1850,
AGED 15.
GERTRUDE MARY, JUNE 6, 1856,
AGED 14.
EDWARD, JULY 18, 1856,
AGED 20.
LOUISA, NOVEMBER 23, 1873,
AGED 50.
"UNTIL THE DAY BREAK."

William Osmond (Sr., 1790-1875)

Osmonds of Burford, Oxfordshire, England

St. John the Baptist, Burford

The magnificent church of St. John the Baptist in Burford, Oxfordshire, England, is almost of cathedral-like proportions, and was built from around 1175 AD. Early Norman construction is evident at the base of the tower, and the upper part of the tower and the spire date back to the 1400's. (Most photos of Salisbury and Burford were taken by Bev Bowerman and Bev Looker in 2009)

Osmonds of Burford, Oxfordshire, England

During the 1500's and 1600's, a number of Osmond families resided in the Burford area, and their children were christened at St. John the Baptist church. Also, during this time, many Osmonds were buried in the churchyard of St. John the Baptist, including John Osmond (1575-1633) and his great-grandson, George Osmond (1663-1694).

Osmonds of Bicester, Oxfordshire, England

Bicester Parish Church is dedicated to St. Edburg, a Saxon saint of local fame who may have been a granddaughter of Alfred the Great. Some older portions of the church structure date back to the 1100's. The original churchyard is no longer used for burials and many of the headstones have been taken up and placed around the outside of the church.

Osmonds of Bicester, Oxfordshire, England

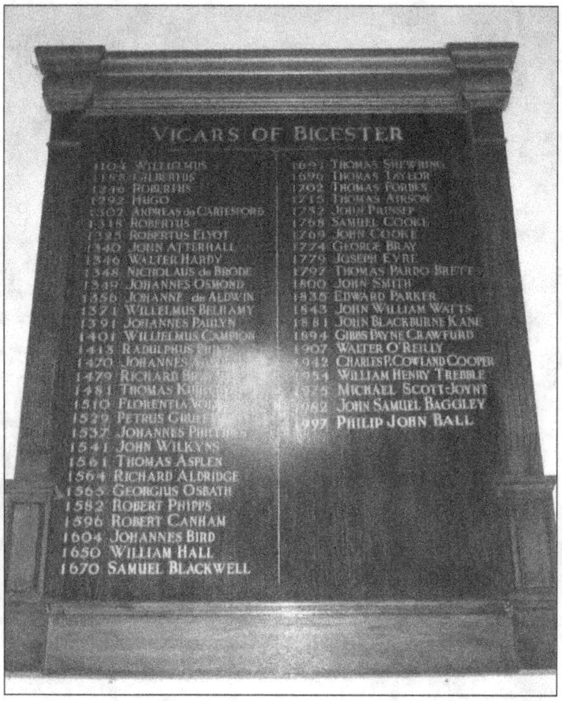

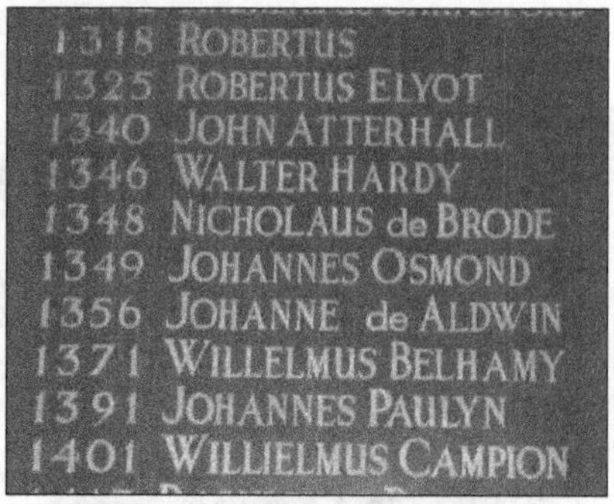

From 1349 to 1355 a Johannes Osmond served as Vicar of St. Edburg, Bicester, Oxfordshire, England. (Photos taken inside St. Edburg's in 2009)

Osmonds of Bicester, Oxfordshire, England

George Osmond Sr. (1808-1860) was a Solicitor (or Lawyer) in Bicester, Oxfordshire, England. George Osmond Sr. was the father of George Osmond Jr. (1837-1913), but never married his son's mother, Nancy Ann Canham. George Osmond Sr. was buried on 6 December 1850 at St. Edburg, Bicester. The inscription on his gravestone reads: "*Sacred to the Memory of George Osmond Esq. who departed this life on the 1st day of December 1860. Aged 52 years.*" (Photos of Bicester taken by Jim and Kathryn Stout in 2009.)

Osmond Pedigree and Descendants

John Osmund, b.abt.1575, Burford, Oxfordshire, England
married Alice
John Osmund, b.abt.1604, Burford, Oxfordshire
married Elizabethe Bery
John Osmund, chr.1635, Burford, Oxfordshire
married Joane Wicks
George Osmund, chr. 1663, Burford, Oxfordshire
married Mary King
John Osmund, chr.1692, Burford, Oxfordshire
Gentleman and Butcher; married Sarah Bly
George Osmond, chr.1716, Bicester, Oxfordshire
Gentleman and Butcher; married Mary Allen
George Osmond, chr.1745, Bicester, Oxfordshire
Gentleman and Esquire; married Anne Phillips

George Osmond (Sr.), chr.1808, Bicester, Oxfordshire
Solicitor; unmarried: Nancy Ann Canham
George Osmond (Jr.), b.1837, Hackney, London
Pioneer; married Amelia Jacobsen (2nd wife)
Rulon Osmond, b.1893, Afton, Wyoming, USA
married Agnes LaVerna Van Noy
George Virl Osmond, b.1917, Etna, Wyoming, USA
married Olive May Davis
Living Descendants: Osmond Singers of Utah

William Osmond, b.1814, Bicester, Oxfordshire
married Elizabeth Jarvis
George Henry Osmond, chr.1839, Bicester, Oxford
Gold Jeweler, married Ann Jarvis (2nd wife)
Henry Cecil Osmond, b.1883, Oxford, Oxfordshire
married Mary Jane Levett
Ronald Thomas Osmond, b.1922, New Zealand
Living descendants: New Zealand

The above *Osmond Pedigree and Descendants* chart was published in 2010

Y-DNA Tests Prove Osmond Relationships

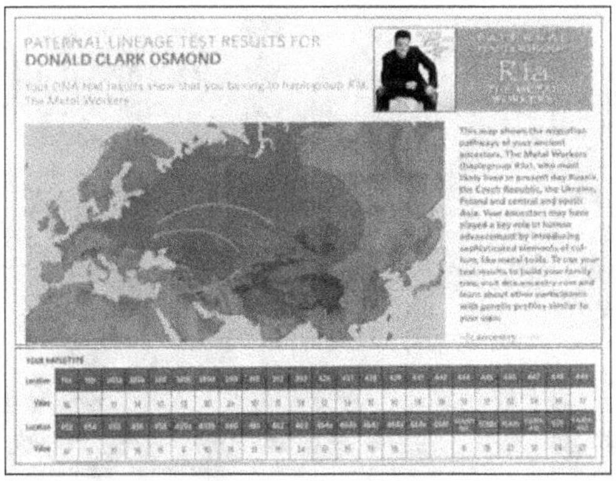

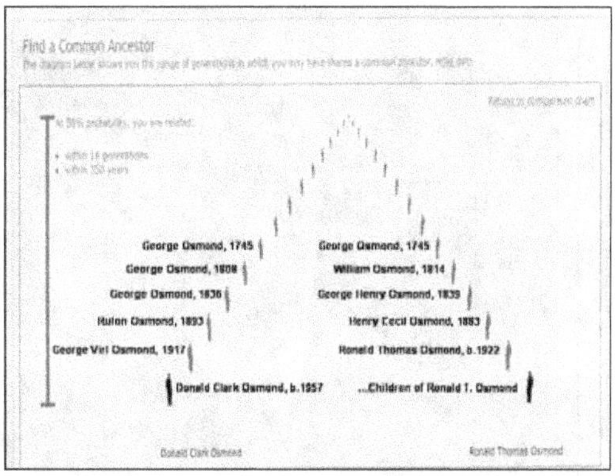

Donny Osmond's Y-DNA Test results were produced in 2008 by Ancestry.com, and are shown here (above left). (Remember: Y-DNA testing for genealogical purposes is not always accurate in pin-pointing precise generational matches or relative time-spans.) Y-DNA tests show that Donny Osmond (b.1957) of Utah, and Ronald Osmond (b.1922) of New Zealand are related through their paternal lines. Their actual genealogies show (above right) that they are "3rd cousins once removed" and that their common paternal ancestor is George Osmond (1745-1821) of Bicester, Oxfordshire, England.

Descendants of George Henry Osmond

George Henry Osmond (1839-1894) and Annie Jarvis (1855-1935)--shown above--lived in Oxford, England, where George Henry Osmond was a well-respected Gold Jeweler.

The family of George Henry Osmond and Ann Jarvis. L-R Back Row: Ronald George Osmond (1884-1947), Henry Cecil Osmond (b.1883); L-R Front Row: Frederick William Osmond (1888-1973), Ann Jarvis Osmond (mother, 1855-1935), Mary Jane Levett (wife of Henry Cecil Osmond).

George Osmond Jr. and his two Wives

Mary Georgina (Georgiana) Huckvale (1835-1922, above, first wife)

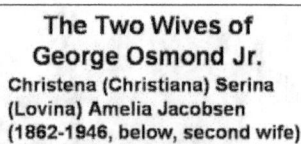

The Two Wives of George Osmond Jr.

Christena (Christiana) Serina (Lovina) Amelia Jacobsen (1862-1946, below, second wife)

George Osmond Jr. was born in London, England, on 23 May 1836/1837, as the son of George Osmond Sr. and Nancy Ann Canham. George Osmond Jr. joined The Church of Jesus Christ of Latter-day Saints (LDS or Mormon Church) in London in 1851, and emigrated to the United States in 1855. In 1855, George Osmond married Mary Georgina Huckvale in St. Louis, Missouri, and they eventually settled in Idaho where they were the parents of ten children. In 1881, George Osmond married his second wife, Christena Amelia Jacobsen, and they eventually settled in Wyoming where they were the parents of seven children. George Osmond Jr. served two two-year LDS missions to England--from 1884 to 1886 and 1890 to 1892. He was a successful farmer, rancher and businessman, a probate judge in Idaho, a state senator in Wyoming, and a beloved LDS Stake President of Star Valley, Wyoming, from 1892 until his death in 1913.

Rulon Osmond & Agnes LaVerna Van Noy

Agnes LaVerna Van Noy and Rulon Osmond were married in 1913 in Salt Lake City, Utah

RulonOsmond 1893-1917

Rulon Osmond was born on 17 August 1893 in Afton, Wyoming, as the fourth son of George Osmond Jr. and Christena Amelia Jacobsen (George's second wife). Rulon Osmond married Agnes LaVerna Van Noy in 1913 in Salt Lake City, Utah. Rulon and Agnes had three sons: Rulon Van Noy Osmond (1914-2001), Ralph Jacobson Osmond (1915-1977), and George Virl Osmond (1917-2007). On 24 November 1917, Rulon suffered a fatal accident while helping others obtain wood from a nearby mountain. In 2008, Cora (Bell) Elizabeth Neyman Osmond (b.1925) was "sealed" (LDS) to Rulon and Agnes LaVerna Osmond. **Above:** the family of Rulon Osmond (1893-1917), L-R: Cora (1925-), Agnes LaVerna (wife of Rulon, 1892-1975), Rulon Jr. (1914-2001), George V. (1917-2007), Ralph J. (1915-1977).

Osmonds in England and America

Lynne D. (1948-) and Pamela Margaret Osmond (1944-2009) are sisters and were born in England, United Kingdom.

Cora (Bell) Elizabeth Neyman Osmond (1928-) married Adelbert (Del) Francis Thinnes in 1953.

Rulon Van Noy Osmond (1914-2001)--the first son of Rulon and Agnes Osmond--married Norma Kennington in 1937.

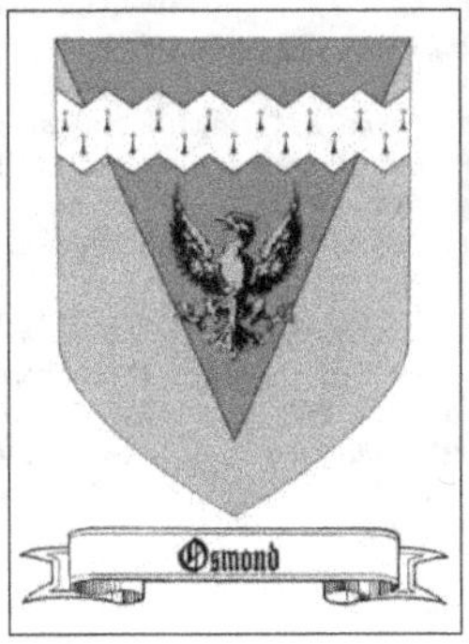

Ralph Jacobson Osmond—the second son of Rulon and Agnes Osmond—married Lydia Tullis in 1938.

The Famous "Singing" Osmonds of America

The family of George Virl Osmond (1917-2007) and Olive May Davis (1925-2004). George married Olive in 1944 in Salt Lake City, Utah. They had nine children: George Virl Jr., Thomas Rulon, Alan Ralph, Melvin Wayne, Merrill Davis, Jay Wesley, Donald Clark, Olive Marie, and James Arthur.

George Virl Osmond was born on 17 August 1893 in Afton, Wyoming, as the third son of Rulon Osmond and Agnes LaVerna Van Noy. George married Olive May Davis in 1944 in Salt Lake City, Utah, and they had nine children: George Virl Jr., Thomas Rulon, Alan Ralph, Melvin Wayne, Merrill Davis, Jay Wesley, Donald Clark, Olive Marie, and James Arthur. George was a veteran of World War II, and worked in real estate, insurance, and as a postmaster. George and Olive taught their children to sing barbershop harmony, and they eventually became known as the famous singing "Osmonds". Olive died in 2004 and George in 2007.

Importance of Genealogy and Family History

Alan Ralph Osmond: ***As I study my genealogy I better understand who I am and why my desires for values and endurance are important to me. I am most thankful to my ancestors for the blood line and heritage they gave me. My mother, Olive, taught her children how to do family research. We published our family history in several magazines and on various websites. We mentioned family history on television shows and during our 50th Anniversary World Tour—where we would greet the audiences from the stage as "Hi Cousin! How are we related?" I know God lives. I wrote a song called "Are You Up There?" I can honestly say, yes, He is! His "Plan of Life" is "The Family". My wife, Suzanne, and I have eight wonderful sons. To date we have sixteen grandchildren and six daughters-in-law. We try to live our lives so that our posterity will always want to remember us.***

Donald (Donny) Clark Osmond: ***Genealogy and family history have always been an interest of mine. I inherited the love of genealogy from my mother and have fond memories of doing research with her and sharing our "finds" together. I remember being in Wales not long ago and as I sat on stage performing, I can still recall looking out into the faces of the crowd, and wondered how many of those people I was distantly related to. At one point I had a feeling inside that many family members beyond the veil were watching my return to their land and performing for our family. I feel a strong sense of responsibility to make sure the "links of the chain" are united and that we can share the eternal blessings that will be ours as a family. I know that my sweet mother who worked so hard on genealogy and temple work has now been united with those ancestors she became familiar with while doing her genealogy work. There are many more for me to find, and someday I will be reunited with those family members I've gotten to know from my research.***

Rulon Robert (Bob) Osmond: ***The principles of loving your neighbor and being of service are powerful. The blessings that come from doing family history encompasses these principles and help us feel the Spirit of God in our lives. With my wife's help and the records my father left me I have been able to be of service to those that I love and that have passed on. I know that God lives and that we are His children and that He loves us. What comfort that gives me!"***

Ancestors of the Osmonds of Utah

Family Group Records containing genealogical and historical information and research documentation with reference sources

Family Group Record

Husband	**Rulon Osmond**					
Born	17 Aug 1893	Place	Afton, Uinta Co., Wyoming	LDS ordinance dates		Temple
Chr.		Place		Baptized	15 Sep 1901	
Died	24 Nov 1917	Place	Afton, Lincoln, Wyoming	Endowed	8 Oct 1913	SLAKE
Buried	26 Nov 1917	Place	Afton, Lincoln, Wyoming	SealPar	BIC	
Married	8 Oct 1913	Place	Salt Lake City, Salt Lake Co., Utah	SealSp	8 Oct 1913	SLAKE
Husband's father	George (Jr.) Osmond					
Husband's mother	Christena (Christiana) Serina (Lovina) Amelia Jacobsen					
Wife	**Agnes LaVerna Van Noy**					
Born	2 Sep 1892	Place	Thayne, Uinta, Wyoming	LDS ordinance dates		Temple
Chr.		Place		Baptized	21 Jul 1900	
Died	14 Jan 1975	Place	Ogden, Weber, Utah	Endowed	8 Oct 1913	SLAKE
Buried	Jan 1975	Place	Afton, Lincoln, Wyoming	SealPar	BIC	
Other Spouse	John Wesley Neyman					
Married	2 Sep 1921	Place		SealSp	DNS	
Other Spouse	Clarence Hoopes					
Married	15 Aug 1932	Place	Logan, Cache, Utah	SealSp	DNS	
Wife's father	Thomas Lorenzo Van Noy					
Wife's mother	Martha Tyresha Vail					

Children	List each child in order of birth.				LDS ordinance dates		Temple
1	M	**Rulon Van Noy Osmond**					
	Born	22 Jun 1914	Place	Thayne, Lincoln, Wyoming	Baptized	6 Mar 1927	
	Chr.		Place		Endowed	29 Sep 1937	LOGAN
	Died	29 Aug 2001	Place	Hyde Park, Cache, Utah	SealPar	BIC	
	Buried	1 Sep 2001	Place	Afton, Lincoln, Wyoming			
	Spouse	Norma Kennington					
	Married	29 Sep 1937	Place	Logan, Cache, Utah	SealSp	29 Sep 1937	LOGAN
2	M	**Ralph Jacobson Osmond**					
	Born	2 Nov 1915	Place	Afton, Lincoln, Wyoming	Baptized	6 Mar 1927	
	Chr.		Place		Endowed	8 May 1952	LOGAN
	Died	3 Aug 1977	Place	Ogden, Weber, Utah	SealPar	BIC	
	Buried	6 Aug 1977	Place	Ogden, Weber, Utah (Aultorest Memorial Park)			
	Spouse	Lydia Tullis					
	Married	11 Jun 1938	Place	Paris, Bear Lake Idaho	SealSp	8 May 1952	LOGAN
3	M	**George Virl Osmond**					
	Born	13 Oct 1917	Place	Etna, Lincoln, Wyoming	Baptized	6 Mar 1927	
	Chr.		Place		Endowed	1 Dec 1944	SLAKE
	Died	6 Nov 2007	Place	Provo, Utah Co., Utah	SealPar	BIC	
	Buried	9 Nov 2007	Place	Provo, Utah Co., Utah (East Lawn Memorial Hills)			
	Spouse	Olive May Davis					
	Married	1 Dec 1944	Place	Salt Lake City, Salt Lake Co., Utah	SealSp	1 Dec 1944	SLAKE
4	F	**Cora (Bell) Elizabeth Neyman Osmond**					
	Born	5 Aug 1925	Place	San Diego City, San Diego Co., California	Baptized	5 Mar 1950	
	Chr.		Place		Endowed	17 Feb 1958	LOGAN
	Died		Place		SealPar	28 Oct 2008	OGDEN
	Buried		Place				
	Spouse	Harold Edgar Womack					
	Married	15 May 1943	Place	Logan, Cache, Utah	SealSp	DNS	
	Spouse	Adelbert (Del) Francis Thinnes					
	Married	3 Feb 1953	Place	Elko, Elko Co., Nevada	SealSp	17 Feb 1958	LOGAN

Notes

HUSBAND - Rulon Osmond

In the 1910 U.S. Census, Rulon Osmond is listed as being about 16 years old (born about 1894) and working as a " Laborer [of] Odd Jobs".

The family history book "George Osmond and Family Pioneers" (1980's) Rulon Osmond is described as follows:

Page XXIII: "Rulon, it seemed had a special destiny. In his younger years he was a model person demonstrating the fine qualities of ambition and integrity. Perhaps his life was cut short for reasons difficult to understand but whatever the caswe may be, his good wife LaVerna raised their three sons to a most remarkable manhood."

Pages 395-397: "Rulon Osmond is the fourth child of George and Amelia [Osmond]. He was born in Afton, Wyoming, on August 17, 1893. Rulon attended the Aften schools for his elementary schooling, his finishing school was at Paris,

Husband **Rulon Osmond**

Wife **Agnes LaVerna Van Noy**

Notes

HUSBAND - Rulon Osmond (Continued)

Idaho, at the school where his father had taught years before. By the time the two older boys were no longer at home, Arthur was married and had a family. Arch had married and shortly afterward had died of appendicitis. President [George] Osmond as usual, was busy with civic and church affairs so the chores and livestock were pretty much in charge of Ruon and Vasco. When work on the farm was caught up Rulon would find work at whatever job was available in the vicinity. He was not one to be idle. At the age of twenty, Rulon married Agnes LaVerna Van Noy. The marriage took place at the Salt Lake Temple on October 8, 1913. Shortly after their marriage they moved to a farm in Etna, Wyoming where he and Vasco tried their luck at farming. It was un-improved land and the boys had to start from scratch. Along with the farm work Rulon held down a couple of side jobs. It takes a little time to get a farm into production and they needed the money to live on. Rulon hauled milk from the neighboring farms to the creamery and also fed cattle on the Wolfley Ranch. President [George] Osmond helped them arrange for their supply of cattle, horses and farm machinery so they could get going on their work. Aunt Mary and Aunt Vernie...gave the boys a hand with the farm work. Land was plowed and prepared and crops planted and harvested. Fences were put up and buildings were improved. Things seemed to be going well with the Osmonds. They had made many friends in Etna and were well liked. They had young and growing families and this was a young and growing community. They had a lot to look forward to and were making long range plans. Things were shaping up well and the farm was now in production and that induced a feeling of security. Three children were born to Rulon.... The oldest was...Rulon but we always called him R.V., the second was Ralph..., and the baby was George. He was still just a baby when things suddenly and drastically changed for the entire family. Font King, a neighbor, and Rulon had gone to the mountains out northwest of Etna for wood and were returning with their wagons loaded. Font needed some help to get his wagon up a steep pitch so Rulon proceded to unhitch his team to go back and double up with Font. During the course of the maneuver the team became excited and Rulon was kicked by his big brown mare 'Bird'. It was immediately apparent that it was serious and the situation was anything but convenient. As fast as possible Rulon was hauled to the nearest farm house, Jake Miller's about two miles away. A doctor was summoned but precious time was slipping away and so was Rulon's life blood. The doctor arrived and immediately recognized he had serious internal hemorrhaging. Immediately surgery was called for but an isolated farm house was no place for so serious an operation. There was no choice but to try to get him to Afton to a hospital in time. He was made as comfortable as possible and the twenty-five miles trip was underway. Two and a half hours over rough country roads really took its toll. Rulon underwent the surgery to sew up his liver which had been severed due to broken ribs. The doctors made the repair as best they could and we all waited for the word that Rulon would be O.K. That word never came. They were unable to stop the bleeding and Rulon died of shock and hemorrhage. It was all so sudden, so unbelieveable. It took time to come to a full realization of what had really happened. He was the kind of fellow everyone liked and the sadness was like a dark cloud over the valley. Now [Rulon's wife] and the boys had to re-armage the whole pattern of their lives. The older boys R.V. and Ralph would remember their dad but George never had the opportunity of really knowing him, being yet a baby. Their mother LaVerna, now alone, faced the overwhelming and frightening task of raising three little boys by herself. Her world had just collapsed and when the numbness of the shock subsided and the reality of the future came into focus she calmly picked up the pieces of a broken life and put together a unity of family, the success of which is brilliantly attested to by what her children and grandchildren have contributed to the world."

On 28 October 2008, The following individuals were "sealed" (in the LDS Ogden Temple) to Rulon and Agnes Osmond: Polly Neyman (b.1921), Peggy Neyman (b.1921), Laverna (Lavina or Lavena, b.1922), John Wesley Neyman Jr. (b.1923), and Cora Elizabeth Neyman (b.1925).

WIFE - Agnes LaVerna Van Noy

Information on the birth and death of Agnes Laverna Van Noy is listed in the IGI via an "LDS Church membership record of a deceased person."

CHILD 2 - Ralph Jacobson Osmond

Research Note: The sealing of Ralph J. Osmond and Lidia Tullis took place on 8 May 1952 in the LDS Logan Temple (FHL Special Collections Film # 178140). The sealings of several of their children (to their parents) took place on 15 May 1952 in the LDS Logan Temple (Special Collections Film # 455067).

Husband	Rulon Osmond
Wife	Agnes LaVerna Van Noy

Notes

CHILD 3 - George Virl Osmond

OBITUARY of George Virl Osmond, Deseret News, November 9, 2007:

George Virl Osmond, father and patriarch of one of the world's most esteemed entertainment families, The Osmonds, passed away peacefully of natural causes the morning of November 6, 2007, at his home in Provo, Utah. He was 90 years old.The father of nine children, Virl, Tom, Alan, Wayne, Merrill, Jay, Donny, Marie and Jimmy. George Osmond was born on October 13, 1917, in Star Valley, Wyoming. He liked to be known as "The Wyoming Cowboy," never forgetting his western roots. A devout Mormon, Osmond served two missions for The Church of Jesus Christ of Latter-day Saints, one in the state of Hawaii and one in the United Kingdom. Osmond was also a respected veteran of World War II. He met and married Olive Davis on Dec. 1, 1944, in the Salt Lake City Temple. As he and Olive began their life together, George worked in real estate, sold insurance and worked as a postmaster for the city of Ogden. Little did he know that from such humble beginnings, what would become one of the world's most renowned musical families. George Osmond loved to sing, and taught his children to sing barbershop harmony. It wasn't long before the community and public took notice of the talented kids and they started performing at church functions and at local civic events. Managing his talented sons, George arranged for them to perform at Disneyland in California, where they caught the eye and were mentioned by Walt Disney himself. History was made when the Osmonds were offered a chance to audition for Andy Williams, an opportunity which would forever change their lives. Living for his childrens' success, George gave up his life and work in Utah and he and his wife Olive soon moved the family to California when it looked as though entertainment would be the future of their talented family. George believed that family was the most important element in his life and he loved each of his children equally. He believed that families are forever eternal and throughout his life, instilled that faith in each of his children. He loved his only wife Olive intensely, who passed away in 2004. George Osmond lived his life true to his faith and true to his family. He was never heard to say a bad word about anyone and he treated everyone equally and with the utmost respect. He and his wife Olive founded The Osmond Foundation, which would later become the Children's Miracle network, the largest charitable organization of its kind serving children's hospitals worldwide. The Osmonds are of the belief that this should be a time of celebration instead of grief. George Osmond leaves nine children: Virl, Tom, Alan, Wayne, Merrill, Jay, Donny, Marie, and Jimmy, 55 grandchildren, and 48 great-grandchildren. His legacy will forever be remembered.

Family Group Record

Husband	George (Jr.) Osmond				
Born	23 May 1836/1837	Place Hackney, London, England	LDS ordinance dates		Temple
Chr.	14 Jun 1837	Place St. Matthew, Bethnal Green, London, England	Baptized	27 Nov 1851	
Died	25 Mar 1913	Place Afton, Lincoln, Wyoming	Endowed	31 Oct 1868	EHOUS
Buried	29 Mar 1913	Place Bloomington, Bear Lake, Idaho	SealPar	5 Jul 1941	LOGAN
Married	Jul 1855	Place St. Louis, St. Louis Co., Missouri	SealSp	31 Oct 1868	EHOUS
Other Spouse	Christena (Christiana) Serina (Lovina) Amelia Jacobsen				
Married	8 Sep 1881	Place Salt Lake City, Salt Lake Co., Utah	SealSp	8 Sep 1881	EHOUS
Husband's father	George (Sr.) Osmond				
Husband's mother	Nancy Ann Canham				

Wife	Mary Georgina (Georgiana) Huckvale				
Born		Place	LDS ordinance dates		Temple
Chr.	12 Apr 1835	Place Chipping Norton, Oxford, England	Baptized	31 Aug 1852	
Died	14 Mar 1922	Place Bloomington, Bear Lake, Idaho	Endowed	31 Oct 1868	EHOUS
Buried	17 Mar 1922	Place Bloomington, Bear Lake, Idaho	SealPar	9 Mar 1945	SLAKE
Wife's father	Joseph Huckvale				
Wife's mother	Mary Worville (Worville)				

Children List each child in order of birth. — LDS ordinance dates — Temple

1	F	**Clara Georginia Osmond**				
	Born	4 Dec 1856	Place Bountiful, Davis, Utah	Baptized	31 Oct 1867	
	Chr.		Place	Endowed	22 Sep 1881	EHOUS
	Died	26 Apr 1936	Place Paris or Bloomington, Bear Lake, Idaho	SealPar	14 Apr 1956	LOGAN
	Buried	30 Apr 1936	Place Bloomington, Bear Lake, Idaho			
	Spouse	Adam Pugh Welker				
	Married	1 Feb 1879	Place Salt Lake City, Salt Lake Co., Utah	SealSp	22 Sep 1881	EHOUS
2	M	**George Anson Osmond**				
	Born	18 Apr 1858	Place Bountiful, Davis, Utah	Baptized	Jul 1868	
	Chr.		Place	Endowed	12 Jun 1883	EHOUS
	Died	19 Nov 1904	Place Portland, Multnomah, Oregon	SealPar	14 Apr 1956	LOGAN
	Buried	Nov 1904	Place Bloomington, Bear Lake, Idaho			
	Spouse	Alice Catharine Hart				
	Married	23 Apr 1883	Place Bloomington, Bear Lake, Idaho	SealSp	12 Jun 1883	EHOUS
3	M	**Alfred Osmond**				
	Born	5 Oct 1861	Place Willard, Box Elder, Utah	Baptized	27 Jan 1878	
	Chr.		Place	Endowed	10 Oct 1889	LOGAN
	Died	1 Apr 1938	Place Logan, Cache, Utah	SealPar	14 Apr 1956	LOGAN
	Buried	5 Apr 1938	Place Provo, Utah Co., Utah (City Cemetery)			
	Spouse	Josephine Frances Nelson				
	Married	29 Dec 1887	Place Bloomington, Bear Lake, Idaho	SealSp	10 Oct 1889	LOGAN
	Spouse	Annie Elizabeth Lloyd				
	Married	16 Jun 1897	Place Logan, Cache, Utah	SealSp	16 Jun 1897	LOGAN
4	F	**Rosebell (Rose) Osmond**				
	Born	8 Jan 1864	Place Willard, Box Elder, Utah	Baptized	2 Sep 1877	
	Chr.		Place	Endowed	9 Sep 1885	LOGAN
	Died	23 Dec 1949	Place Boise, Ada, Idaho	SealPar	14 Apr 1956	LOGAN
	Buried		Place			
	Spouse	Benjamin Erastus Rich				
	Married	12 Sep 1885	Place Salt Lake City, Salt Lake Co., Utah	SealSp	28 Feb 1992	DENVE
	Spouse	William John Starkey				
	Married	10 Nov 1888	Place Ogden, Weber, Utah	SealSp		
5	M	**Ira Osmond**				
	Born	2 Mar 1866	Place Bloomington, Bear Lake, Idaho	Baptized	8 May 1954	
	Chr.		Place	Endowed	1 Feb 1956	
	Died	21 Jun 1946	Place Montpeliler, Bear Lake, Idaho	SealPar	14 Apr 1956	LOGAN
	Buried	Jun 1946	Place Bloomington, Bear Lake, Idaho			
	Spouse					
	Married		Place	SealSp		
6	F	**Ida Ann Osmond**				
	Born	26 Feb 1869	Place Bloomington, Bear Lake, Idaho	Baptized	10 Oct 1889	
	Chr.		Place	Endowed	30 Oct 1889	LOGAN
	Died	30 Oct 1943	Place Paris, Bear Lake, Idaho	SealPar	14 Apr 1956	LOGAN
	Buried	1 Nov 1943	Place Bloomington, Bear Lake, Idaho			
	Spouse	Oliver Cowdery Dunford				
	Married	30 Oct 1889	Place Logan, Cache, Utah	SealSp	30 Oct 1889	LOGAN

25 Jul 2010

Family Group Record

Husband	George (Jr.) Osmond				
Wife	Mary Georgina (Georgiana) Huckvale				
Children	List each child in order of birth.			LDS ordinance dates	Temple
7 F	**Ella Osmond**				
Born	18 Jan 1872	Place	Bloomington, Bear Lake, Idaho	Baptized 7 Jul 1881	
Chr.		Place		Endowed 19 Jan 1956	LOGAN
Died	2 Jan 1938	Place		SealPar BIC	
Buried		Place			
Spouse	Louis Charles Newman				
Married	5 Jun 1893	Place	Bloomington, Bear Lake, Idaho	SealSp 24 Jun 1998	SLAKE
8 F	**Nellie Osmond**				
Born	2 Jul 1874	Place	Bloomington, Bear Lake, Idaho	Baptized 3 Jul 1884	
Chr.		Place		Endowed 9 Jun 1897	LOGAN
Died	1 Sep 1968	Place	Pocatello, Bannock, Idaho	SealPar BIC	
Buried	1968	Place	Bloomington, Bear Lake, Idaho		
Spouse	Eugene Scheib Hart				
Married	16 Jun 1897	Place	Logan, Cache, Utah	SealSp 16 Jun 1897	LOGAN
9 F	**Georgina Osmond**				
Born	2 Jul 1877	Place	Bloomington, Bear Lake, Idaho	Baptized Child	
Chr.		Place		Endowed Child	
Died	18 Dec 1877	Place	Bloomington, Bear Lake, Idaho	SealPar BIC	
Buried	Jan 1878	Place	Bloomington, Bear Lake, Idaho		
Spouse					
Married		Place		SealSp	
10 F	**Alice Maud Osmond**				
Born	16 Sep 1879	Place	Bloomington, Bear Lake, Idaho	Baptized 12 Jun 1892	
Chr.		Place		Endowed 12 Dec 1966	SLAKE
Died	22 Jan 1947	Place	Hollywood, Los Angeles Co., California	SealPar BIC	
Buried	25 Jan 1947	Place	Hollywood, Los Angeles Co., California		
Spouse	Forrest Eldridge Reed				
Married	12 Oct 1908	Place	Pocatello, Bannock, Idaho	SealSp 11 Aug 1971	OAKLA

Notes

HUSBAND - George (Jr.) Osmond

Genealogical Data on George (Jr.) Osmond (1836/1837-1913):

1) George Osmond was christened in the Church of England on two separate occasions: 1) as "George Osmond" at St. Matthew's church, Bethnal Green, London, Middlesex, (FHL Film # 855942) on 14 June 1837, and recorded as born on 23 May 1837, the son of George and Ann Osmond, of Howards Place, Gent.; and 2) as "George Canham Flight" at Christ Church, St. George in the East, Watney Street, Stepney, London, Middlesex (viewable on Ancestry.com), on 20 October 1843, and recorded as born 23 May 1836, as the son of Hanson and Ann Flight, of Jane Street, Coal Merchant.

2) George Osmond's living LDS endowment record (FHL Film 1239501, Entry #26, Special Collections) states that he was born on 23 May 1836 in London, Middlesex, England, and that his parents were George Osmond and Nancy Canham.

3) The Woolwich LDS. Branch Records of the LDS British Mission lists George Osmond as "George Flight", and states that he was born on 23 May 1836 in Hackney and baptized into the LDS Church on 27 November 1851.

4) In the 1851 Census, George Osmond is listed as "George Flight", age 14 (born about 1837), born in Middlesex, and working as a "Shipwright apprentice" while residing in the home of William White in Charlton, Kent, England.

5) "George Osmond" was an 18 year old passenger and "Shipwright" aboard the passenger ship "Clara Wheeler" that left Liverpool, England, in November 1854, and arrived in New Orleans, Lousiana, on 12 January 1855. (LDS church members aboard the "Clara Wheeler" sailed under the direction of LDS church leader Henry E. Phelps.)

6) In the 1910 U.S. Census, George Osmond is listed as being naturalized in 1857--probably in Utah.

7) The burial gravestone of George Osmond in Bloomington, Bear Lake, Idaho, lists him as being born on May 23, 1837, and having died on 25 March 1913.

8) Because George Osmond Jr. had two christening records that listed different birth years--1836 and 1837--a number of his descendants have used both dates as his year of birth. However, George Osmond appears to have favored the year 1836--stating in his diary entry of 23 May 1886: "I am fifty years old today".

Research Note, September 2008:

In September 2008, Y-DNA 46-Chromosome test results (via Ancestry.com) were provided on Donald (Donny)

Husband **George (Jr.) Osmond**

Wife **Mary Georgina (Georgiana) Huckvale**

Notes

HUSBAND - George (Jr.) Osmond (Continued)

Clark Osmond (of Utah) and Ronald Thomas Osmond (of New Zealand). These results showed a "50% probability" that these two individuals were related "within 14 generations" or "within 350 years", although it is known that such Y-DNA testing for genealogical purposes is not always accurate in pin-pointing precise generational matches or relative time-spans. However, according to their actual genealogies, these two individuals are "3rd cousins 1 time removed", with their common male ancestor being George Osmond of Bicester, England (b.1745-d.1821). The Y-DNA comparison of Donny Osmond and Ronald Osmond is important to Osmond family historians because it proves that the American pioneer, George Osmond (who was born in 1836 in London, England, and who died in Afton, Wyoming in 1913) was the son of George Osmond (b.1808-d.1860) of Bicester, England, and Nancy Ann Canham, and not the son of Hanson Flight and Nancy Ann Canham, as some people had previously thought possible.

Research Note, September 2008:

In September 2008, Lynne D. Osmond stated the following: "I think that George Osmond was re-christened as George Canham Flight. I've misplaced one part of the LDS records for the church at Eltham but the part I do have states he was George Flight until at least June 6, 1853, when he became an Elder. I think it's possible that when it was known he was to emigrate [to America] he was told his real name, and changed it to Osmond as found on the passenger list for the ship Clara Wheeler. As I said, this cannot be proved and [now] doesn't really matter, as George is proved [through DNA to be an] Osmond."

Historical Note: The family history book "George Osmond and Family Pioneers" (1980's) states that when George Osmond (1837-1913) joined the LDS Church in 1850, his "relatives and friends all turned against him. His mother pleaded with him to give up this new strange religion, but to no avail. His relatives felt bitter toward him and accused him of disgracing the family name. ...To his surprise he [George Osmond] was never able to convert any of his relatives to the truth of the Gospel. ...It was said that George broke his mother's heart when he joined up with the 'Deluded Mormons.' He grieved to cause her sorrow, but he could not give up what he believed to be the truth. ... George gave up family and friends, financial security, and even his mother, who was living alone at the time he left to come to America. ...George parted from his relatives, his mother, his brothers and sister, in bitterness. They said, 'We don't want to see or hear from you until you have left the Mormons.' Records show that his mother soon repented and would have been happy to hear from her son in America" (pages 4-5). Also, in his LDS mission diary entry dated November 13, 1884, George Osmond wrote: "The trip to Brighton will remain in my memory as long as life lasts. I saw the house where my mother died. My brother and sister told me many anecdotes of her which proved that 'Her son in America' as she ever loved to call me, was always uppermost in her mind and affections. God bless her and grant that I may yet be able to prove to her how much I love her. I did not visit her grave. It may have been weakness, but I felt I would rather not."

Brief History of George Osmond (1836-1913):

George Osmond was a native of England, convert to the LDS Church, emigrant to Utah, pioneer of Bear Lake Valley, Bishop of Bloomington Ward, and President of Star Valley Stake.

George Osmond was born in London, England, on May 23, 1836. He was the son of George and Nancy Ann (Canham) Osmond.

When he was 14 years of age, he was apprenticed to learn the ship-building trade at the government dockyard in Woolwich, near London. It was while he was there that he was invited by a friend to attend an LDS meeting. He heard the gospel message, believed, and was baptized on November 27, 1850, six months before his 15th birthday.

When he was 18 years of age he emigrated to America with the object of joining the Saints in Utah. He sailed to New Orleans and then traveled by steamboat to St. Louis. At St. Louis, in June 1855, he married Mary Georgina Huckvale (b. 1835), a convert to the LDS Church whom he had known in England. Together they crossed the plains and arrived in Salt Lake City in September of 1855.

The first home of George Osmond was in Bountiful, where he operated a small farm and was employed as a school teacher. He then moved to Willard and obtained a homestead. In 1865, he moved to Bear Lake Valley and settled at Bloomington, Idaho. He became presiding elder of the Bloomington Branch in 1871 and in 1875 Bishop of the ward. When Bear Lake Stake was organized in 1877, George Osmond was chosen as second counselor to President William Budge. He served with diligence in this capacity and assisted in building up the settlements in Bear Lake Valley. On September 8, 1881, George Osmond married his second wife, Christena Serina Amelia Jacobsen (b.

Husband	George (Jr.) Osmond
Wife	Mary Georgina (Georgiana) Huckvale

Notes

HUSBAND - George (Jr.) Osmond (Continued)

1862).

In 1884, George Osmond was called on a two-year LDS mission to England, where he served as assistant editor of the Millennial Star. In 1890, he was again called on a two-year LDS mission to the British Isles, where he served as president of the Scottish and London Districts.

When the Star Valley Stake was organized in August 1892, George Osmond was chosen as the first president. He moved to Afton the same year and there established a permanent home with his second wife, Amelia. He met all the problems incident to the establishment of L.D.S. communities in the fertile valley. He also took part in civic life and served as Justice of the Peace, Probate Judge, and as State Senator in the Wyoming Legislature for two terms. He died in Afton, Wyoming, on March 25, 1913.

Obituary of George Osmond (Jr.):□The Paris Post
Paris, Idaho, Printed April 4, 1913
Funeral Services for President George Osmond

Bloomington, April 3-Impressive and inspirational funeral services were held over the remains of President George Osmond in the meeting house at Bloomington Saturday, March 29th at two P.M. Appropriate musical selections were rendered by the Bloomington choir under the able leadership of Abraham O. Christensen.

It was one of the largest funerals ever held in Bloomington. In addition to the greatest part of the adult population of Bloomington being present a great many friends from St. Charles, Paris, Montpelier and other parts of the stake came to pay their last tribute of respect to the great and good man who was so universally loved.

The speakers were F.M. Winters, Bishop E.M. Pugmire, Clarence Gardner, W.W. Burton, President Wm. L. Rich, Bishop Alma Findlay, and President Jos. R. Shepherd. These men were nearly all life-long friends of the deceased, and their remarks were listened to with breathless appreciation by the large congregation. The speeches were not formal and conventional funeral sermons, but simple and sincere tributes of affection to the friend that they dearly loved. Sense of loss was felt in every heart, but they were all grateful for the long life that was so rich in service and devotion.

President George Osmond was born in London England May 23rd 1837. He was apprenticed in 1850 to the ship building trade in the Government dock yard at Woolwich, near London. He possessed such great natural aptitude for this work and studied so persistently that he soon placed himself at the head of the classes in the school. This proposition would have entitled him to a splendid college education free of charge, had he continued in the service. At this time however he heard Mormon Elders preach and was at once converted. He therefore gave up his position in the school and began preaching the gospel. In 1884, when President Osmond returned to England he called on his friend who had taken the place in school left vacant by him. In addition to the college education that his friend had received, he had a splendid pension, and a magnificent home, all of which had been given him by the shipyard company.

Four years after his conversion he immigrated to New Orleans and then worked his way Northway to St. Louis. The following year he married Georgiana Huckvale, and with her came across the plains to Salt Lake City. After having lived in Bountiful, Davis County, and Willard, Box Elder County, for a while, he, in 1864, came to Bear Lake Valley, Idaho, where he spent many years of the most valuable part of his life. He served as Bishop of Bloomington for many years and later was chosen counselor to President Budge of the Bear Lake Stake.

In addition to his many positions in the Church, he was very active in civil interests of life. He was probate judge of Bear Lake county and also state senator of the Wyoming legislature during the sessions 1898-99 and 1900-01.

He filled two missions to Great Britain, during which time he traveled extensively through England and on the continent. He was also President of the Liverpool Conference and editor of the Millennial Star. After returning from his last mission to Great Britain in 1892 he was called to Star Valley to be president of that stake, a position that he held until his death, which occurred in Afton Wyoming, March 25th 1913.

President Osmond was a remarkable man, in any environment and among any people he would have been eminent; but, like the Apostle Paul, his greatness was manifested as a servant of Jesus Christ. His life was kindly, chaste and genial and bright as the noon-day sun. He could make himself at home in all kinds of company and had a wonderful aptitude for service in all relations of life. He was particularly devoted to the plain people and consecrated the best efforts of his life to their interests. As an example of his devotion to them, he at one time contracted with the government, through its agent, to furnish a large amount of oats for the mail stations that were located in the Snake

Husband	George (Jr.) Osmond
Wife	Mary Georgina (Georgiana) Huckvale

Notes

HUSBAND - George (Jr.) Osmond (Continued)

River Valley. After the contract was signed and sealed President said to the agent "what do I get out of this?" The agent replied that he, of course would deduct a liberal commission from the contract price. President Osmond responded, "That is not my way of doing business, the people shall have every cent of the contract price, but you ought to give me something for my work."

The agent being wholly unacquainted with such methods of doing business, was perplexed but finally agreed to give a small compensation for President Osmond's work. In succeeding years after the contract was made, the agent would jokingly say, "Well, Mr. Osmond, what is your present to be?"

President Osmond was passionately fond of music and possessed rare literary ability. Some of his poems and masters pieces of verse, and it is only in the matter of quantity that he was not one of the great literary artists of his age. While he has passed to the great beyond, his numerous friends believe that his memory can never die.

Services at Afton

At the funeral services held at Afton, Wyoming, Counselor Clarence Gardner presided. In speaking of the deceased, he said among other things, "President Osmond was always striving to do his duty and to accomplish good in the earth. His last words were 'God bless you brother,' with instructions and suggestions respecting stake matters. He has given counsel enough to make us a good people. He gained the confidence and love of all. Those who lived a Christian life like President Osmond, can safely say,"O grave where is thy victory, O death where is thy sting." His death is our loss. But this loss is his infinite gain, for he died unto the Lord ad he shall rest from his labors."

Other speakers Bishop Hyde of Auburn, Bishop Bracken of Freedom, Thomas Walton, C. H. Haderlie, Thomas F. Burton, and Bishop Low, all paid high tributes to the work and worth of the deceased.

Contributed by Thomas Sleight

When the news reached Paris of the death of President George Osmond, many sympathetic hearts were touched because of the love and respect they had for him. He was but a young man when he came to this country, in 1864, having a few years before immigrated to America from England. Because of his natural makeup t was easy for him to become an American of the best type; his physical and mental powers had never been abused and they were so well balanced that the obstacles of life were made easy to overcome.

In 1865 and '66 he taught school in Paris and instead of carrying a whip and a cross look to enforce his rules, he studied the disposition of his pupils, won their love and respect, and made a success of the school.

As a journalist, he was above the average in early days and at one time was editor of the Paris newspaper, then called the Democrat. I well remember one of his editorials on the timber question, which if adhered to, would have saved this country thousands of dollars. He told the wood haulers and loggers when working in the canyon not to cut thrifty saplings to use for a binder every time they loaded their wagons, but make one do for the season. This advice has since been given by Roosevelt and others who have been interested in the timber question.

As farmer and a horticulturist, he was always expected to enlighten us on these subjects at our conferences, because of his many experiments in producing grains and fruits. He could eat apples grown on his own lot when many of us had given up in despair. He was the first to file a possessory claim to a small spring in Lanark, since know as the "Osmond Springs," which name should be retained on the county map in honor of George Osmond, the friend of Peace.

From the Star Valley Independent

Like a wave of gloom engulfing everyone, was the news of the passing away of the great leader and Stake President, George Osmond. It came as a personal loss to thousands, because not alone has his position placed him as a spiritual adviser to the Latter Day Saints of Star Valley Stake, but his kindness of heart, his unselfishness and his wide experience, have brought him in very close touch with the masses and they loved him for they never found him wanting when they have made a call on him.

The Tabernacle was perhaps the laurel in his crown in which he took great pleasure and he was pleased to see its completion. True to his Priesthood and his callings he has been a worthy friend and counselor to many; he had a gift of clear thought and well defined expression, and as a public speaker, he carried his audiences with his clear annunciation of facts, and forceful arguments, coupled with his inspiring and soul lifting expression. His life has been an inspiration to all, his death has left a gloom in the hearts of all who knew him.

After an illness of three weeks George Osmond, President of the Star Valley Stake passed away at his home in Afton, on Tuesday March 25th, 1913, surrounded by his family and friends.

George Osmond was born in England, May 23, 1835 and in his youth immigrated to Zion. He shortly afterward located at Bloomington, Idaho, where he became very active in church matters. After his second mission spent in

Husband	George (Jr.) Osmond
Wife	Mary Georgina (Georgiana) Huckvale

Notes

HUSBAND - George (Jr.) Osmond (Continued)

England, where he held the position as editor of the Millennial Star some of the time, he returned home in May 1892, and the following August the Star Valley Stake was organized and he was selected to fill the office of President, which position he had filled well and nobly.

Funeral services were held in the Tabernacle, Thursday afternoon, and a large concourse of people assembled to pay their last respects to the honored leader. President Clarence Gardner conducted the services. The speakers were Clarence Gardner, Thomas Walton, C.H. Haderlie, Bishop Hyde, Bishop Bracken, Arthur F. Burton and Bishop Oz Low. The choir sang special selections, and Mark Hurd and Thomas Burton sang a duet. The tabernacle was draped in white. There was an abundance of floral offerings both in the hall and on the casket.

After the services the remains were taken back to the home and will be taken to Bloomington today and funeral services held tomorrow in the Bloomington meeting house, interment taking place in the cemetery there.

He leaves a large family and a legion of friends to mourn his loss.

WIFE - Mary Georgina (Georgiana) Huckvale

The christening of Mary Georgiana Huckvale is listed in the IGI (via the LDS Extraction Program, FHL Film # 95229), which states that she was christened on 12 April 1835, Chipping Norton, Oxfordshire, England, and that her parents were Joseph Huckvale and Mary.

"Georiana Huckwill" (born 1836) departed from Liverpool on 26 April 1855 on the ship "William Stetson", which arrived on 27 May 1855 in New York. The LDS church leader was Aaron Smethurst. (FHL Film #175508).

Brief History of Mary Georgina (Georgiana) Huckvale, written by Sandy Douglas, a great-grand-daughter, February 2009:

Mary Georgina Huckvale was born at Oxford, England, March 7, 1836 [actually 1835]. Her parents were James and Mary Worvill Huckvale. Mary had been a maid to James' first wife, who was a semi-invalid for several years before her death. There were three children: Alfred, who died in childhood, Mary Georgina (or Georgia as she was called) and her younger brother John. Her people were quiet, refined folk, who read their Bible and attended church services every Sunday.

At the age of 13, Georgina was apprenticed to a dressmaker where she learned dressmaking as well as to knit lace and other handicraft.

When Georgina met her husband George, probably in her early teens, he became converted to the L.D.S. Church and later converted her. Her parents were not angry with her, they felt she should be allowed to do as she pleased. George left for America in 1854, and she followed him the following summer along with her best friend Carrie and her husband. They were married in St. Louis.

When crossing the plains, she and Carrie did not want to wear the ugly sunbonnet the pioneers wore, and they wore their pretty bonnets instead. They were severely burned and blistered, and the bonnets were ruined.

During those early days, her dressmaking ability came in handy, and she also worked in the early Relief Society, helping to nurse the sick. It was often said of her that she had great patience and endurance and made an excellent nurse.

Nellie Hart related a few memories of her mother. She stated, "She was very conscientious, quiet, loveable, capable, dependable, and industrious. She was a splendid homemaker and an immaculate housekeeper. She was truly a helpmate to her husband, and she was a wonderful mother, also a kind and thoughtful neighbor. She was never idle, and she often worked outside in the garden and kept the place beautiful and home both inside and outside.

She was a beautiful seamstress, and she kept the family clothed neat and attractive by her diligence and ability to make use of any available material they could acquire.

She was ever careful and mindful of the feelings of others, and as a neighbor, she was kind and considerate. Many were the hours she spent with the sick or the unfortunate in the community, and she was ever ready to share the best she had with others less fortunate than she. She cared tenderly for her mother who lived to be 92 years of age.

She was very particular in her speech. Although she had received very little schooling, she was careful to avoid grammatical errors. Even in her everyday association with her family she was never known to use careless or imperfect language.

Family Group Record

Husband **George (Jr.) Osmond**

Wife **Mary Georgina (Georgiana) Huckvale**

Notes

WIFE - Mary Georgina (Georgiana) Huckvale (Continued)

It is doubtful that she was ever really converted to plural marriage, but when it was required of her, she accepted it because of the great love she had for her husband and her desire to sustain him in his ecclesiastical callings. Several names of eligible women were presented to her. On these none were acceptable until Milly Jacobsen came to her attention. This girl she accepted and took into her home as a plural wife for her husband. Here they lived peacefully, and we hope happily."

George built Georgina a beautiful home in Bloomington. Georgina loved to entertain, and she was a wonderful hostess. She entertained many church officials such as President Brigham Young, President John Taylor, Brigham Young Jr and his wife Amelia Folsom Young, President Young's daughters Zina Young Card and Susan Young Gates, and Apostle Moses Thatcher.

Georgina loved to garden and planted all kinds of berries and some apple seeds which grew to finally produce after 15 years. Bear Lakers were in awe that fruit was produced in the cold climate.

In her later years Georgina's health began to fail. Arthritis settled in her back, and she was soon badly bent. A broken hip, never set, contributed to her trouble. Her hands were drawn out of shape, yet she insisted on doing her work. She was never free from pain yet she bore up and seldom complained.

On Georgina's 86th birthday, her daughters arranged a luncheon and spent the day with her. She was up and seemed to feel better. She told of many incidents of early days. Her sight and hearing were almost gone, yet her mind was clear except events that happened long ago seemed more recent.

When Clara wished her many happy returns she said, "I want no more birthdays, I'm tired of pain and I want to go." One week later her wish was granted and she was at rest. She passed away March 14, 1922, and is buried in Bloomington, Idaho..

Family Group Record

Husband	**George (Jr.) Osmond**				
Born	23 May 1836/1837	Place Hackney, London, England	LDS ordinance dates		Temple
Chr.	14 Jun 1837	Place St. Matthew, Bethnal Green, London, England	Baptized	27 Nov 1851	
Died	25 Mar 1913	Place Afton, Lincoln, Wyoming	Endowed	31 Oct 1868	EHOUS
Buried	29 Mar 1913	Place Bloomington, Bear Lake, Idaho	SealPar	5 Jul 1941	LOGAN
Married	8 Sep 1881	Place Salt Lake City, Salt Lake Co., Utah	SealSp	8 Sep 1881	EHOUS
Other Spouse	Mary Georgina (Georgiana) Huckvale				
Married	Jul 1855	Place St. Louis, St. Louis Co., Missouri	SealSp	31 Oct 1868	EHOUS
Husband's father	George (Sr.) Osmond				
Husband's mother	Nancy Ann Canham				
Wife	**Christena (Christiana) Serina (Lovina) Amelia Jacobsen**				
Born	9 Nov 1862	Place Brigham City, Box Elder, Utah	LDS ordinance dates		Temple
Chr.		Place	Baptized	30 Jul 1876	
Died	23 Sep 1946	Place Logan, Cache, Utah	Endowed	8 Sep 1881	EHOUS
Buried	26 Sep 1946	Place Afton, Lincoln, Wyoming	SealPar	7 Jun 1968	IFALL
Wife's father	Frederick Jacobsen				
Wife's mother	Elizabeth Pedersen				
Children	List each child in order of birth.		LDS ordinance dates		Temple
1 M	**James Arthur Osmond**				
Born	7 Jun 1882	Place Bloomington, Bear Lake, Idaho	Baptized	7 Jun 1890	
Chr.		Place	Endowed	29 Aug 1901	SLAKE
Died	17 Jan 1965	Place Salt Lake City, Salt Lake Co., Utah	SealPar	BIC	
Buried	Jan 1965	Place Afton, Lincoln, Wyoming			
Spouse	Lucy Isabel Call				
Married	29 Aug 1901	Place Salt Lake City, Salt Lake Co., Utah	SealSp	29 Aug 1901	SLAKE
2 M	**William Archer Osmond**				
Born	5 Sep 1884	Place Bloomington, Bear Lake, Idaho	Baptized	5 Sep 1892	
Chr.		Place	Endowed	13 Mar 1907	SLAKE
Died	9 Jul 1907	Place Salt Lake City, Salt Lake Co., Utah (St. Mark's Hospital)	SealPar	BIC	
Buried	Jul 1907	Place Afton, Uinta, Wyoming			
Spouse	Amy Lucille Hale				
Married	13 Mar 1907	Place Salt Lake City, Salt Lake Co., Utah	SealSp	13 Mar 1907	SLAKE
3 M	**Vasco Osmond**				
Born	9 Sep 1889	Place Bloomington, Bear Lake, Idaho	Baptized	9 Sep 1897	
Chr.		Place	Endowed	3 Oct 1912	SLAKE
Died	3 Jan 1971	Place Thayne, Lincoln, Wyoming	SealPar	BIC	
Buried	Jan 1971	Place Thayne, Lincoln, Wyoming			
Spouse	Mary Anna Moser				
Married	3 Oct 1912	Place Salt Lake City, Salt Lake Co., Utah	SealSp	3 Oct 1912	SLAKE
4 M	**Rulon Osmond**				
Born	17 Aug 1893	Place Afton, Uinta Co., Wyoming	Baptized	15 Sep 1901	
Chr.		Place	Endowed	8 Oct 1913	SLAKE
Died	24 Nov 1917	Place Afton, Lincoln, Wyoming	SealPar	BIC	
Buried	26 Nov 1917	Place Afton, Lincoln, Wyoming			
Spouse	Agnes LaVerna Van Noy				
Married	8 Oct 1913	Place Salt Lake City, Salt Lake Co., Utah	SealSp	8 Oct 1913	SLAKE
5 F	**Elizabeth Mary Osmond**				
Born	4 Jun 1896	Place Afton, Unita Co., Wyoming	Baptized	4 Jun 1906	
Chr.		Place	Endowed	17 Aug 1921	SLAKE
Died	18 Nov 1974	Place Bountiful, Davis, Utah	SealPar	BIC	
Buried	21 Nov 1974	Place Kaysville, Davis, Utah (City Cemetery)			
Spouse	Darwin Joshua Willis				
Married	17 Aug 1921	Place Salt Lake City, Salt Lake Co., Utah	SealSp	17 Aug 1921	SLAKE
6 F	**Leona Osmond**				
Born	9 May 1899	Place Afton, Unita Co., Wyoming	Baptized	9 May 1907	
Chr.		Place	Endowed	20 Oct 1992	ARIZO
Died	24 Nov 1990	Place Phoenix, Maricopa, Arizona	SealPar	BIC	
Buried		Place			
Spouse	Guy Leonard Umscheid				
Married	1 May 1937	Place	SealSp	22 Oct 1992	ARIZO
7 M	**Wesley Osmond**				
Born	31 Mar 1901	Place Afton, Unita Co., Wyoming	Baptized	31 Mar 1909	
Chr.		Place	Endowed	10 Apr 1976	OGDEN
Died	18 Nov 1971	Place Perry, Box Elder, Utah	SealPar	BIC	
Buried	Nov 1971	Place Bloomington, Bear Lake, Idaho			

25 Jul 2010

Family Group Record

Husband	George (Jr.) Osmond			
Wife	Christena (Christiana) Serina (Lovina) Amelia Jacobsen			
Children	List each child in order of birth.		LDS ordinance dates	Temple
7 M	Wesley Osmond			
Spouse	Vera Leona Dray			
Married	8 Feb 1922 (D)	Place Smott, Lincoln, Wyoming	SealSp 21 Apr 1995	IFALL
Spouse	Ruby Josephine Nelson			
Married	16 Sep 1934	Place Bloomington, Bear Lake, Idaho	SealSp 10 Apr 1976	OGDEN

Notes

HUSBAND - George (Jr.) Osmond

Genealogical Data on George (Jr.) Osmond (1836/1837-1913):

1) George Osmond was christened in the Church of England on two separate occasions: 1) as "George Osmond" at St. Matthew's church, Bethnal Green, London, Middlesex, (FHL Film # 855942) on 14 June 1837, and recorded as born on 23 May 1837, the son of George and Ann Osmond, of Howards Place, Gent.; and 2) as "George Canham Flight" at Christ Church, St. George in the East, Watney Street, Stepney, London, Middlesex (viewable on Ancestry.com), on 20 October 1843, and recorded as born 23 May 1836, as the son of Hanson and Ann Flight, of Jane Street, Coal Merchant.

2) George Osmond's living LDS endowment record (FHL Film 1239501, Entry #26, Special Collections) states that he was born on 23 May 1836 in London, Middlesex, England, and that his parents were George Osmond and Nancy Canham.

3) The Woolwich LDS. Branch Records of the LDS British Mission lists George Osmond as "George Flight", and states that he was born on 23 May 1836 in Hackney and baptized into the LDS Church on 27 November 1851.

4) In the 1851 Census, George Osmond is listed as "George Flight", age 14 (born about 1837), born in Middlesex, and working as a "Shipwright apprentice" while residing in the home of William White in Charlton, Kent, England.

5) "George Osmond" was an 18 year old passenger and "Shipwright" aboard the passenger ship "Clara Wheeler" that left Liverpool, England, in November 1854, and arrived in New Orleans, Lousiana, on 12 January 1855. (LDS church members aboard the "Clara Wheeler" sailed under the direction of LDS church leader Henry E. Phelps.)

6) In the 1910 U.S. Census, George Osmond is listed as being naturalized in 1857--probably in Utah.

7) The burial gravestone of George Osmond in Bloomington, Bear Lake, Idaho, lists him as being born on May 23, 1837, and having died on 25 March 1913.

8) Because George Osmond Jr. had two christening records that listed different birth years--1836 and 1837--a number of his descendants have used both dates as his year of birth. However, George Osmond appears to have favored the year 1836--stating in his diary entry of 23 May 1886: "I am fifty years old today".

Research Note, September 2008:

In September 2008, Y-DNA 46-Chromosome test results (via Ancestry.com) were provided on Donald (Donny) Clark Osmond (of Utah) and Ronald Thomas Osmond (of New Zealand). These results showed a "50% probability" that these two individuals were related "within 14 generations" or "within 350 years", although it is known that such Y-DNA testing for genealogical purposes is not always accurate in pin-pointing precise generational matches or relative time-spans. However, according to their actual genealogies, these two individuals are "3rd cousins 1 time removed", with their common male ancestor being George Osmond of Bicester, England (b.1745-d.1821). The Y-DNA comparison of Donny Osmond and Ronald Osmond is important to Osmond family historians because it proves that the American pioneer, George Osmond (who was born in 1836 in London, England, and who died in Afton, Wyoming in 1913) was the son of George Osmond (b.1808-d.1860) of Bicester, England, and Nancy Ann Canham, and not the son of Hanson Flight and Nancy Ann Canham, as some people had previously thought possible.

Research Note, September 2008:

In September 2008, Lynne D. Osmond stated the following: "I think that George Osmond was re-christened as George Canham Flight. I've misplaced one part of the LDS records for the church at Eltham but the part I do have states he was George Flight until at least June 6, 1853, when he became an Elder. I think it's possible that when it was known he was to emigrate [to America] he was told his real name, and changed it to Osmond as found on the passenger list for the ship Clara Wheeler. As I said, this cannot be proved and [now] doesn't really matter, as George is proved [through DNA to be an] Osmond."

Historical Note: The family history book "George Osmond and Family Pioneers" (1980's) states that when George Osmond (1837-1913) joined the LDS Church in 1850, his "relatives and friends all turned against him. His mother

Husband **George (Jr.) Osmond**

Wife **Christena (Christiana) Serina (Lovina) Amelia Jacobsen**

Notes

HUSBAND - George (Jr.) Osmond (Continued)

pleaded with him to give up this new strange religion, but to no avail. His relatives felt bitter toward him and accused him of disgracing the family name. ...To his surprise he [George Osmond] was never able to convert any of his relatives to the truth of the Gospel. ...It was said that George broke his mother's heart when he joined up with the 'Deluded Mormons.' He grieved to cause her sorrow, but he could not give up what he believed to be the truth. ... George gave up family and friends, financial security, and even his mother, who was living alone at the time he left to come to America. ...George parted from his relatives, his mother, his brothers and sister, in bitterness. They said, 'We don't want to see or hear from you until you have left the Mormons.' Records show that his mother soon repented and would have been happy to hear from her son in America" (pages 4-5). Also, in his LDS mission diary entry dated November 13, 1884, George Osmond wrote: "The trip to Brighton will remain in my memory as long as life lasts. I saw the house where my mother died. My brother and sister told me many anecdotes of her which proved that 'Her son in America' as she ever loved to call me, was always uppermost in her mind and affections. God bless her and grant that I may yet be able to prove to her how much I love her. I did not visit her grave. It may have been weakness, but I felt I would rather not."

Brief History of George Osmond (1836-1913):

George Osmond was a native of England, convert to the LDS Church, emigrant to Utah, pioneer of Bear Lake Valley, Bishop of Bloomington Ward, and President of Star Valley Stake.

George Osmond was born in London, England, on May 23, 1836. He was the son of George and Nancy Ann (Canham) Osmond.

When he was 14 years of age, he was apprenticed to learn the ship-building trade at the government dockyard in Woolwich, near London. It was while he was there that he was invited by a friend to attend an LDS meeting. He heard the gospel message, believed, and was baptized on November 27, 1850, six months before his 15th birthday. When he was 18 years of age he emigrated to America with the object of joining the Saints in Utah. He sailed to New Orleans and then traveled by steamboat to St. Louis. At St. Louis, in June 1855, he married Mary Georgina Huckvale (b. 1835), a convert to the LDS Church whom he had known in England. Together they crossed the plains and arrived in Salt Lake City in September of 1855.

The first home of George Osmond was in Bountiful, where he operated a small farm and was employed as a school teacher. He then moved to Willard and obtained a homestead. In 1865, he moved to Bear Lake Valley and settled at Bloomington, Idaho. He became presiding elder of the Bloomington Branch in 1871 and in 1875 Bishop of the ward. When Bear Lake Stake was organized in 1877, George Osmond was chosen as second counselor to President William Budge. He served with diligence in this capacity and assisted in building up the settlements in Bear Lake Valley. On September 8, 1881, George Osmond married his second wife, Christena Serina Amelia Jacobsen (b. 1862).

In 1884, George Osmond was called on a two-year LDS mission to England, where he served as assistant editor of the Millennial Star. In 1890, he was again called on a two-year LDS mission to the British Isles, where he served as president of the Scottish and London Districts.

When the Star Valley Stake was organized in August 1892, George Osmond was chosen as the first president. He moved to Afton the same year and there established a permanent home with his second wife, Amelia. He met all the problems incident to the establishment of L.D.S. communities in the fertile valley. He also took part in civic life and served as Justice of the Peace, Probate Judge, and as State Senator in the Wyoming Legislature for two terms. He died in Afton, Wyoming, on March 25, 1913.

Obituary of George Osmond (Jr.):□The Paris Post
Paris, Idaho, Printed April 4, 1913
Funeral Services for President George Osmond

Bloomington, April 3-Impressive and inspirational funeral services were held over the remains of President George Osmond in the meeting house at Bloomington Saturday, March 29th at two P.M. Appropriate musical selections were rendered by the Bloomington choir under the able leadership of Abraham O. Christensen.

It was one of the largest funerals ever held in Bloomington. In addition to the greatest part of the adult population of Bloomington being present a great many friends from St. Charles, Paris, Montpelier and other parts of the stake came to pay their last tribute of respect to the great and good man who was so universally loved.

The speakers were F.M. Winters, Bishop E.M. Pugmire, Clarence Gardner, W.W. Burton, President Wm. L.

Husband George (Jr.) Osmond

Wife Christena (Christiana) Serina (Lovina) Amelia Jacobsen

Notes

HUSBAND - George (Jr.) Osmond (Continued)

Rich, Bishop Alma Findlay, and President Jos. R. Shepherd. These men were nearly all life-long friends of the deceased, and their remarks were listened to with breathless appreciation by the large congregation. The speeches were not formal and conventional funeral sermons, but simple and sincere tributes of affection to the friend that they dearly loved. Sense of loss was felt in every heart, but they were all grateful for the long life that was so rich in service and devotion.

President George Osmond was born in London England May 23rd 1837. He was apprenticed in 1850 to the ship building trade in the Government dock yard at Woolwich, near London. He possessed such great natural aptitude for this work and studied so persistently that he soon placed himself at the head of the classes in the school. This proposition would have entitled him to a splendid college education free of charge, had he continued in the service. At this time however he heard Mormon Elders preach and was at once converted. He therefore gave up his position in the school and began preaching the gospel. In 1884, when President Osmond returned to England he called on his friend who had taken the place in school left vacant by him. In addition to the college education that his friend had received, he had a splendid pension, and a magnificent home, all of which had been given him by the shipyard company.

Four years after his conversion he immigrated to New Orleans and then worked his way Northway to St. Louis. The following year he married Georgiana Huckvale, and with her came across the plains to Salt Lake City. After having lived in Bountiful, Davis County, and Willard, Box Elder County, for a while, he, in 1864, came to Bear Lake Valley, Idaho, where he spent many years of the most valuable part of his life. He served as Bishop of Bloomington for many years and later was chosen counselor to President Budge of the Bear Lake Stake.

In addition to his many positions in the Church, he was very active in civil interests of life. He was probate judge of Bear Lake county and also state senator of the Wyoming legislature during the sessions 1898-99 and 1900-01.

He filled two missions to Great Britain, during which time he traveled extensively through England and on the continent. He was also President of the Liverpool Conference and editor of the Millennial Star. After returning from his last mission to Great Britain in 1892 he was called to Star Valley to be president of that stake, a position that he held until his death, which occurred in Afton Wyoming, March 25th 1913.

President Osmond was a remarkable man, in any environment and among any people he would have been eminent; but, like the Apostle Paul, his greatness was manifested as a servant of Jesus Christ. His life was kindly, chaste and genial and bright as the noon-day sun. He could make himself at home in all kinds of company and had a wonderful aptitude for service in all relations of life. He was particularly devoted to the plain people and consecrated the best efforts of his life to their interests. As an example of his devotion to them, he at one time contracted with the government, through its agent, to furnish a large amount of oats for the mail stations that were located in the Snake River Valley. After the contract was signed and sealed President said to the agent "what do I get out of this?" The agent replied that he, of course would deduct a liberal commission from the contract price. President Osmond responded, "That is not my way of doing business, the people shall have every cent of the contract price, but you ought to give me something for my work."

The agent being wholly unacquainted with such methods of doing business, was perplexed but finally agreed to give a small compensation for President Osmond's work. In succeeding years after the contract was made, the agent would jokingly say, "Well, Mr. Osmond, what is your present to be?"

President Osmond was passionately fond of music and possessed rare literary ability. Some of his poems and masters pieces of verse, and it is only in the matter of quantity that he was not one of the great literary artists of his age. While he has passed to the great beyond, his numerous friends believe that his memory can never die.

Services at Afton

At the funeral services held at Afton, Wyoming, Counselor Clarence Gardner presided. In speaking of the deceased, he said among other things, "President Osmond was always striving to do his duty and to accomplish good in the earth. His last words were 'God bless you brother,' with instructions and suggestions respecting stake matters. He has given counsel enough to make us a good people. He gained the confidence and love of all. Those who lived a Christian life like President Osmond, can safely say,"O grave where is thy victory, O death where is thy sting." His death is our loss. But this loss is his infinite gain, for he died unto the Lord ad he shall rest from his labors."

Other speakers Bishop Hyde of Auburn, Bishop Bracken of Freedom, Thomas Walton, C. H. Haderlie, Thomas F. Burton, and Bishop Low, all paid high tributes to the work and worth of the deceased.

Contributed by Thomas Sleight

Husband	George (Jr.) Osmond
Wife	Christena (Christiana) Serina (Lovina) Amelia Jacobsen

Notes

HUSBAND - George (Jr.) Osmond (Continued)

When the news reached Paris of the death of President George Osmond, many sympathetic hearts were touched because of the love and respect they had for him. He was but a young man when he came to this country, in 1864, having a few years before immigrated to America from England. Because of his natural makeup t was easy for him to become an American of the best type; his physical and mental powers had never been abused and they were so well balanced that the obstacles of life were made easy to overcome.

In 1865 and '66 he taught school in Paris and instead of carrying a whip and a cross look to enforce his rules, he studied the disposition of his pupils, won their love and respect, and made a success of the school.

As a journalist, he was above the average in early days and at one time was editor of the Paris newspaper, then called the Democrat. I well remember one of his editorials on the timber question, which if adhered to, would have saved this country thousands of dollars. He told the wood haulers and loggers when working in the canyon not to cut thrifty saplings to use for a binder every time they loaded their wagons, but make one do for the season. This advice has since been given by Roosevelt and others who have been interested in the timber question.

As farmer and a horticulturist, he was always expected to enlighten us on these subjects at our conferences, because of his many experiments in producing grains and fruits. He could eat apples grown on his own lot when many of us had given up in despair. He was the first to file a possessory claim to a small spring in Lanark, since know as the "Osmond Springs," which name should be retained on the county map in honor of George Osmond, the friend of Peace.

From the Star Valley Independent

Like a wave of gloom engulfing everyone, was the news of the passing away of the great leader and Stake President, George Osmond. It came as a personal loss to thousands, because not alone has his position placed him as a spiritual adviser to the Latter Day Saints of Star Valley Stake, but his kindness of heart, his unselfishness and his wide experience, have brought him in very close touch with the masses and they loved him for they never found him wanting when they have made a call on him.

The Tabernacle was perhaps the laurel in his crown in which he took great pleasure and he was pleased to see its completion. True to his Priesthood and his callings he has been a worthy friend and counselor to many; he had a gift of clear thought and well defined expression, and as a public speaker, he carried his audiences with his clear annunciation of facts, and forceful arguments, coupled with his inspiring and soul lifting expression. His life has been an inspiration to all, his death has left a gloom in the hearts of all who knew him.

After an illness of three weeks George Osmond, President of the Star Valley Stake passed away at his home in Afton, on Tuesday March 25th, 1913, surrounded by his family and friends.

George Osmond was born in England, May 23, 1835 and in his youth immigrated to Zion. He shortly afterward located at Bloomington, Idaho, where he became very active in church matters. After his second mission spent in England, where he held the position as editor of the Millennial Star some of the time, he returned home in May 1892, and the following August the Star Valley Stake was organized and he was selected to fill the office of President, which position he had filled well and nobly.

Funeral services were held in the Tabernacle, Thursday afternoon, and a large concourse of people assembled to pay their last respects to the honored leader. President Clarence Gardner conducted the services. The speakers were Clarence Gardner, Thomas Walton, C.H. Haderlie, Bishop Hyde, Bishop Bracken, Arthur F. Burton and Bishop Oz Low. The choir sang special selections, and Mark Hurd and Thomas Burton sang a duet. The tabernacle was draped in white. There was an abundance of floral offerings both in the hall and on the casket.

After the services the remains were taken back to the home and will be taken to Bloomington today and funeral services held tomorrow in the Bloomington meeting house, interment taking place in the cemetery there.

He leaves a large family and a legion of friends to mourn his loss.

WIFE - Christena (Christiana) Serina (Lovina) Amelia Jacobsen

The birth date and place of Christena Sernia (Lovina) Amelia Jacobsen was personally supplied by her at the time she took out her own (living) LDS Endowment, which took place in the Endowment House (Salt Lake City, Utah) on 8 September 1881. At this time, Christena stated that she was born on 9 November 1862 in Brigham City, Box Elder, Utah; that she was baptized into the LDS Church in 1871, and that her parents were Frederick Jacobsen and Elizabeth Petersen. (See: FHL "Special Collections" Film # 183408, page 205.)

Brief History of Christena (Christiana) Sernia (Lovina) Amelia Jacobsen, written by Rulon Robert (Bob) Osmond, a

Husband **George (Jr.) Osmond**

Wife **Christena (Christiana) Serina (Lovina) Amelia Jacobsen**

Notes

WIFE - Christena (Christiana) Serina (Lovina) Amelia Jacobsen (Continued)

great-grandson, in February 2009:

Christiana Lovina Amelia Jacobson

Amelia was born 9 November 1861 in Brigham City, Utah to Fredrick Jacobson Sr. and Elizabeth Pedersen. Her childhood was not easy because her mother never was strong and she had to become the mother at an early age.

On the 8th of September 1881 she married George Osmond, and while they lived in Bloomington, Idaho, James Arthur, William Archer and Vosco were born. In December of 1890 George was called to return again to England to serve a second LDS mission. This meant two more long, lean and lonely years for Amelia.

She was a wonderful housekeeper and kept her children immaculate. She helped care for and comfort her lonely and aging mother whose husband had deserted her.

When George returned from his mission in 1892 he was immediately called to go to Star Valley, Wyoming, to preside over the new LDS stake created there. Amelia now was called to leave the land of her childhood, her new home, her widowed mother, her brothers and her childhood friends and go with her husband and her three small sons to preside over his home while he presided over the new Star Valley Stake.

Living in Star Valley at that time was very hard. When they first arrived they lived in a one room house with a dirt roof. When it rained or the snow melted she used pots, pans and umbrellas to keep the water off of the dirt floor. In the spring they found a better house. The village blacksmith moved out of his shop and let them live in it. It had shingles and kept the water out but it still had a dirt floor and she could never get the smell out no matter how much she dug it out. The second winter found them living in a new house which was clean, warm with no leaks or bugs.

In 1893 a fourth son, Rulon, was born which brought their children to four. With their little family and all of the friends and visitors (both political and ecclesiastical) that George had (and with no hotels or restaurants nearby), as well as always helping those in need, Amelia always seemed to be preparing food and beds for everyone.

Elizabeth Mary was born in 1896, and three years later--in 1899--Leona was born in 1899. In 1901, Wesley--their last child--was born.

Throughout the years Amelia saw that her children attended church and helped others. President Osmond was so very busy that many times she had to attend meetings with her sons. She was a faithful Relief Society teacher and was in the Stake Primary Presidency for many years. She did everything she could to help others and often repeated a statement of her mother "No one will ask how long it took to do it, but how well it was done". She was very independent, would not impose on others, rarely if ever asked for a favor, and seldom accepted one.

Amelia's lungs were never strong and she suffered at times with pneumonia which brought about real trials with little children. She also suffered with ulcers on her legs which seemed to be incurable. An experimenting doctor cut the veins in her legs and "bled her" which was a very cruel act and caused her untold agony throughout her life. She was left a widow when she was 51 years old and her youngest child was twelve years old.

In her sixty's Amelia moved to Logan, Utah, where she lived close to her son Arthur. She enjoyed spending time with Arthur, especially when he came home from working in the temple. From the 1920's until her death in 1946, she spent much of her time visiting and living with her children and grand children, who loved her very much.

Amelia Osmond was the mother of five sons and two daughters, eighteen grandchildren and thirty four great grand children. All of her descendants are Latter Day Saints and are the kind of people she would be proud to claim as her own.

CHILD 2 - William Archer Osmond

Died from an appendix attack.

CHILD 4 - Rulon Osmond

In the 1910 U.S. Census, Rulon Osmond is listed as being about 16 years old (born about 1894) and working as a " Laborer [of] Odd Jobs".

The family history book "George Osmond and Family Pioneers" (1980's) Rulon Osmond is described as follows:

Page XXIII: "Rulon, it seemed had a special destiny. In his younger years he was a model person demonstrating the fine qualities of ambition and integrity. Perhaps his life was cut short for reasons difficult to understand but whatever the caswe may be, his good wife LaVerna raised their three sons to a most remarkable manhood."

Husband	**George (Jr.) Osmond**
Wife	**Christena (Christiana) Serina (Lovina) Amelia Jacobsen**

Notes

CHILD 4 - Rulon Osmond (Continued)

Pages 395-397: "Rulon Osmond is the fourth child of George and Amelia [Osmond]. He was born in Afton, Wyoming, on August 17, 1893. Rulon attended the Aften schools for his elementary schooling, his finishing school was at Paris, Idaho, at the school where his father had taught years before. By the time the two older boys were no longer at home, Arthur was married and had a family. Arch had married and shortly afterward had died of appendicitis. President [George] Osmond as usual, was busy with civic and church affairs so the chores and livestock were pretty much in charge of Ruon and Vasco. When work on the farm was caught up Rulon would find work at whatever job was available in the vicinity. He was not one to be idle. At the age of twenty, Rulon married Agnes LaVerna Van Noy. The marriage took place at the Salt Lake Temple on October 8, 1913. Shortly after their marriage they moved to a farm in Etna, Wyoming where he and Vasco tried their luck at farming. It was un-improved land and the boys had to start from scratch. Along with the farm work Rulon held down a couple of side jobs. It takes a little time to get a farm into production and they needed the money to live on. Rulon hauled milk from the neighboring farms to the creamery and also fed cattle on the Wolfley Ranch. President [George] Osmond helped them arrange for their supply of cattle, horses and farm machinery so they could get going on their work. Aunt Mary and Aunt Vernie...gave the boys a hand with the farm work. Land was plowed and prepared and crops planted and harvested. Fences were put up and buildings were improved. Things seemed to be going well with the Osmonds. They had made many friends in Etna and were well liked. They had young and growing families and this was a young and growing community. They had a lot to look forward to and were making long range plans. Things were shaping up well and the farm was now in production and that induced a feeling of security. Three children were born to Rulon.... The oldest was...Rulon but we always called him R.V., the second was Ralph..., and the baby was George. He was still just a baby when things suddenly and drastically changed for the entire family. Font King, a neighbor, and Rulon had gone to the mountains out northwest of Etna for wood and were returning with their wagons loaded. Font needed some help to get his wagon up a steep pitch so Rulon proceded to unhitch his team to go back and double up with Font. During the course of the maneuver the team became excited and Rulon was kicked by his big brown mare 'Bird'. It was immediately apparent that it was serious and the situation was anything but convenient. As fast as possible Rulon was hauled to the nearest farm house, Jake Miller's about two miles away. A doctor was summoned but precious time was slipping away and so was Rulon's life blood. The doctor arrived and immediately recognized he had serious internal hemorrhaging. Immediately surgery was called for but an isolated farm house was no place for so serious an operation. There was no choice but to try to get him to Afton to a hospital in time. He was made as comfortable as possible and the twenty-five miles trip was underway. Two and a half hours over rough country roads really took its toll. Rulon underwent the surgery to sew up his liver which had been severed due to broken ribs. The doctors made the repair as best they could and we all waited for the word that Rulon would be O.K. That word never came. They were unable to stop the bleeding and Rulon died of shock and hemorrhage. It was all so sudden, so unbelieveable. It took time to come to a full realization of what had really happened. He was the kind of fellow everyone liked and the sadness was like a dark cloud over the valley. Now [Rulon's wife] and the boys had to re-arrnage the whole pattern of their lives. The older boys R.V. and Ralph would remember their dad but George never had the opportunity of really knowing him, being yet a baby. Their mother LaVerna, now alone, faced the overwhelming and frightening task of raising three little boys by herself. Her world had just collapsed and when the numbness of the shock subsided and the reality of the future came into focus she calmly picked up the pieces of a broken life and put together a unity of family, the success of which is brilliantly attested to by what her children and grandchildren have contributed to the world."

On 28 October 2008, The following individuals were "sealed" (in the LDS Ogden Temple) to Rulon and Agnes Osmond: Polly Neyman (b.1921), Peggy Neyman (b.1921), Laverna (Lavina or Lavena, b.1922), John Wesley Neyman Jr. (b.1923), and Cora Elizabeth Neyman (b.1925).

When was George Osmond Jr. born: 1836 or 1837 ?

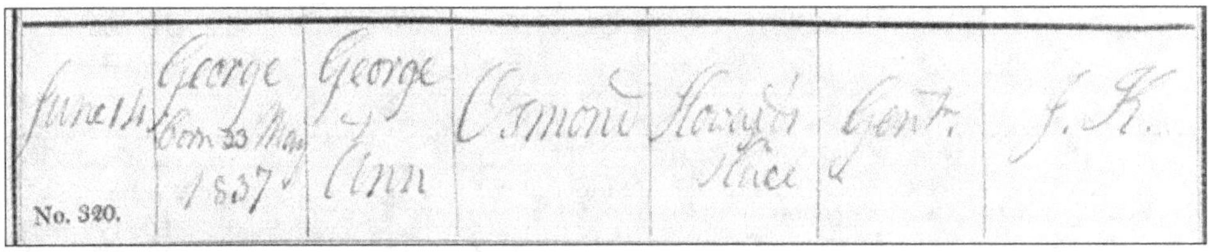

June 14th	George born 23 May 1837	George & Ann	Osmond	Howards Place	Gent.	J. K.

No. 320.

George Osmond Jr. was christened in the Church of England on two separate occasions. 1) Top Photo: as "George Osmond" at St. Matthew's church, Bethnal Green, London, Middlesex, (FHL Film # 855942) on 14 June 1837, and recorded as born on 23 May 1837, the son of George and Ann Osmond, of Howards Place, Gent.; and 2) Bottom Photo: as "George Canham Flight" at Christ Church, St. George in the East, Watney Street, Stepney, London, Middlesex (viewable on Ancestry.com), on 20 October 1843, and recorded as born 23 May 1836, as the son of Hanson and Ann Flight, of Jane Street, Coal Merchant.

Because George Osmond Jr. had two christening records that listed different birth years--1836 and 1837--a number of his descendants have used both dates as his year of birth. However, George Osmond appears to have favored the year 1836--stating in his diary entry of 23 May 1886: "I am fifty years old today".

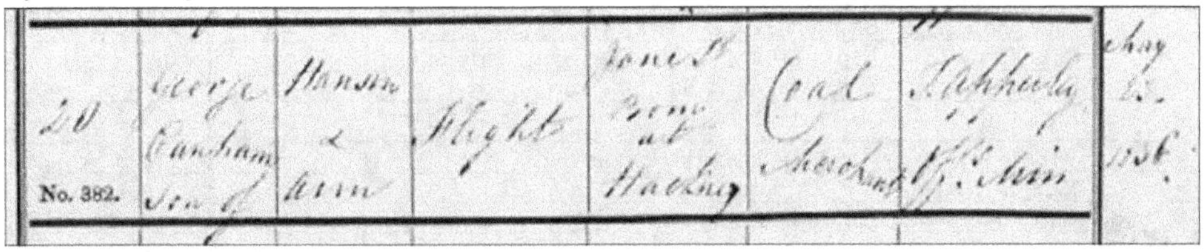

No. 382.

Ann Canham Osmond
1805-1876
Mother of George Osmond

George Osmond Jr. (left, 1836/1837-1913) left England in 1854 and sailed to the United States, eventually residing at different times in Utah, Idaho and Wyoming. In the 1970's, George's descendants formed the *George Osmond Family Organization*, and in the 1980's a book was published (top right) on George and his two wives and their families. The mother of George Osmond was Nancy Ann Canham (above center, 1805-1876), whose picture was printed in 1973 in the book: *The Autobiography of Melvin A. Cook* (1973, Volume 1, p.312; FHL # 921.73, C772c).

Family Group Record

Husband George (Sr.) Osmond

	Date		Place	LDS ordinance dates		Temple
Born		Place				
Chr.	6 Mar 1808	Place	Bicester, Oxfordshire, England	Baptized	17 Jul 1937	
Died	1 Dec 1860	Place	Sheep Street, Market End, Bicester, Oxfordshire, England	Endowed	15 Sep 1937	LOGAN
Buried	6 Dec 1860	Place	St. Edburg, Bicester, Oxfordshire, England	SealPar	5 Aug 1977	LANGE
Married		Place	(This couple were never married)	SealSp	6 May 1939	LOGAN
Husband's father	George Osmond					
Husband's mother	Anne Phillips					

Wife Nancy Ann Canham

	Date		Place	LDS ordinance dates		Temple
Born	12 Dec 1805	Place	of Blackheath, London, England			
Chr.	26 Jan 1806	Place	St. Mary, Woolwich, Kent, England	Baptized	17 Jul 1937	
Died	5 Nov 1876	Place	17 Marlborough Place, Brighton, Sussex, England	Endowed	15 Sep 1937	
Buried	Nov 1876	Place	Woodvale Cemetery, Brighton, Sussex, England	SealPar	25 Nov 1957	
Other Spouse	Hanson Flight					
Married	10 Jun 1827	Place	St. Michael, Crooked Lane, London, London, England	SealSp	14 Mar 1979	IFALL
Wife's father	George Canham					
Wife's mother	Elizabeth White					

Children List each child in order of birth.

1 M George (Jr.) Osmond

	Date		Place	LDS ordinance dates		Temple
Born	23 May 1836/1837	Place	Hackney, London, England	Baptized	27 Nov 1851	
Chr.	14 Jun 1837	Place	St. Matthew, Bethnal Green, London, England	Endowed	31 Oct 1868	EHOUS
Died	25 Mar 1913	Place	Afton, Lincoln, Wyoming	SealPar	5 Jul 1941	LOGAN
Buried	29 Mar 1913	Place	Bloomington, Bear Lake, Idaho			
Spouse	Mary Georgina (Georgiana) Huckvale					
Married	Jul 1855	Place	St. Louis, St. Louis Co., Missouri	SealSp	31 Oct 1868	EHOUS
Spouse	Christena (Christiana) Serina (Lovina) Amelia Jacobsen					
Married	8 Sep 1881	Place	Salt Lake City, Salt Lake Co., Utah	SealSp	8 Sep 1881	EHOUS

2 M John Osmond

	Date		Place	LDS ordinance dates		Temple
Born	23 May 1836/1837	Place	Hackney, London, England	Baptized	1 Oct 1958	
Chr.		Place		Endowed	9 Dec 1958	
Died	Abt 1843	Place	London, Middlesex, England	SealPar	5 Jul 1941	LOGAN
Buried		Place				
Spouse						
Married		Place		SealSp		

Notes

MARRIAGE

Research Note: No evidence has been found that George Osmond and Nancy Ann Canham were ever married.

Note: The IGI contains an LDS proxy marriage sealing for George Osmond and Nancy Ann Canham, which was done on 6 May 1939 in the LDS Logan Temple.

HUSBAND - George (Sr.) Osmond

The christening of George Osmond is listed in the parish registers of Bicester (FHL Book #: British, 942.57/B1, K29ce, Vol.2, p.207), which states that he was christened on 6 March 1808 as "George [the] son [of] George and Ann Osmond".

In September 2009, the Osmond Family Organization of Utah obtained a copy of the death certificate of George Osmond from England, which stated that he died at the age of 52 years of "Diseased Bladder [and] Exhaustion" on 1 December 1860, at Sheep Street, Bicester, and that he was "Soliciter".

The burial of George (Sr.) Osmond is listed in the Monumental Inscriptions (published in April 1992) for St. Edburg, Bicester, Oxfordshire, England (FHL Microfiche # 6400193), and states that George Osmond was buried in plot # 273 and that (in 1992) his "tomb [was] half buried". The Monumental Inscription reads: "Sacred to the Memory of George Osmond Esq. who departed this life on the 1st day of December 1860. Aged 52 years." In 2009, the gravestone of George (Sr.) Osmond at St. Edburg, Bicester, Oxford, England, was located and photographed by Kathryn and Jim Stout (professional genealogists in Lancashire, England); and in 2010 the gravestone was visited and again photographed by James (Jimmy) A. Osmond (of Utah). Photographs of George Osmond's gravestone and other related items are in possession of the Osmond Family Organization of Utah.

In the 1841 Census, George Osmond is listed as being about 35 years old (born about 1807-1811), born in Oxfordshire, England, an "Attorney" and residing with his mother "Ann" (about 61 years old) in Bicester, Oxfordshire,

Husband **George (Sr.) Osmond**

Wife **Nancy Ann Canham**

Notes

HUSBAND - George (Sr.) Osmond (Continued)

England.

In the 1851 Census, George Osmond is listed as being about 44 years old (born about 1807), born in Bicester, Oxfordshire, unmarried and working as a "Solicitor", while residing in the household of Wellington and Ann Ellis located at: 4 White Rock, St. Mary Magdalen, Hastings, Sussex, England.

Historical Note: The family history book "George Osmond and Family Pioneers" (1980's, p.2-3) states that George Osmond Jr.'s (1837-1913) "father was George Osmond, the attorney.... George Sr. was born in Bicester, Oxfordshire, England, and died December 1st, 1860, while residing at Sheep Street, Market End, Bicester, England.... Rumors are that the Osmond family was one of considerable wealth and high social standing. George Sr. seems to have alienated himself to some extent from the family traditions, perhaps a free spirit seeking self expression. Who knows. The records do not give the answer. Indications are that he was 'cut off' from what normally would have been his inheritance. Whether he ever received it or not is still in question. He, George Sr. apparently established a law practice at Bicester, as certain documents from that area bear his signature and reference is made to him in that capacity. It is said that he had a 'good bit' of money and we do find Nancy living in her own home and caring for her family, yet no reference is made to him at this time."

Historical Note: The family history book "George Osmond and Family Pioneers" (1980's) states that when George Osmond (1837-1913) joined the LDS Church in 1850, his "relatives and friends all turned against him. His mother pleaded with him to give up this new strange religion, but to no avail. His relatives felt bitter toward him and accused him of disgracing the family name. ...To his surprise he [George Osmond] was never able to convert any of his relatives to the truth of the Gospel. ...It was said that George broke his mother's heart when he joined up with the 'Deluded Mormons.' He grieved to cause her sorrow, but he could not give up what he believed to be the truth. ... George gave up family and friends, financial security, and even his mother, who was living alone at the time he left to come to America. ...George parted from his relatives, his mother, his brothers and sister, in bitterness. They said, 'We don't want to see or hear from you until you have left the Mormons.' Records show that his mother soon repented and would have been happy to hear from her son in America" (pages 4-5). Also, in his LDS mission diary entry dated November 13, 1884, George Osmond wrote: "The trip to Brighton will remain in my memory as long as life lasts. I saw the house where my mother died. My brother and sister told me many anecdotes of her which proved that 'Her son in America' as she ever loved to call me, was always uppermost in her mind and affections. God bless her and grant that I may yet be able to prove to her how much I love her. I did not visit her grave. It may have been weakness, but I felt I would rather not."

WIFE - Nancy Ann Canham

In the 1871 Census, "Anne Flight" is listed as being about 64 years old (born about 1807), born in Woolwich, Kent, a widow and lodger, who was living off "Income from rent of houses", and residing at: 60 Albion Hill, Brighton, Sussex, with Edward and Margarett Barns.

The death of "Nancy Flight" is listed in the on-line FreeBMD as having taken place during October-December 1876 in the district of Brighton (Volume 2b, Page 129).

The burial site of Nancy Ann Canham Flight is located in Woodvale Cemetery on Lewes Road in Brighton, Sussex, England. Nancy is buried in Plot # 17649 in Woodvale Cemetery. Unfortunately, no gravestone is visible as her plot area is now covered by grass (2009).

Research Note, April 2008: Mark E. Gardner, a professional genealogist, stated the following in April 2008: "George Osmond married in the Endowment House in Salt Lake City, Utah, on 31 October 1868, and stated at that time that he was the son of George Osmond and Nancy Ann Canham. This George we know was born out of wedlock. Nancy Ann Canham married Hanson Flight in 1828 and never married George Osmond. We actually find George with the last name of Flight in a later baptism record and in the 1851 British Census as learning a trade as a shipwright in the Woolwich area."

Husband	George (Sr.) Osmond
Wife	Nancy Ann Canham

Notes

WIFE - Nancy Ann Canham (Continued)

Research Note: The on-line FreeBMD contains the 1876 death listing of "Nancy Flight".

Historical Note: The family history book "George Osmond and Family Pioneers" (1980's, p.3) states that "George [Osmond's] mother Nancy [Canham], was fairly well educated and desired George should have a good education...."

Historical Note: The family history book "George Osmond and Family Pioneers" (1980's) states that when George Osmond (1837-1913) joined the LDS Church in 1850, his "relatives and friends all turned against him. His mother pleaded with him to give up this new strange religion, but to no avail. His relatives felt bitter toward him and accused him of disgracing the family name. ...To his surprise he [George Osmond] was never able to convert any of his relatives to the truth of the Gospel. ...It was said that George broke his mother's heart when he joined up with the 'Deluded Mormons.' He grieved to cause her sorrow, but he could not give up what he believed to be the truth. ... George gave up family and friends, financial security, and even his mother, who was living alone at the time he left to come to America [in 1854]. ...George parted from his relatives, his mother, his brothers and sister, in bitterness. They said, 'We don't want to see or hear from you until you have left the Mormons.' Records show that his mother soon repented and would have been happy to hear from her son in America" (pages 4-5). Also, in his LDS mission diary entry dated November 13, 1884, George Osmond wrote: "The trip to Brighton will remain in my memory as long as life lasts. I saw the house where my mother died. My brother and sister told me many anecdotes of her which proved that 'Her son in America' as she ever loved to call me, was always uppermost in her mind and affections. God bless her and grant that I may yet be able to prove to her how much I love her. I did not visit her grave. It may have been weakness, but I felt I would rather not."

CHILD 1 - George (Jr.) Osmond

Genealogical Data on George (Jr.) Osmond (1836/1837-1913):

1) George Osmond was christened in the Church of England on two separate occasions: 1) as "George Osmond" at St. Matthew's church, Bethnal Green, London, Middlesex, (FHL Film # 855942) on 14 June 1837, and recorded as born on 23 May 1837, the son of George and Ann Osmond, of Howards Place, Gent.; and 2) as "George Canham Flight" at Christ Church, St. George in the East, Watney Street, Stepney, London, Middlesex (viewable on Ancestry.com), on 20 October 1843, and recorded as born 23 May 1836, as the son of Hanson and Ann Flight, of Jane Street, Coal Merchant.

2) George Osmond's living LDS endowment record (FHL Film 1239501, Entry #26, Special Collections) states that he was born on 23 May 1836 in London, Middlesex, England, and that his parents were George Osmond and Nancy Canham.

3) The Woolwich LDS. Branch Records of the LDS British Mission lists George Osmond as "George Flight", and states that he was born on 23 May 1836 in Hackney and baptized into the LDS Church on 27 November 1851.

4) In the 1851 Census, George Osmond is listed as "George Flight", age 14 (born about 1837), born in Middlesex, and working as a "Shipwright apprentice" while residing in the home of William White in Charlton, Kent, England.

5) "George Osmond" was an 18 year old passenger and "Shipwright" aboard the passenger ship "Clara Wheeler" that left Liverpool, England, in November 1854, and arrived in New Orleans, Lousiana, on 12 January 1855. (LDS church members aboard the "Clara Wheeler" sailed under the direction of LDS church leader Henry E. Phelps.)

6) In the 1910 U.S. Census, George Osmond is listed as being naturalized in 1857--probably in Utah.

7) The burial gravestone of George Osmond in Bloomington, Bear Lake, Idaho, lists him as being born on May 23, 1837, and having died on 25 March 1913.

8) Because George Osmond Jr. had two christening records that listed different birth years--1836 and 1837--a number of his descendants have used both dates as his year of birth. However, George Osmond appears to have favored the year 1836--stating in his diary entry of 23 May 1886: "I am fifty years old today".

Research Note, September 2008:

In September 2008, Y-DNA 46-Chromosome test results (via Ancestry.com) were provided on Donald (Donny) Clark Osmond (of Utah) and Ronald Thomas Osmond (of New Zealand). These results showed a "50% probability" that these two individuals were related "within 14 generations" or "within 350 years", although it is known that such Y-DNA testing for genealogical purposes is not always accurate in pin-pointing precise generational matches or relative time-spans. However, according to their actual genealogies, these two individuals are "3rd cousins 1 time removed",

Family Group Record

Husband **George (Sr.) Osmond**

Wife **Nancy Ann Canham**

Notes

CHILD 1 - George (Jr.) Osmond (Continued)

with their common male ancestor being George Osmond of Bicester, England (b.1745-d.1821). The Y-DNA comparison of Donny Osmond and Ronald Osmond is important to Osmond family historians because it proves that the American pioneer, George Osmond (who was born in 1836 in London, England, and who died in Afton, Wyoming in 1913) was the son of George Osmond (b.1808-d.1860) of Bicester, England, and Nancy Ann Canham, and not the son of Hanson Flight and Nancy Ann Canham, as some people had previously thought possible.

Research Note, September 2008:

In September 2008, Lynne D. Osmond stated the following: "I think that George Osmond was re-christened as George Canham Flight. I've misplaced one part of the LDS records for the church at Eltham but the part I do have states he was George Flight until at least June 6, 1853, when he became an Elder. I think it's possible that when it was known he was to emigrate [to America] he was told his real name, and changed it to Osmond as found on the passenger list for the ship Clara Wheeler. As I said, this cannot be proved and [now] doesn't really matter, as George is proved [through DNA to be an] Osmond."

Historical Note: The family history book "George Osmond and Family Pioneers" (1980's) states that when George Osmond (1837-1913) joined the LDS Church in 1850, his "relatives and friends all turned against him. His mother pleaded with him to give up this new strange religion, but to no avail. His relatives felt bitter toward him and accused him of disgracing the family name. ...To his surprise he [George Osmond] was never able to convert any of his relatives to the truth of the Gospel. ...It was said that George broke his mother's heart when he joined up with the 'Deluded Mormons.' He grieved to cause her sorrow, but he could not give up what he believed to be the truth. ... George gave up family and friends, financial security, and even his mother, who was living alone at the time he left to come to America. ...George parted from his relatives, his mother, his brothers and sister, in bitterness. They said, 'We don't want to see or hear from you until you have left the Mormons.' Records show that his mother soon repented and would have been happy to hear from her son in America" (pages 4-5). Also, in his LDS mission diary entry dated November 13, 1884, George Osmond wrote: "The trip to Brighton will remain in my memory as long as life lasts. I saw the house where my mother died. My brother and sister told me many anecdotes of her which proved that 'Her son in America' as she ever loved to call me, was always uppermost in her mind and affections. God bless her and grant that I may yet be able to prove to her how much I love her. I did not visit her grave. It may have been weakness, but I felt I would rather not."

Brief History of George Osmond (1836-1913):

George Osmond was a native of England, convert to the LDS Church, emigrant to Utah, pioneer of Bear Lake Valley, Bishop of Bloomington Ward, and President of Star Valley Stake.

George Osmond was born in London, England, on May 23, 1836. He was the son of George and Nancy Ann (Canham) Osmond.

When he was 14 years of age, he was apprenticed to learn the ship-building trade at the government dockyard in Woolwich, near London. It was while he was there that he was invited by a friend to attend an LDS meeting. He heard the gospel message, believed, and was baptized on November 27, 1850, six months before his 15th birthday.

When he was 18 years of age he emigrated to America with the object of joining the Saints in Utah. He sailed to New Orleans and then traveled by steamboat to St. Louis. At St. Louis, in June 1855, he married Mary Georgina Huckvale (b. 1835), a convert to the LDS Church whom he had known in England. Together they crossed the plains and arrived in Salt Lake City in September of 1855.

The first home of George Osmond was in Bountiful, where he operated a small farm and was employed as a school teacher. He then moved to Willard and obtained a homestead. In 1865, he moved to Bear Lake Valley and settled at Bloomington, Idaho. He became presiding elder of the Bloomington Branch in 1871 and in 1875 Bishop of the ward. When Bear Lake Stake was organized in 1877, George Osmond was chosen as second counselor to President William Budge. He served with diligence in this capacity and assisted in building up the settlements in Bear Lake Valley. On September 8, 1881, George Osmond married his second wife, Christena Serina Amelia Jacobsen (b. 1862).

In 1884, George Osmond was called on a two-year LDS mission to England, where he served as assistant editor of the Millennial Star. In 1890, he was again called on a two-year LDS mission to the British Isles, where he served as president of the Scottish and London Districts.

Husband **George (Sr.) Osmond**

Wife **Nancy Ann Canham**

Notes

CHILD 1 - George (Jr.) Osmond (Continued)

When the Star Valley Stake was organized in August 1892, George Osmond was chosen as the first president. He moved to Afton the same year and there established a permanent home with his second wife, Amelia. He met all the problems incident to the establishment of L.D.S. communities in the fertile valley. He also took part in civic life and served as Justice of the Peace, Probate Judge, and as State Senator in the Wyoming Legislature for two terms. He died in Afton, Wyoming, on March 25, 1913.

Obituary of George Osmond (Jr.):□The Paris Post
Paris, Idaho, Printed April 4, 1913
Funeral Services for President George Osmond

Bloomington, April 3-Impressive and inspirational funeral services were held over the remains of President George Osmond in the meeting house at Bloomington Saturday, March 29th at two P.M. Appropriate musical selections were rendered by the Bloomington choir under the able leadership of Abraham O. Christensen.

It was one of the largest funerals ever held in Bloomington. In addition to the greatest part of the adult population of Bloomington being present a great many friends from St. Charles, Paris, Montpelier and other parts of the stake came to pay their last tribute of respect to the great and good man who was so universally loved.

The speakers were F.M. Winters, Bishop E.M. Pugmire, Clarence Gardner, W.W. Burton, President Wm. L. Rich, Bishop Alma Findlay, and President Jos. R. Shepherd. These men were nearly all life-long friends of the deceased, and their remarks were listened to with breathless appreciation by the large congregation. The speeches were not formal and conventional funeral sermons, but simple and sincere tributes of affection to the friend that they dearly loved. Sense of loss was felt in every heart, but they were all grateful for the long life that was so rich in service and devotion.

President George Osmond was born in London England May 23rd 1837. He was apprenticed in 1850 to the ship building trade in the Government dock yard at Woolwich, near London. He possessed such great natural aptitude for this work and studied so persistently that he soon placed himself at the head of the classes in the school. This proposition would have entitled him to a splendid college education free of charge, had he continued in the service. At this time however he heard Mormon Elders preach and was at once converted. He therefore gave up his position in the school and began preaching the gospel. In 1884, when President Osmond returned to England he called on his friend who had taken the place in school left vacant by him. In addition to the college education that his friend had received, he had a splendid pension, and a magnificent home, all of which had been given him by the shipyard company.

Four years after his conversion he immigrated to New Orleans and then worked his way Northway to St. Louis. The following year he married Georgiana Huckvale, and with her came across the plains to Salt Lake City. After having lived in Bountiful, Davis County, and Willard, Box Elder County, for a while, he, in 1864, came to Bear Lake Valley, Idaho, where he spent many years of the most valuable part of his life. He served as Bishop of Bloomington for many years and later was chosen counselor to President Budge of the Bear Lake Stake.

In addition to his many positions in the Church, he was very active in civil interests of life. He was probate judge of Bear Lake county and also state senator of the Wyoming legislature during the sessions 1898-99 and 1900-01.

He filled two missions to Great Britain, during which time he traveled extensively through England and on the continent. He was also President of the Liverpool Conference and editor of the Millennial Star. After returning from his last mission to Great Britain in 1892 he was called to Star Valley to be president of that stake, a position that he held until his death, which occurred in Afton Wyoming, March 25th 1913.

President Osmond was a remarkable man, in any environment and among any people he would have been eminent; but, like the Apostle Paul, his greatness was manifested as a servant of Jesus Christ. His life was kindly, chaste and genial and bright as the noon-day sun. He could make himself at home in all kinds of company and had a wonderful aptitude for service in all relations of life. He was particularly devoted to the plain people and consecrated the best efforts of his life to their interests. As an example of his devotion to them, he at one time contracted with the government, through its agent, to furnish a large amount of oats for the mail stations that were located in the Snake River Valley. After the contract was signed and sealed President said to the agent "what do I get out of this?" The agent replied that he, of course would deduct a liberal commission from the contract price. President Osmond responded, "That is not my way of doing business, the people shall have every cent of the contract price, but you ought to give me something for my work."

Husband	George (Sr.) Osmond
Wife	Nancy Ann Canham

Notes

CHILD 1 - George (Jr.) Osmond (Continued)

The agent being wholly unacquainted with such methods of doing business, was perplexed but finally agreed to give a small compensation for President Osmond's work. In succeeding years after the contract was made, the agent would jokingly say, "Well, Mr. Osmond, what is your present to be?"

President Osmond was passionately fond of music and possessed rare literary ability. Some of his poems and masters pieces of verse, and it is only in the matter of quantity that he was not one of the great literary artists of his age. While he has passed to the great beyond, his numerous friends believe that his memory can never die.

Services at Afton

At the funeral services held at Afton, Wyoming, Counselor Clarence Gardner presided. In speaking of the deceased, he said among other things, "President Osmond was always striving to do his duty and to accomplish good in the earth. His last words were 'God bless you brother,' with instructions and suggestions respecting stake matters. He has given counsel enough to make us a good people. He gained the confidence and love of all. Those who lived a Christian life like President Osmond, can safely say,"O grave where is thy victory, O death where is thy sting." His death is our loss. But this loss is his infinite gain, for he died unto the Lord ad he shall rest from his labors."

Other speakers Bishop Hyde of Auburn, Bishop Bracken of Freedom, Thomas Walton, C. H. Haderlie, Thomas F. Burton, and Bishop Low, all paid high tributes to the work and worth of the deceased.

Contributed by Thomas Sleight

When the news reached Paris of the death of President George Osmond, many sympathetic hearts were touched because of the love and respect they had for him. He was but a young man when he came to this country, in 1864, having a few years before immigrated to America from England. Because of his natural makeup t was easy for him to become an American of the best type; his physical and mental powers had never been abused and they were so well balanced that the obstacles of life were made easy to overcome.

In 1865 and '66 he taught school in Paris and instead of carrying a whip and a cross look to enforce his rules, he studied the disposition of his pupils, won their love and respect, and made a success of the school.

As a journalist, he was above the average in early days and at one time was editor of the Paris newspaper, then called the Democrat. I well remember one of his editorials on the timber question, which if adhered to, would have saved this country thousands of dollars. He told the wood haulers and loggers when working in the canyon not to cut thrifty saplings to use for a binder every time they loaded their wagons, but make one do for the season. This advice has since been given by Roosevelt and others who have been interested in the timber question.

As farmer and a horticulturist, he was always expected to enlighten us on these subjects at our conferences, because of his many experiments in producing grains and fruits. He could eat apples grown on his own lot when many of us had given up in despair. He was the first to file a possessory claim to a small spring in Lanark, since know as the "Osmond Springs," which name should be retained on the county map in honor of George Osmond, the friend of Peace.

From the Star Valley Independent

Like a wave of gloom engulfing everyone, was the news of the passing away of the great leader and Stake President, George Osmond. It came as a personal loss to thousands, because not alone has his position placed him as a spiritual adviser to the Latter Day Saints of Star Valley Stake, but his kindness of heart, his unselfishness and his wide experience, have brought him in very close touch with the masses and they loved him for they never found him wanting when they have made a call on him.

The Tabernacle was perhaps the laurel in his crown in which he took great pleasure and he was pleased to see its completion. True to his Priesthood and his callings he has been a worthy friend and counselor to many; he had a gift of clear thought and well defined expression, and as a public speaker, he carried his audiences with his clear annunciation of facts, and forceful arguments, coupled with his inspiring and soul lifting expression. His life has been an inspiration to all, his death has left a gloom in the hearts of all who knew him.

After an illness of three weeks George Osmond, President of the Star Valley Stake passed away at his home in Afton, on Tuesday March 25th, 1913, surrounded by his family and friends.

George Osmond was born in England, May 23, 1835 and in his youth immigrated to Zion. He shortly afterward located at Bloomington, Idaho, where he became very active in church matters. After his second mission spent in England, where he held the position as editor of the Millennial Star some of the time, he returned home in May 1892, and the following August the Star Valley Stake was organized and he was selected to fill the office of President, which position he had filled well and nobly.

Funeral services were held in the Tabernacle, Thursday afternoon, and a large concourse of people

Family Group Record

Husband	George (Sr.) Osmond
Wife	Nancy Ann Canham

Notes

CHILD 1 - George (Jr.) Osmond (Continued)

assembled to pay their last respects to the honored leader. President Clarence Gardner conducted the services. The speakers were Clarence Gardner, Thomas Walton, C.H. Haderlie, Bishop Hyde, Bishop Bracken, Arthur F. Burton and Bishop Oz Low. The choir sang special selections, and Mark Hurd and Thomas Burton sang a duet. The tabernacle was draped in white. There was an abundance of floral offerings both in the hall and on the casket.

After the services the remains were taken back to the home and will be taken to Bloomington today and funeral services held tomorrow in the Bloomington meeting house, interment taking place in the cemetery there.

He leaves a large family and a legion of friends to mourn his loss.

CHILD 2 - John Osmond

Historical Note: The family history book "George Osmond and Family Pioneers" (1980's, p.1-2) states that George Osmond (1837-1913) had a "twin brother John" and that they "were born in London, England, May 23rd, 1836" [which could have been 1837]. Also, George Osmond "remembers the time his father brought home two broad rimmed sailor hats, the wind blew them off and the boys, George and John, ran down the street after them. At the age of seven, the boys had measles which caused the death of John. George tells of the night when their nice new house burned to the ground and all that was saved was John's body. George indicates in his diary that he knew and associated with the other children as he refers to his sister Rosebelle and his brothers Henry and James. He mentions their being together as children but details are lacking."

Research Note, May-September 2008:

Some family sources and the IGI have suggested that George Osmond (1836-1913) also had a twin brother, John Osmond. However, according to Lynne D. Osmond (of: 120 Alessandra Ct., Apt. 104, Frederick, MD., 21702-4022) there is "no evidence of a twin to George Osmond (1836-1913). ...I think--but will never be able to prove--that there was a John Flight, and he and George Osmond were brought up together and have been referred to [by some family members] as twins."

LDS Ordinance Report:

Genealogical information about John Osmond is listed in FHL Film # 457501 (Special Collections), and was supplied in the late 1950's by Lucy Osmond (of: 357 Center Street, Salt Lake City, Utah) based on information from James Arthur Osmond and from "correspondence [with] Somerset House, London, England". Lucy Osmond's record stated that John Osmond was born on 23 May 1836 in Hackney, London, and that he was a "twin" to George Osmond.

CERTIFIED COPY OF AN ENTRY OF DEATH

GIVEN AT THE **GENERAL REGISTER OFF**

Application Number 1608796-28

REGISTRATION DISTRICT					BICESTER UNION			
1860 DEATH in the Sub-district of Bicester					in the Counties of Oxford and Buckingham			

Columns:–	1	2	3	4	5	6	7	8	9
No.	When and where died	Name and surname	Sex	Age	Occupation	Cause of death	Signature, description and residence of informant	When registered	Signature of registrar
194	First December 1860 Sheep Street Bicester	George Osmond	Male	52 years	Solicitor	Diseased Bladder Exhaustion Certified	Sarah Shrewsbury Present at Death Sheep Street Bicester	Fifth December 1860	George Reynolds Registrar

CERTIFIED to be a true copy of an entry in the certified copy of a Register of Deaths in the District above mentioned.

Given at the GENERAL REGISTER OFFICE, under the Seal of the said Office, the 14th day of September 2009

DYC 446656

See note overleaf

CAUTION: THERE ARE OFFENCES RELATING TO FALSIFYING OR ALTERING A CERTIFICATE AND USING OR POSSESSING A FALSE CERTIFICATE

WARNING: A CERTIFICATE IS NOT EVIDENCE OF IDENTITY.

APJ

1013256 16847 10/08 3MSPSL 021426

Family Group Record

Husband	**Hanson Flight**				
Born	Abt 1807/1808	Place Stratford, Essex, England	LDS ordinance dates		Temple
Chr.		Place	Baptized	2 Sep 1955	
Died	29 Oct 1858	Place St. Mary, St. George in the East, Middlesex, England	Endowed	7 May 1957	
Buried		Place	SealPar	18 Jun 1970	SLAKE
Married	10 Jun 1827	Place St. Michael, Crooked Lane, London, London, England	SealSp	14 Mar 1979	IFALL
Other Spouse	Maria				
Married	Abt 1841	Place	SealSp	8 Jan 2010	MTIMP
Other Spouse	Martha Hopkinson				
Married	19 Aug 1858	Place St. Phillips, Bethnal Green, Middlesex, England	SealSp	8 Jan 2010	MTIMP
Husband's father	Joseph Flight				
Husband's mother	Jane Greenwood				
Wife	**Nancy Ann Canham**				
Born	12 Dec 1805	Place of Blackheath, London, England	LDS ordinance dates		Temple
Chr.	26 Jan 1806	Place St. Mary, Woolwich, Kent, England	Baptized	17 Jul 1937	
Died	5 Nov 1876	Place 17 Marlborough Place, Brighton, Sussex, England	Endowed	15 Sep 1937	
Buried	Nov 1876	Place Woodvale Cemetery, Brighton, Sussex, England	SealPar	25 Nov 1957	
Other Spouse	George (Sr.) Osmond				
Married		Place (This couple were never married)	SealSp	6 May 1939	LOGAN
Wife's father	George Canham				
Wife's mother	Elizabeth White				
Children	List each child in order of birth.		LDS ordinance dates		Temple
1 F	**Rosabella (Rosebelle) (Sarah Ann) Flight**				
Born	26 May 1841	Place Sheerness, Kent, England	Baptized	2 Sep 1955	
Chr.	20 Oct 1843	Place Church, Stepney, Middlesex, England	Endowed	10 Sep 1956	SLAKE
Died	21 Sep 1924	Place 70 Nightingale Road, Wood Green, Middlesex, England	SealPar	9 Mar 1960	SLAKE
Buried	Sep 1924	Place Woodvale Cemetery, Brighton, Sussex, England			
Spouse	Thomas Croker				
Married	12 Mar 1860	Place St. George The Martyr, Southwark, Surrey, England	SealSp	20 May 2009	OGDEN
2 M	**Robert Henry (Hy) Canham (Canhan) Flight**				
Born	21 Aug 1847	Place London, Middlesex, England	Baptized	2 Sep 1955	
Chr.	17 Feb 1869	Place St. Mary, Newington, Surrey, England	Endowed	7 May 1957	SLAKE
Died	10 May 1917	Place 3A Rymer Road, South Croydon, Croydon Co., England	SealPar	9 Mar 1960	SLAKE
Buried	May 1917	Place Woodvale Cemetery, Brighton, Sussex, England			
Spouse					
Married		Place	SealSp		

Notes

MARRIAGE

The marriage of Hanson Flight and Nancy Canham is listed in the parish register for St. Michael, Crooked Lane, London (FHL Film # 535713), which stated that the marriage was by "Licence" and took place on 10 June 1827, and that Hanson Flight was a Bachelor and Minor "of this parish" and that "Jane Flight [a] Widow [was the] natural mother of said [Hanson Flight, a] minor", and that Nancy Canham was a Spinster "of this parish of Greenwich in the County of Kent". The marriage was witnessed by John Eaton and Sarah Smith.

The on-line "London Examiner" newspaper--incorrectly dated as 16 March 1828--contains the following marriage announcement: "On the 10th instant [10 June 1827], at St. Michael's, Mr. Hansen Flight, second son of the late Mr. J. Flight, of Westham Abbey-mills, to Miss Ann Canham, of Blackheath, Kent".

In addition, this marriage is also listed in the IGI (via the LDS Extraction Program).

Some of the genealogical information on this individual(s) and/or event was provided by Lynne D. Osmond (2008): 120 Alessandra Ct., Apt. 104, Frederick, MD., 21702-4022 (Phone: 301-694-0056). Her Email: ct65as@yahoo.com.

HUSBAND - Hanson Flight

The birth and parentage of Hanson Flight is listed in the IGI (via Patron submission).

The death of Hanson Flight is listed in the on-line FreeBMD.

In February 2009, Mark E. Gardner obtained a copy of the death certificate of Hanson Flight from England, which stated that Hanson Flight died on 29 October 1858 at "15 Upper King Street" in "St. Mary in the Parish of St. George in the East" in the "County of Middlesex", England, at about the age of 50 years (born about 1808), and that his

Family Group Record

Husband **Hanson Flight**

Wife **Nancy Ann Canham**

Notes

HUSBAND - Hanson Flight (Continued)

occupation was "Collecting Clerk to a Draper", and that he died of "Cancer in the Neck, 8 months". The informant was Elizabeth Masters.

In the 1841 Census, Hanson Flight is listed as being about 30 years old (born about 1811), born in Middlesex, and working as a Draper, and residing with "Maria".

In the 1851 Census, Hanson Flight is listed as being about 44 years old (born about 1807), born in Stratford, Essex, and residing with his wife, Martha, and their daughter, Martha.

WIFE - Nancy Ann Canham

In the 1871 Census, "Anne Flight" is listed as being about 64 years old (born about 1807), born in Woolwich, Kent, a widow and lodger, who was living off "Income from rent of houses", and residing at: 60 Albion Hill, Brighton, Sussex, with Edward and Margarett Barns.

The death of "Nancy Flight" is listed in the on-line FreeBMD as having taken place during October-December 1876 in the district of Brighton (Volume 2b, Page 129).

The burial site of Nancy Ann Canham Flight is located in Woodvale Cemetery on Lewes Road in Brighton, Sussex, England. Nancy is buried in Plot # 17649 in Woodvale Cemetery. Unfortunately, no gravestone is visible as her plot area is now covered by grass (2009).

Research Note, April 2008: Mark E. Gardner, a professional genealogist, stated the following in April 2008: "George Osmond married in the Endowment House in Salt Lake City, Utah, on 31 October 1868, and stated at that time that he was the son of George Osmond and Nancy Ann Canham. This George we know was born out of wedlock. Nancy Ann Canham married Hanson Flight in 1828 and never married George Osmond. We actually find George with the last name of Flight in a later baptism record and in the 1851 British Census as learning a trade as a shipwright in the Woolwich area."

Research Note: The on-line FreeBMD contains the 1876 death listing of "Nancy Flight".

Historical Note: The family history book "George Osmond and Family Pioneers" (1980's, p.3) states that "George [Osmond's] mother Nancy [Canham], was fairly well educated and desired George should have a good education...."

Historical Note: The family history book "George Osmond and Family Pioneers" (1980's) states that when George Osmond (1837-1913) joined the LDS Church in 1850, his "relatives and friends all turned against him. His mother pleaded with him to give up this new strange religion, but to no avail. His relatives felt bitter toward him and accused him of disgracing the family name. ...To his surprise he [George Osmond] was never able to convert any of his relatives to the truth of the Gospel. ...It was said that George broke his mother's heart when he joined up with the 'Deluded Mormons.' He grieved to cause her sorrow, but he could not give up what he believed to be the truth. ... George gave up family and friends, financial security, and even his mother, who was living alone at the time he left to come to America [in 1854]. ...George parted from his relatives, his mother, his brothers and sister, in bitterness. They said, 'We don't want to see or hear from you until you have left the Mormons.' Records show that his mother soon repented and would have been happy to hear from her son in America" (pages 4-5). Also, in his LDS mission diary entry dated November 13, 1884, George Osmond wrote: "The trip to Brighton will remain in my memory as long as life lasts. I saw the house where my mother died. My brother and sister told me many anecdotes of her which proved that 'Her son in America' as she ever loved to call me, was always uppermost in her mind and affections. God bless her and grant that I may yet be able to prove to her how much I love her. I did not visit her grave. It may have been weakness, but I felt I would rather not."

CHILD 1 - Rosabella (Rosebelle) (Sarah Ann) Flight

In September 2009, Lynne Osmond stated the following: "I have suspected for years but have just come across the proof...[that] Rosabelle Flight and Sarah Ann Flight are the same person. Sarah Ann was christened at the same time

Husband	Hanson Flight
Wife	Nancy Ann Canham

Notes

CHILD 1 - Rosabella (Rosebelle) (Sarah Ann) Flight (Continued)

as George Canham Flight, [on] 20 October 1843, [and] her birth is listed as 26 May 1841. The London Births and Baptisms [registry for] 1813-1906, list Rosabelle Flight's adult baptism as 11 March 1860, one day before she married. Her birth is listed as 26 May 1841."

The birth and first christening of "Sarah Ann" Flight is listed in the parish register for Christ Church, Stepney, Middlesex, England, and in the Family History Library (Salt Lake City, Utah) CD for Christ Church, Stepney, Middlesex, England. According to the christening record, Sarah Ann Flight's parents were "Hanson and Ann Flight" and Hanson was a "Coal Merchant".

The second christening of "Rosabella an adult daughter of Hanson and Ann Flight" is listed in the parish register of St. Mary, Newington, Surrey, as provided by Mark E. Gardner, a professional genealogist in Salt Lake City, Utah, in November 2009. According to this christening record, Rosabella was christened on 11 March 1860, and born on 26 May 1841.

In the 1871 Census, Rosabelle (Corker) is listed as being about 29 years old (born about 1842), born in Bow, Middlesex, and residing with her husband, Thomas Croker in Brighton, Sussex.

In the 1881 Census, Rosabella Flight is listed as being about 39 years old (born about 1842), born in London, Middlesex, England, married and working as a "Manageress [in a] Boot Shop" while residing at 214 Western Road, Brighton, Sussex, England.

In the 1891 Census, Rosabella (Flight) Croker is listed as being about 49 years old (born about 1842), born in St. George in The East, Midlesex, married but residing with her brother, Robert H.C. Flight, at: 7 Bedford Hill Road, St. Mary, London, England.

In the 1901 Census, Rosabelle (Flight) Croker is listed as being about 59 years old (born about 1842), born in London, Middlesex, a "Widow" and "Living on own means" while residing with her brother, Robert Henry Canham Flight, at: 39 Egremont Place, St. Mary, Brighton, Sussex, England.

In February 2009, Mark E. Gardner obtained a copy of the death certificate of Rosabelle Croker from England, which stated that Rosabelle Croker died on 21 September 1924 at "70 Nightingale Road" in "Wood Green, Middlesex, England, at about the age of 83 years (born about 1841), and that her occupation was a "Widow of Thomas Croker, a Solicitor", and that she died of "Senile Decay [and] Cardiac disease". The informant was L. Riddell.

In December 2009, Lynne Osmond stated that "Robert Henry Canham Flight and Rosabelle [Flight] Croker are buried in the same grave as their mother Nancy, in Brighton."

The IGI (via patron submission) lists this individual as Rosabelle Flight, who was born about 1841 in Kent, England, and died on 21 September 1924 in Edmonton, London, England.

In February 2009, Mark E. Gardner obtained a copy of the marriage certificate of Thomas Croker and Rosabella Flight from England, which stated that they were married by Banns on 12 March 1863 at St. Judes church in the parish of St. George the Martyr in the country of Surrey, England, and that Thomas Croker was about 23 years old (born about 1837), a Bachelor and Clerk of 5 Richmond Terrace, and that his father was Joseph Croker, a Shipowner; and that Rosabella Flight was about 18 years old (born about 1845), a Spinster of 5 Richmond Terrace, and that her father was Hanson Flight, a Coal Merchant. The witnesses were George Canham and Martha Burton.

Historical Note: The family history book "George Osmond and Family Pioneers" (1980's, p.1-2) states that George Osmond (1837-1913) had a "twin brother John" and that they "were born in London, England, May 23rd, 1836". Also, George Osmond "remembers the time his father brought home two broad rimmed sailor hats, the wind blew them off and the boys, George and John, ran down the street after them. At the age of seven, the boys had measles which caused the death of John. George tells of the night when their nice new house burned to the ground and all that was

Husband **Hanson Flight**

Wife **Nancy Ann Canham**

Notes

CHILD 1 - Rosabella (Rosebelle) (Sarah Ann) Flight (Continued)

saved was John's body. George indicates in his diary that he knew and associated with the other children as he refers to his sister Rosebelle and his brothers Henry and James. He mentions their being together as children but details are lacking."

Historical Note: A copy of a letter send by "R.H.C. Flight" of "15 Wymdham Street, Marine Parade, Brighton, England", on "18 May 1897" to George Osmond (then in the United States) was published in the 1980's book "George Osmond and Family Pioneers", page 526. In the letter, R.H.C. Flight states that "Rosabelle and I are in fairly good health tho of course not feeling as young as we used to. We have been in Brighton some years and have a nice house a few doors from the sea and parade and are still engaged in letting apartments. ...I have sold the house at Balham that you saw us in...."

CHILD 2 - Robert Henry (Hy) Canham (Canhan) Flight

The birth and christening of Robert Henry Canham Flight is listed in the parish register of St. Mary, Newington, Surrey, as provided by Mark E. Gardner, a professional genealogist in Salt Lake City, Utah, in November 2009.

In September 2009, Lynne Osmond stated: "At [the parish church of] St. Mary, Newington, Surrey, the adult baptism of Robert Henry Canham Flight [is listed as], 17 February 1869, [and his] birth [as] 21 August 1847.

In the 1881 Census, Robert Hy. Flight is listed as being about 33 years old (born about 1848), born in London, Middlesex, England, unmarried and working as a "Solicitors Clerk, Unemployed" while residing at 214 Western Road, Brighton, Sussex, England.

In the 1891 Census, Robert H.C. Flight is listed as being about 45 years old (born about 1846), born in St. George in The East, Midlesex, single and "Living on own means" while residing with his sister, Rosabella (Flight) Croker, at: 7 Bedford Hill Road, St. Mary, London, England.

In the 1901 Census, "Robert Henry Canhan Flight" is listed as being about 54 years old (born about 1847), born in London, Middlesex, single and "Living on own means" while residing with his sister, Rosabella (Flight) Croker, at: 39 Egremont Place, St. Mary, Brighton, Sussex, England.

In February 2009, Mark E. Gardner obtained a copy of the death certificate of Robert Henry Canham Flight from England, which stated that Robert Henry Canham Flight died on 10 May 1917 at "3A Rymer Road" in "south Croydon, Croydon Co., England, at about the age of 68 years (born about 1849), and that his occupation was a "Solicitors Clerk" , and that he died of "Syncope from exastion with a dilated heart". The informant was Thomas Jackson, Coroner.

In December 2009, Lynne Osmond stated that "Robert Henry Canham Flight and Rosabelle [Flight] Croker are buried in the same grave as their mother Nancy, in Brighton."

Historical Note: A copy of a letter send by "R.H.C. Flight" of "15 Wymdham Street, Marine Parade, Brighton, England", on "18 May 1897" to George Osmond (then in the United States) was published in the 1980's book "George Osmond and Family Pioneers", page 526. In the letter, R.H.C. Flight states that "Rosabelle and I are in fairly good health tho of course not feeling as young as we used to. We have been in Brighton some years and have a nice house a few doors from the sea and parade and ar still engaged in letting apartments. ...I have sold the house at Balham that you saw us in...."

Family Group Record

Husband	George Osmond					
	Born		Place		LDS ordinance dates	Temple
	Chr.	15 Oct 1745	Place Bicester, Oxfordshire, England	Baptized	1 Nov 1977	PROVO
	Died	10 Oct 1821	Place Bicester, Oxfordshire, England	Endowed	22 Nov 1977	PROVO
	Buried	16 Oct 1821	Place Market End, Bicester, Oxfordshire, England	SealPar	25 Jan 1978	PROVO
	Married	25 Nov 1807	Place Bicester, Oxfordshire, England	SealSp	14 Mar 1972	LANGE
	Husband's father	George Osmond				
	Husband's mother	Mary Allen				
Wife	**Anne Phillips**					
	Born		Place		LDS ordinance dates	Temple
	Chr.	25 Jul 1779	Place Stoke Lyne, Oxfordshire, England	Baptized	19 Dec 1980	SGEOR
	Died	1842	Place Bicester, Oxfordshire, England	Endowed	18 Feb 1981	SGEOR
	Buried	4 May 1842	Place Market End, Bicester, Oxfordshire, England	SealPar	19 Feb 1981	SGEOR
	Wife's father	Joseph Phillips				
	Wife's mother	Hannah Ashton				
Children	List each child in order of birth.				LDS ordinance dates	Temple
1 M	**George (Sr.) Osmond**					
	Born		Place	Baptized	17 Jul 1937	
	Chr.	6 Mar 1808	Place Bicester, Oxfordshire, England	Endowed	15 Sep 1937	LOGAN
	Died	1 Dec 1860	Place Sheep Street, Market End, Bicester, Oxfordshire, England	SealPar	5 Aug 1977	LANGE
	Buried	6 Dec 1860	Place St. Edburg, Bicester, Oxfordshire, England			
	Spouse	Nancy Ann Canham				
	Married		Place (This couple were never married)	SealSp	6 May 1939	LOGAN
2 F	**Ann (Anne) Osmond**					
	Born		Place	Baptized	6 Feb 1971	LANGE
	Chr.	7 May 1809	Place Bicester, Oxfordshire, England	Endowed	8 Jun 1971	LANGE
	Died	15 Jul 1864	Place Weston-Super-Mare, Soms., England	SealPar	14 Mar 1972	LANGE
	Buried		Place			
	Spouse	George Osmond				
	Married	8 Sep 1832	Place Holy Trinity, Clapham, Surrey, England	SealSp	1 May 1980	MANTI
	Spouse	Wellington Ellis				
	Married	12 Sep 1840	Place Bicester, Oxfordshire, England	SealSp	20 Jan 1978	PROVO
3 M	**John Osmond**					
	Born		Place	Baptized	8 Jul 1977	LANGE
	Chr.	4 Jul 1811	Place Bicester, Oxfordshire, England	Endowed	5 Aug 1977	LANGE
	Died	23 Mar 1848	Place Sheep Street, Bicester, Oxfordshire, England	SealPar	22 Nov 1977	LANGE
	Buried	30 Mar 1848	Place Bicester, Oxfordshire, England			
	Spouse					
	Married		Place	SealSp		
4 M	**William Osmond**					
	Born	31 Aug 1814	Place Bicester, Oxfordshire, England	Baptized	11 Nov 1972	MANTI
	Chr.	1 Sep 1814	Place Bicester, Oxfordshire, England	Endowed	21 Mar 1973	MANTI
	Died	Bef Jun 1855	Place	SealPar	22 Mar 1973	MANTI
	Buried		Place			
	Spouse	Elizabeth Jarvis				
	Married	11 Sep 1837	Place St. Mary Magdalene, Woodstock, Oxfordshire, England	SealSp	27 Nov 2009	MTIMP

Notes

MARRIAGE

The marriage of George Osmond and Ann Phillips is listed in the "Oxfordshire Marriage Index: 1538-1837" by the Oxfordshire Family History Society, p.73, which states that this couple was married in Bicester on 25 December 1807.

HUSBAND - George Osmond

The christening of George Osmond is listed in the parish registers of Bicester (FHL Book #: British, 942.57/B1, K29ce, Vol.2, p.142), which states that he was christened on 15 October 1745.

The burial of George Osmond is listed in the parish registers of Bicester (FHL Book #: British, 942.57/B1, K29ce, Vol.2, p.181), which states that he was buried on 16 October 1821 at the age of 75 (born about 1746).

Research Notes Prior to 2008:

There was some question about his age when he married Ann PHILLIPS; however, the information is correct. He was about 62 when he married her.

Sources of information: 1. PRs Bicester, Oxford, Eng. (by corr). 2. CR for Death info. (by corr) 1842. 3. Will of

Husband **George Osmond**

Wife **Anne Phillips**

Notes

HUSBAND - George Osmond (Continued)

George Osmond 1860,PPR. 4. Death Record 1860 for child 1, George, at Bicester 5. Death Record 1864 for child 2, Mrs. Ann Ellis at Weston-Super-Mare.

Research Note: August 2009:

It appears that George Osmond (1745-1821) had several occupations during his life of 76 years. For example, he was listed as a "Draper" in the 1814 christening of his fourth child, William Osmond, and also on the 1842 death certificate of his wife, Ann. He was additionally listed as an "Esquire" in the 1821 newspaper account of his death (which appeared in the Jackson's Oxford Journal of October 13, 1821 and that read: "On Wednesday last, died at Bicester, in the 76th year of his age, George Osmond, Esq., who so fulfilled the duties of husband, father and friend, as to obtain the esteem of all who knew him"), and as a "Gentleman" in his Will which was proved on 2 January 1822 (FHL Film # 156244).

WIFE - Anne Phillips

Research Notes Prior to 2008:

Ann Phillips married George Osmond in Bicester parish Oxford county 25 November 1807 by license. George was much older than Ann. Ann was recorded in the marriage record as being a spinster of Bicester, yet no christening for her was found in the Bicester parish registers. However, her christening was located in the nearby parish of Stoke Lyne, 21 November 1779. Her parents were Joseph Phillips and Hannah Ashton.

In the 1841 Census, "Ann Osmond" is listed as being about 61 years old (born about 1780), born in Oxfordshire, England, and living "Ind"[ependently] with her son, George Osmond, an Attorney (about 30 years old) in Bicester, Oxfordshire, England.

In September 2009, the Osmond Family Organization obtained a copy of the death certificate of "Ann Osmond" from England, which stated that she died when she was about 64 years old from "Natural Decay" on 26 February 1842 in Market End, Bicester, and that she was the "Widow of George Osmond, [a] Draper". Also, although Anne left no will, an Administration was made dated 26 February 1842.

CHILD 1 - George (Sr.) Osmond

The christening of George Osmond is listed in the parish registers of Bicester (FHL Book #: British, 942.57/B1, K29ce, Vol.2, p.207), which states that he was christened on 6 March 1808 as "George [the] son [of] George and Ann Osmond".

In September 2009, the Osmond Family Organization of Utah obtained a copy of the death certificate of George Osmond from England, which stated that he died at the age of 52 years of "Diseased Bladder [and] Exhaustion" on 1 December 1860, at Sheep Street, Bicester, and that he was "Soliciter".

The burial of George (Sr.) Osmond is listed in the Monumental Inscriptions (published in April 1992) for St. Edburg, Bicester, Oxfordshire, England (FHL Microfiche # 6400193), and states that George Osmond was buried in plot # 273 and that (in 1992) his "tomb [was] half buried". The Monumental Inscription reads: "Sacred to the Memory of George Osmond Esq. who departed this life on the 1st day of December 1860. Aged 52 years." In 2009, the gravestone of George (Sr.) Osmond at St. Edburg, Bicester, Oxford, England, was located and photographed by Kathryn and Jim Stout (professional genealogists in Lancashire, England); and in 2010 the gravestone was visited and again photographed by James (Jimmy) A. Osmond (of Utah). Photographs of George Osmond's gravestone and other related items are in possession of the Osmond Family Organization of Utah.

In the 1841 Census, George Osmond is listed as being about 35 years old (born about 1807-1811), born in Oxfordshire, England, an "Attorney" and residing with his mother "Ann" (about 61 years old) in Bicester, Oxfordshire, England.

In the 1851 Census, George Osmond is listed as being about 44 years old (born about 1807), born in Bicester,

Family Group Record

Husband	George Osmond
Wife	Anne Phillips

Notes

CHILD 1 - George (Sr.) Osmond (Continued)

Oxfordshire, unmarried and working as a "Solicitor", while residing in the household of Wellington and Ann Ellis located at: 4 White Rock, St. Mary Magdalen, Hastings, Sussex, England.

Historical Note: The family history book "George Osmond and Family Pioneers" (1980's, p.2-3) states that George Osmond Jr.'s (1837-1913) "father was George Osmond, the attorney.... George Sr. was born in Bicester, Oxfordshire, England, and died December 1st, 1860, while residing at Sheep Street, Market End, Bicester, England.... Rumors are that the Osmond family was one of considerable wealth and high social standing. George Sr. seems to have alienated himself to some extent from the family traditions, perhaps a free spirit seeking self expression. Who knows. The records do not give the answer. Indications are that he was 'cut off' from what normally would have been his inheritance. Whether he ever received it or not is still in question. He, George Sr. apparently established a law practice at Bicester, as certain documents from that area bear his signature and reference is made to him in that capacity. It is said that he had a 'good bit' of money and we do find Nancy living in her own home and caring for her family, yet no reference is made to him at this time."

Historical Note: The family history book "George Osmond and Family Pioneers" (1980's) states that when George Osmond (1837-1913) joined the LDS Church in 1850, his "relatives and friends all turned against him. His mother pleaded with him to give up this new strange religion, but to no avail. His relatives felt bitter toward him and accused him of disgracing the family name. ...To his surprise he [George Osmond] was never able to convert any of his relatives to the truth of the Gospel. ...It was said that George broke his mother's heart when he joined up with the 'Deluded Mormons.' He grieved to cause her sorrow, but he could not give up what he believed to be the truth. ... George gave up family and friends, financial security, and even his mother, who was living alone at the time he left to come to America. ...George parted from his relatives, his mother, his brothers and sister, in bitterness. They said, 'We don't want to see or hear from you until you have left the Mormons.' Records show that his mother soon repented and would have been happy to hear from her son in America" (pages 4-5). Also, in his LDS mission diary entry dated November 13, 1884, George Osmond wrote: "The trip to Brighton will remain in my memory as long as life lasts. I saw the house where my mother died. My brother and sister told me many anecdotes of her which proved that 'Her son in America' as she ever loved to call me, was always uppermost in her mind and affections. God bless her and grant that I may yet be able to prove to her how much I love her. I did not visit her grave. It may have been weakness, but I felt I would rather not."

CHILD 2 - Ann (Anne) Osmond

The christening of Ann Osmond is listed in the parish registers of Bicester (FHL Book #: British, 942.57/B1, K29ce, Vol. 2, p.209), which states that she was christened on 7 May 1809.

CHILD 3 - John Osmond

The christening of John Osmond is listed in the parish registers of Bicester (FHL Book #: British, 942.57/B1, K29ce, Vol.2, p.212), which states that he was christened on 4 July 1811.

In September 2009, the Osmond Family Organization obtained a copy of the death certificate of John Osmond from England, which stated that he died at the age of 36 years from "Affliction of the Stomach" on 23 March 1848 at Sheep Street, Bicester, and that he was a "Surgeon".

Some of the genealogical information on this individual(s) and/or event was provided by Lynne D. Osmond (2008): 120 Alessandra Ct., Apt. 104, Frederick, MD., 21702-4022.

CHILD 4 - William Osmond

The christening of William Osmond is listed in the parish registers of Bicester (FHL Book #: British, 942.57/B1, K29ce, Vol.2, p.218), which states that he was christened on 1 September 1814 as "William [the] son [of] George and Ann Osmond, draper, b. Aug. 31".

In the 1841 Census, William Osmond is listed as being about 25 years old (born about 1816), born in Oxfordshire, working as a "Auctioneer", and residing with his wife, Elizabeth, and their one-year son, George, in Wendlebury,

Family Group Record

Husband **George Osmond**

Wife **Anne Phillips**

Notes

CHILD 4 - William Osmond (Continued)

Oxfordshire.

Research Note: In April 2008, Mark E. Gardner, a professional genealogist, stated that it appears that William Osmond and Elizabeth Jarvis had only one child--George Henry Osmond.

Research Note: In April 2008, Lynne D. Osmond (of: 120 Alessandra Ct., Apt. 104, Frederick, MD., 21702) stated that "George Henry Osmond's father was William Osmond, who I discovered come to the United States of America in 1852 and possibly naturalised in 1857, but I have found no further evidence of him."

CERTIFIED COPY OF AN ENTRY OF DEATH

GIVEN AT THE **GENERAL REGISTER OFF**

Application Number 1608796-26

REGISTRATION DISTRICT	BICESTER UNION
1842 DEATH in the Sub-district of Bicester	in the Counties of Oxford and Buckingham

Columns:– 1	2	3	4	5	6	7	8	9
No. When and where died	Name and surname	Sex	Age	Occupation	Cause of death	Signature, description and residence of informant	When registered	Signature of registrar
267 Twenty sixth February 1842 Bicester Market End	Ann Osmond	Female	64 years	Widow of George Osmond Draper	Natural Decay	Martha Scarsbrook Present at Death Bicester Market End	Fourth March 1842	Joseph Reynolds Registrar

CERTIFIED to be a true copy of an entry in the certified copy of a Register of Deaths in the District above mentioned.

Given at the GENERAL REGISTER OFFICE, under the Seal of the said Office, the 14th day of September 2009

DYC 446874

See note overleaf

WARNING: A CERTIFICATE IS NOT EVIDENCE OF IDENTITY.

1013256 16847 10/08 3MSPSL 021426

CM

Family Group Record

Husband George Osmond

			LDS ordinance dates	Temple
Born		Place		
Chr.	25 Dec 1716	Place Bicester, Oxfordshire, England	Baptized 1 Nov 1977	PROVO
Died	Jul 1754	Place Bicester, Oxfordshire, England	Endowed 22 Nov 1977	PROVO
Buried	16 Jul 1754	Place Bicester, Oxfordshire, England	SealPar 25 Jan 1977	PROVO
Married	26 Jun 1742	Place Bicester, Oxfordshire, England	SealSp 9 Nov 1990	LOGAN
Husband's father	John Osmund			
Husband's mother	Sarah Bly			

Wife Mary Allen

			LDS ordinance dates	Temple
Born		Place		
Chr.	12 Jun 1721	Place Bicester, Oxfordshire, England	Baptized 13 Jan 1979	LONDO
Died		Place	Endowed 6 Apr 1979	LONDO
Buried		Place	SealPar 10 May 1979	LONDO
Other Spouse	William White			
Married	10 Sep 1759	Place Bicester, Oxfordshire, England	SealSp 14 Mar 1972	LANGE
Wife's father	Thomas Allin			
Wife's mother	Elizabeth Wootten (Wotten)			

Children List each child in order of birth.

1 M **John Osmond**

			LDS ordinance dates	Temple
Born		Place	Baptized 1 Nov 1977	PROVO
Chr.	3 Dec 1743	Place Bicester, Oxfordshire, England	Endowed 22 Nov 1977	PROVO
Died		Place	SealPar 25 Jan 1978	PROVO
Buried	9 Oct 1805	Place Bicester, Oxfordshire, England		
Spouse	Elizabeth Phillips			
Married	19 May 1766	Place Blockley, Worcestershire, England	SealSp 1 Apr 2009	OGDEN
Spouse	Ann Tidmas			
Married	14 Aug 1799	Place Bourton-On-Dunsmore, Warwickshire, England	SealSp 14 Mar 1972	LANGE

2 M **George Osmond**

			LDS ordinance dates	Temple
Born		Place	Baptized 1 Nov 1977	PROVO
Chr.	15 Oct 1745	Place Bicester, Oxfordshire, England	Endowed 22 Nov 1977	PROVO
Died	10 Oct 1821	Place Bicester, Oxfordshire, England	SealPar 25 Jan 1978	PROVO
Buried	16 Oct 1821	Place Market End, Bicester, Oxfordshire, England		
Spouse	Anne Phillips			
Married	25 Nov 1807	Place Bicester, Oxfordshire, England	SealSp 14 Mar 1972	LANGE

3 F **Sarah Osmond**

			LDS ordinance dates	Temple
Born		Place	Baptized 20 Jan 1979	LONDO
Chr.	8 Aug 1748	Place Bicester, Oxfordshire, England	Endowed 11 Apr 1979	LONDO
Died		Place	SealPar 18 May 1979	LONDO
Buried		Place		
Spouse				
Married		Place	SealSp	

4 M **William Osmond**

			LDS ordinance dates	Temple
Born		Place	Baptized 6 Mar 1971	LANGE
Chr.	30 Jul 1750	Place Bicester, Oxfordshire, England	Endowed 22 Sep 1971	LANGE
Died		Place Wandsworth, Surrey, England	SealPar 15 Mar 1972	LANGE
Buried	7 Feb 1832	Place Bicester, Oxfordshire, England		
Spouse				
Married		Place	SealSp	

5 M **Thomas Osmond**

			LDS ordinance dates	Temple
Born		Place	Baptized 6 Mar 1971	LANGE
Chr.	8 Feb 1753	Place Bicester, Oxfordshire, England	Endowed 22 Sep 1971	LANGE
Died		Place	SealPar 15 Mar 1972	LANGE
Buried		Place		
Spouse	Mary			
Married	Abt 1788	Place of Oxford or Warwickshire, England	SealSp 11 Aug 2009	MTIMP

Notes

MARRIAGE

The marriage of George Osmond and Mary Allen is listed in the "Oxfordshire Marriage Index: 1538-1837" by the Oxfordshire Family History Society, p.29, which states that this couple was married in Bicester on 26 Jun 1742.

A copy of the marriage license of George Osmond and Mary Allen was published in the 1980's book: "George Osmond and Family Pioneers", on page 529.

Family Group Record

Husband **George Osmond**

Wife **Mary Allen**

Notes

HUSBAND - George Osmond

The christening of George Osmond is listed in the parish registers of Bicester (FHL Book #: British, 942.57/B1, K29ce, Vol.2, p.118), which states that he was christened on 25 Dec 1716.

The burial of George Osmond is listed in the parish registers of Bicester (FHL Book #: British, 942.57/B1, K29ce, Vol.2, p.124), which states that he was buried on 16 July 1754.

George Osmond was a "Butcher" and left a Probate Record in 1755 (FHL Book # 942.57, B40, V.61: Index to the probate records of the courts of the bishop and archdeacon of Oxford, 1733-1857 : and of the Oxfordshire peculiars, 1547-1856).

WIFE - Mary Allen

Research Notes Prior to 2008:
She married (second husband) William WHITE in 1759.
Marriage to George found in Biceseter parish transcripts -marriage FHL# 942.57/B1 K29c
Died young.

CHILD 1 - John Osmond

The christening of John Osmond is listed in the parish registers of Bicester (FHL Book #: British, 942.57/B1, K29ce, Vol.2, p.141), which states that he was christened on 3 December 1743.

The burial of John Osmond is listed in the parish registers of Bicester (FHL Book #: British, 942.57/B1, K29ce, Vol.2, p. 167), which states that he was buried on 9 October 1805.

Research Note: In August 2008, Lynne Osmond stated the following: "John Osmond, b.1743, of Chipping Norton, married Ann Tidmas at Bourton-On-Dunsmore, Warwickshire, in 1799 (Pallot's Marriage Index). This Ann "died [in 1853] at her residence, Peers-Row, St. Giles, in this city, aged 88 [born about 1765], Mrs. Ann Osmond, formerly of Forest Hill, in this county." (Oxford, from JOJ of Sat. Dec. 10th, 1853). In the 1851 Census she was living at 30, Peer's Row, aged 86, b. Wincott, Worcestershire. From the Osmondology paper, John was previously married to an Elizabeth who died in 1787, although I have no more info on her. John was a Bookseller in Chipping Norton (from Universal British Directory, 1791). On the 1841 Census, there is a John Osmond in Chipping Norton that I think may be the son of the above John and Elizabeth...."

Historical Notes taken from the 1980's book "George Osmond and Family Pioneers", p.523-524:

"29 September 1772 [taken from the Jackson's Oxford Journal]: Housebreaking: On Tuesday evening 29th September, the shop window belonging to Mr. John Osmand of Chipping Norton was broke open, and two large table spoons and eight paris of silver wrought shoe buckles were stolen. Whoever will give the said Mr. John Osmand information whereby the offending party may be convicted shall receive one guinea reward."

"5 June 1773 [taken from the Jackson's Oxford Journal]: We hear from Bicester that on Monday last the Friendly Society of that place met...and walked to church preceded by the Gentlemen of the Music Society. A Choir Service was performed and an excellent sermon preached.... The organ [was played] by Mr. John Osmond."

CHILD 2 - George Osmond

The christening of George Osmond is listed in the parish registers of Bicester (FHL Book #: British, 942.57/B1, K29ce, Vol.2, p.142), which states that he was christened on 15 October 1745.

The burial of George Osmond is listed in the parish registers of Bicester (FHL Book #: British, 942.57/B1, K29ce, Vol.2, p.181), which states that he was buried on 16 October 1821 at the age of 75 (born about 1746).

Research Notes Prior to 2008:

There was some question about his age when he married Ann PHILLIPS; however, the information is correct. He was about 62 when he married her.

Sources of information: 1. PRs Bicester, Oxford, Eng. (by corr). 2. CR for Death info. (by corr) 1842. 3. Will of

Family Group Record

Husband **George Osmond**

Wife **Mary Allen**

Notes

CHILD 2 - George Osmond (Continued)

George Osmond 1860,PPR. 4. Death Record 1860 for child 1, George, at Bicester 5. Death Record 1864 for child 2, Mrs. Ann Ellis at Weston-Super-Mare.

Research Note: August 2009:

It appears that George Osmond (1745-1821) had several occupations during his life of 76 years. For example, he was listed as a "Draper" in the 1814 christening of his fourth child, William Osmond, and also on the 1842 death certificate of his wife, Ann. He was additionally listed as an "Esquire" in the 1821 newspaper account of his death (which appeared in the Jackson's Oxford Journal of October 13, 1821 and that read: "On Wednesday last, died at Bicester, in the 76th year of his age, George Osmond, Esq., who so fulfilled the duties of husband, father and friend, as to obtain the esteem of all who knew him"), and as a "Gentleman" in his Will which was proved on 2 January 1822 (FHL Film # 156244).

CHILD 3 - Sarah Osmond

The christening of Sarah Osmond is listed in the parish registers of Bicester (FHL Book #: British, 942.57/B1, K29ce, Vol.2, p.145), which states that she was christened on 8 August 1748.

CHILD 4 - William Osmond

The christening of William Osmond is listed in the parish registers of Bicester (FHL Book #: British, 942.57/B1, K29ce, Vol.2, p.147), which states that he was christened on 30 July 1750.

The burial of William Osmond is listed in the parish registers of Bicester (FHL Book #: British, 942.57/B1, K29ce, Vol.2, p.192), which states that he was buried on 7 February 1832 at the age of 82 (born about 1750) and that he was "from Wandsworth in Surrey".

CHILD 5 - Thomas Osmond

The christening of Thomas Osmond is listed in the parish registers of Bicester (FHL Book #: British, 942.57/B1, K29ce, Vol.2, p.149), which states that he was christened on 8 February 1753.

In April-July 2008, Lynne D. Osmond (of: 120 Alessandra Ct., Apt. 104, Frederick, MD., 21702-4022;) stated the following: "Thomas Osmond b. 1753 in Bicester and the father of George Osmond b. 1793, settled in Coventry and was in business as a currier."

Family Group Record

Husband John Osmund

Born		Place		LDS ordinance dates	Temple
Chr.	29 Oct 1692	Place	Burford, Oxfordshire, England	Baptized 9 Jan 1993	PORTL
Died	10 Mar 1767	Place	Bicester, Oxfordshire, England	Endowed 9 Jan 1993	PORTL
Buried	13 Mar 1767	Place	Bicester, Oxfordshire, England	SealPar 1 Jun 1995	SLAKE
Married	5 Feb 1715	Place	Piddington, Oxfordshire, England	SealSp 24 Apr 1973	SLAKE
Other Spouse	Elizabeth Harding Cross				
Married	28 Feb 1730	Place	Bicester, Oxfordshire, England	SealSp 14 Mar 1972	LANGE
Husband's father	George Osmund				
Husband's mother	Mary King				

Wife Sarah Bly

Born		Place		LDS ordinance dates	Temple
Chr.	29 Oct 1688	Place	Piddington, Oxfordshire, England	Baptized 6 Jun 1986	PROVO
Died		Place		Endowed 5 Sep 1986	PROVO
Buried	16 Aug 1722	Place	Bicester, Oxfordshire, England	SealPar 6 Sep 1986	PROVO
Wife's father	John Bly				
Wife's mother	Joane (Johanna)				

Children List each child in order of birth.

LDS ordinance dates — Temple

1 M George Osmond

Born		Place		Baptized 1 Nov 1977	PROVO
Chr.	25 Dec 1716	Place	Bicester, Oxfordshire, England	Endowed 22 Nov 1977	PROVO
Died	Jul 1754	Place	Bicester, Oxfordshire, England	SealPar 25 Jan 1977	PROVO
Buried	16 Jul 1754	Place	Bicester, Oxfordshire, England		
Spouse	Mary Allen				
Married	26 Jun 1742	Place	Bicester, Oxfordshire, England	SealSp 9 Nov 1990	LOGAN

2 M John Osmond

Born		Place		Baptized Child	
Chr.	31 Mar 1718	Place	Bicester, Oxfordshire, England	Endowed Child	
Died		Place		SealPar 25 Jan 1978	PROVO
Buried	25 May 1720	Place	Bicester, Oxfordshire, England		
Spouse					
Married		Place		SealSp	

3 M William Osmond

Born		Place		Baptized Child	
Chr.	2 Oct 1719	Place	Bicester, Oxfordshire, England	Endowed Child	
Died		Place		SealPar 1 May 1986	PROVO
Buried	13 Mar 1719/1720	Place	Bicester, Oxfordshire, England		
Spouse					
Married		Place		SealSp	

4 F Sarah Osmond

Born		Place		Baptized 1 Nov 1977	PROVO
Chr.	16 Sep 1721	Place	Bicester, Oxfordshire, England	Endowed 29 Nov 1977	PROVO
Died		Place		SealPar 25 Jan 1978	PROVO
Buried	22 Apr 1753	Place	Bicester, Oxfordshire, England		
Spouse					
Married		Place		SealSp	

Notes

MARRIAGE

The marriage of John Osmond and Sarah Bly is listed in the "Oxfordshire Marriage Index: 1538-1837" by the Oxfordshire Family History Society, p.139, which states that this couple was married in Piddington on 5 February 1715, and that John Osmond was of Caversfield, and Sarah Bly was of Bicester.

This marriage (with the year only) is listed in the IGI.

HUSBAND - John Osmund

The christening of John Osmund is listed in the parish register of Burford (FHL Microfiche # 6142017, Part 2 of 6, Baptisms for the period 1661-1709), which states that he was christened on 29 October 1692 as "Osmund, John s. o. George".

The burial of John Osmund is listed in the parish registers of Bicester (FHL Book #: British, 942.57/B1, K29ce, Vol.2, p. 135), which states that he was buried on 13 March 1767.

Family Group Record

Husband	John Osmund
Wife	Sarah Bly

Notes

HUSBAND - John Osmund (Continued)

Research Notes Prior to 2008:

Will dated 3 Sep 1766 - proved 20 Mar 1767 (Arch of Oxford). Information that his wife was Sarah Bly - that he had a sister, Mary who married a Mr. Brown. Mary his sister received cottages in the parish of Burford.

Parish records Bicester, Oxfordshire, England(by corr). 2.

Will of husband dated 3 Sep 1766, Proved 20 May 1767.

Will dated 3 Sep 1766; Proved 20 May 1767. (John Osmond)

Research Note, April 2008:

The Will of John Osmund (FHL Film # 95082) states that he was a "Gentleman", and that he had a half-sister by the name of Mary Brown--who was probably Mary Butler who was christened in 1702 and who later married a Mr. Brown.

Historical Notes taken from the 1980's book "George Osmond and Family Pioneers", p.523:

"Friday, 21 January 1757 [taken from the Jackson's Oxford Journal]: We hear from Burford in this County, that on Friday the 21st Instant, John Osman, Isaac Coburn, Stephen Palmer, William Beechy, William Wickens, Thomas Roaf, Simon Jeffs, and Thomas May, rung the Whole Peal of Grandshire Triples [or the ringing of church bells], five thousand and forty Changes in three hours and eighteen minutes, a thing never before performed in that Town."

"Tuesday, 10 March 1767 [taken from the Jackson's Oxford Journal]: Last Tuesday morning died at Bicester in this County, aged 74, Mr. John Osmond, formerly an eminent Butcher of that Place, in which Business he had acquired an ample fortune and had retired from Trade many Years. He was greatly esteemed for the Honesty of his Dealings: and what was very much to his Honour, was universally acknowledged to be remarkably clean in his business."

WIFE - Sarah Bly

The burial of Sarah (Osmond) John Osmond is listed in the parish registers of Bicester (FHL Book #: British, 942.57/B1, K29ce, Vol.2, p.96), which states that "Sarah [the] wife [of] John Osmond" was buried on 16 August 1722.

CHILD 1 - George Osmond

The christening of George Osmond is listed in the parish registers of Bicester (FHL Book #: British, 942.57/B1, K29ce, Vol.2, p.118), which states that he was christened on 25 Dec 1716.

The burial of George Osmond is listed in the parish registers of Bicester (FHL Book #: British, 942.57/B1, K29ce, Vol.2, p.124), which states that he was buried on 16 July 1754.

George Osmond was a "Butcher" and left a Probate Record in 1755 (FHL Book # 942.57, B40, V.61: Index to the probate records of the courts of the bishop and archdeacon of Oxford, 1733-1857 : and of the Oxfordshire peculiars, 1547-1856).

CHILD 2 - John Osmond

The christening of John Osmond is listed in the parish registers of Bicester (FHL Book #: British, 942.57/B1, K29ce, Vol.2, p.119), which states that he was christened on 31 March 1718.

CHILD 3 - William Osmond

The christening of William Osmond is listed in the parish registers of Bicester (FHL Book #: British, 942.57/B1, K29ce, Vol.2, p.120), which states that he was christened on 2 October 1719.

CHILD 4 - Sarah Osmond

The christening of Sarah Osmond is listed in the parish registers of Bicester (FHL Book #: British, 942.57/B1, K29ce, Vol.2, p.122), which states that she was christened on 16 September 1721. In addition, the register states "BT has " Osborne", PR had Osborn crossed out and inserted 'Osmond'."

The burial of Sarah Osmond is listed in the parish registers of Bicester (FHL Book #: British, 942.57/B1, K29ce, Vol.2, p.123), which states that "Sarah [the] daughter [of] John Osmond" was buried on 22 April 1753.

Family Group Record

Husband George Osmund

Born		Place		LDS ordinance dates		Temple
Chr.	21 Feb 1663	Place	Burford, Oxfordshire, England	Baptized	9 Jan 1993	PORTL
Died		Place		Endowed	9 Jan 1993	PORTL
Buried	15 Jan 1694	Place	Burford, Oxfordshire, England	SealPar	18 Mar 1993	PORTL
Married	16 Nov 1691	Place	Burford, Oxfordshire, England	SealSp	7 Dec 1993	PORTL
Husband's father	John Osmund					
Husband's mother	Joane Wicks					

Wife Mary King

Born		Place		LDS ordinance dates		Temple
Chr.	13 Mar 1665	Place	Burford, Oxfordshire, England	Baptized	26 Feb 1998	PROVO
Died		Place		Endowed	21 Oct 1998	PROVO
Buried		Place		SealPar	25 Jun 1999	ARIZO
Other Spouse	Edward (Jr.) Butler (Butller)					
Married	2 Feb 1701	Place	Oddington, Oxford, England	SealSp	2 May 2008	MTIMP
Wife's father	William (Jr.) King					
Wife's mother						

Children List each child in order of birth. — LDS ordinance dates — Temple

1 M **John Osmund**

Born		Place		Baptized	9 Jan 1993	PORTL
Chr.	29 Oct 1692	Place	Burford, Oxfordshire, England	Endowed	9 Jan 1993	PORTL
Died	10 Mar 1767	Place	Bicester, Oxfordshire, England	SealPar	1 Jun 1995	SLAKE
Buried	13 Mar 1767	Place	Bicester, Oxfordshire, England			
Spouse	Sarah Bly					
Married	5 Feb 1715	Place	Piddington, Oxfordshire, England	SealSp	24 Apr 1973	SLAKE
Spouse	Elizabeth Harding Cross					
Married	28 Feb 1730	Place	Bicester, Oxfordshire, England	SealSp	14 Mar 1972	LANGE

2 M **George Osmund**

Born		Place		Baptized	Child	
Chr.	2 Sep 1694	Place	Burford, Oxfordshire, England	Endowed	Child	
Died		Place		SealPar	18 Mar 1993	PORTL
Buried	7 Dec 1694	Place	Burford, Oxfordshire, England			
Spouse						
Married		Place		SealSp		

Notes

MARRIAGE

The marriage of George Osmun and Mary King is listed in the parish register of Burford (FHL Microfiche # 6142017, Part 3 of 6, Marriages 1620 to 1714), which states that they were married on 16 November 1691 as "George Osmun and Mary King".

HUSBAND - George Osmund

The christening of George Osmund is listed in the parish register of Burford (FHL Microfiche # 6142017, Part 2 of 6, Baptisms for the period 1661-1709), which states that he was christened on 21 February 1663 as "Osmund, George s. o. John O. jun".

The burial of George Osmund is listed in the parish register of Burford (FHL Microfiche # 6142017, Part 4 of 6, Burials for the period 1630-1695), which states that he was buried on 15 January 1694 as "Osmund, George".

WIFE - Mary King

The christening of Mary King is listed in the IGI.

The christening of Mary King is listed in the Burford Parish Register (FHL Microfiche # 6142017).

Mary King is the first person who married an Osmond in Bicester, Oxford, and was the first "Osmond" mentioned in Bicester with the surname of Butler.

CHILD 1 - John Osmund

The christening of John Osmund is listed in the parish register of Burford (FHL Microfiche # 6142017, Part 2 of 6, Baptisms for the period 1661-1709), which states that he was christened on 29 October 1692 as "Osmund, John s. o. George".

Family Group Record

Husband	George Osmund
Wife	Mary King

Notes

CHILD 1 - John Osmund (Continued)

The burial of John Osmund is listed in the parish registers of Bicester (FHL Book #: British, 942.57/B1, K29ce, Vol.2, p. 135), which states that he was buried on 13 March 1767.

Research Notes Prior to 2008:

Will dated 3 Sep 1766 - proved 20 Mar 1767 (Arch of Oxford). Information that his wife was Sarah Bly - that he had a sister, Mary who married a Mr. Brown. Mary his sister received cottages in the parish of Burford.

Parish records Bicester, Oxfordshire, England(by corr). 2.

Will of husband dated 3 Sep 1766, Proved 20 May 1767.

Will dated 3 Sep 1766; Proved 20 May 1767. (John Osmond)

Research Note, April 2008:

The Will of John Osmund (FHL Film # 95082) states that he was a "Gentleman", and that he had a half-sister by the name of Mary Brown--who was probably Mary Butler who was christened in 1702 and who later married a Mr. Brown.

Historical Notes taken from the 1980's book "George Osmond and Family Pioneers", p.523:

"Friday, 21 January 1757 [taken from the Jackson's Oxford Journal]: We hear from Burford in this County, that on Friday the 21st Instant, John Osman, Isaac Coburn, Stephen Palmer, William Beechy, William Wickens, Thomas Roaf, Simon Jeffs, and Thomas May, rung the Whole Peal of Grandshire Triples [or the ringing of church bells], five thousand and forty Changes in three hours and eighteen minutes, a thing never before performed in that Town."

"Tuesday, 10 March 1767 [taken from the Jackson's Oxford Journal]: Last Tuesday morning died at Bicester in this County, aged 74, Mr. John Osmond, formerly an eminent Butcher of that Place, in which Business he had acquired an ample fortune and had retired from Trade many Years. He was greatly esteemed for the Honesty of his Dealings: and what was very much to his Honour, was universally acknowledged to be remarkably clean in his business."

CHILD 2 - George Osmund

The christening of George Osmund is listed in the parish register of Burford (FHL Microfiche # 6142017, Part 2 of 6, Baptisms for the period 1661-1709), which states that he was christened on 2 September 1694 as "Osmund, George s. o. George".

The burial of George Osmund is listed in the Burford Parish Register (FHL Microfiche # 6142017, Part 4 of 6, Burials for the period 1630-1695), which states that he was buried on 7 December 1694 as "Osmund, George, ch. o. George".

Family Group Record

Husband John Osmund

				LDS ordinance dates		Temple
Born		Place				
Chr.	14 Feb 1635	Place	Burford, Oxfordshire, England	Baptized	9 Jan 1993	PORTL
Died		Place		Endowed	9 Jan 1993	PORTL
Buried		Place		SealPar	18 Mar 1993	PORTL
Married	15 Oct 1660	Place	Burford, Oxfordshire, England	SealSp	24 Apr 1973	SLAKE
Husband's father	John Osmund					
Husband's mother	Elizabethe Bery					

Wife Joane Wicks

				LDS ordinance dates		Temple
Born	Abt 1638	Place	of Burford, Oxfordshire, England			
Chr.		Place		Baptized	13 Feb 1993	PORTL
Died		Place		Endowed	22 Jan 1994	PORTL
Buried		Place		SealPar		
Wife's father						
Wife's mother						

Children List each child in order of birth.

1 M **George Osmund**

				LDS ordinance dates		Temple
Born		Place		Baptized	9 Jan 1993	PORTL
Chr.	21 Feb 1663	Place	Burford, Oxfordshire, England	Endowed	9 Jan 1993	PORTL
Died		Place		SealPar	18 Mar 1993	PORTL
Buried	15 Jan 1694	Place	Burford, Oxfordshire, England			
Spouse	Mary King					
Married	16 Nov 1691	Place	Burford, Oxfordshire, England	SealSp	7 Dec 1993	PORTL

2 M **John Osmond**

				LDS ordinance dates		Temple
Born		Place		Baptized	9 Jan 1993	PORTL
Chr.	16 Apr 1666	Place	Burford, Oxfordshire, England	Endowed	9 Jan 1993	PORTL
Died		Place		SealPar	18 Mar 1993	PORTL
Buried		Place				
Spouse	Katharine Pattin					
Married	12 Oct 1714	Place	Burford, Oxfordshire, England	SealSp	24 Apr 1973	SLAKE

Notes

MARRIAGE

The marriage of John Osman and Joane Wicks is listed in the parish register of Burford (FHL Microfiche # 6142017, Part 3 of 6, Marriages 1620 to 1714), which states that they were married on 15 October 1660 as "John Osman and Joane Wicks".

HUSBAND - John Osmund

The christening of John Osmund is listed in the parish register of Burford (FHL Microfiche # 6142017, Part 1 of 6, Baptisms for the period 1612-1660), which states that he was christened on 14 February 1635 as "Osmund, John, s. o. John".

John Osmund's occupation was that of a "Slatter", and he was called a "jun" (or junior) in one of the christenings of his two sons.

CHILD 1 - George Osmund

The christening of George Osmund is listed in the parish register of Burford (FHL Microfiche # 6142017, Part 2 of 6, Baptisms for the period 1661-1709), which states that he was christened on 21 February 1663 as "Osmund, George s. o. John O. jun".

The burial of George Osmund is listed in the parish register of Burford (FHL Microfiche # 6142017, Part 4 of 6, Burials for the period 1630-1695), which states that he was buried on 15 January 1694 as "Osmund, George".

CHILD 2 - John Osmond

The christening of John Osmond is listed in the parish register of Burford (FHL Microfiche # 6142017, Part 2 of 6, Baptisms for the period 1661-1709), which states that he was christened on 16 April 1666 as "Osmond, John s. o. John O. [a] Slatter".

Family Group Record

Husband John Osmund

Born	Abt 1604	Place of Burford, Oxfordshire, England	LDS ordinance dates	Temple
Chr.		Place	Baptized 9 Jan 1993	PORTL
Died		Place	Endowed 9 Jan 1993	PORTL
Buried	4 Mar 1664/1665	Place Burford, Oxfordshire, England	SealPar 18 Mar 1993	PORTL
Married	14 Oct 1629	Place Burford, Oxfordshire, England	SealSp 24 Apr 1973	SLAKE
Husband's father	John Osmund			
Husband's mother	Alice			

Wife Elizabethe Bery

Born		Place	LDS ordinance dates	Temple
Chr.	2 Oct 1598	Place Brize Norton, Oxford, England	Baptized 9 Jul 1982	LOGAN
Died		Place	Endowed 18 Sep 1982	LOGAN
Buried	5 Mar 1667	Place Burford, Oxfordshire, England	SealPar 3 Dec 1982	LOGAN
Wife's father	Franncis Berye			
Wife's mother				

Children List each child in order of birth. — LDS ordinance dates — Temple

1 F **Ann Osmonde**

Born		Place	Baptized 23 Jan 1993	PORTL
Chr.	30 Sep 1628	Place Burford, Oxfordshire, England	Endowed 27 Jan 1993	PORTL
Died		Place	SealPar 15 Apr 1993	PORTL
Buried		Place		
Spouse	Simon Hayter			
Married	21 Jun 1658	Place Burford, Oxfordshire, England	SealSp 16 Jul 2010	MTIMP

2 M **Frances Osman**

Born		Place	Baptized 9 Jan 1993	PORTL
Chr.	24 Jan 1629/1630	Place Burford, Oxfordshire, England	Endowed 9 Jan 1993	PORTL
Died		Place	SealPar 13 Jan 1994	PORTL
Buried	30 Dec 1655	Place Burford, Oxfordshire, England		
Spouse	Joane Freeman			
Married	27 Feb 1653	Place Burford, Oxfordshire, England	SealSp 13 Jan 1994	PORTL

3 F **Elizabeth Osman**

Born	Bef 28 Mar 1630	Place of Burford, Oxfordshire, England	Baptized Child	
Chr.		Place	Endowed Child	
Died		Place	SealPar 16 Jul 2010	MTIMP
Buried	28 Mar 1630	Place Burford, Oxfordshire, England		
Spouse				
Married		Place	SealSp	

4 F **Jane Osman**

Born		Place	Baptized Child	
Chr.	21 Feb 1631	Place Burford, Oxfordshire, England	Endowed Child	
Died		Place	SealPar 7 Dec 1993	PORTL
Buried	22 Feb 1631	Place Burford, Oxfordshire, England		
Spouse				
Married		Place	SealSp	

5 F **Margery Osman**

Born		Place	Baptized Child	
Chr.	21 Feb 1631	Place Burford, Oxfordshire, England	Endowed Child	
Died		Place	SealPar 7 Dec 1993	PORTL
Buried	22 Feb 1631	Place Burford, Oxfordshire, England		
Spouse				
Married		Place	SealSp	

6 F **Jane Osmund**

Born		Place	Baptized 23 Jan 1993	PORTL
Chr.	26 May 1633	Place Burford, Oxfordshire, England	Endowed 27 Jan 1993	PORTL
Died		Place	SealPar 15 Apr 1993	PORTL
Buried	23 May 1695	Place Burford, Oxfordshire, England		
Spouse				
Married		Place	SealSp	

7 M **John Osmund**

Born		Place	Baptized 9 Jan 1993	PORTL
Chr.	14 Feb 1635	Place Burford, Oxfordshire, England	Endowed 9 Jan 1993	PORTL
Died		Place	SealPar 18 Mar 1993	PORTL
Buried		Place		
Spouse	Joane Wicks			
Married	15 Oct 1660	Place Burford, Oxfordshire, England	SealSp 24 Apr 1973	SLAKE

26 Jul 2010

Family Group Record

Husband	John Osmund				
Wife	Elizabethe Bery				
Children	List each child in order of birth.			LDS ordinance dates	Temple
8 M	Robert Osmund				
Born		Place		Baptized 9 Jan 1993	PORTL
Chr.	2 Sep 1638	Place	Burford, Oxfordshire, England	Endowed 22 Jan 1994	PORTL
Died		Place		SealPar 22 Jan 1994	PORTL
Buried		Place			
Spouse					
Married		Place		SealSp	

Notes

MARRIAGE

The marriage of John Osmond and Elizabeth Bery is listed in the parish register of Burford (FHL Microfiche # 6142017, Part 3 of 6, Marriages 1620 to 1714), which states that they were married on 14 October 1629 as "John Osmond and Elizabeth Bery" and "by license from Doctor Barker".

The marriage of John Osmond and Elizabeth Bery is listed in the "Oxfordshire Marriage Index: 1538-1837" by the Oxfordshire Family History Society, p.103, which states that this couple was married in Burford on 14 October 1629.

This marriage is listed in the IGI, which contains the following information: "Record extracted from Oxfordshire Marriage Transcripts, 1538-1837, compiled by J. S. W. Gibson. (The index was based on the groom index, film numbers 54,396 to 54,397.)"

HUSBAND - John Osmund

Christening records for Burford begin in 1612. However, the early parish records of Burford (FHL Microfiche # 6142017, Parts 1 through 6) and the patronymics (or naming patterns) of Osmond descendants were used in determining the possible parentage and approximate birth year of John Osmund.

The burial of John Osmund is listed in the parish register of Burford (FHL Microfiche # 6142017, Part 4 of 6, Burials for the period 1630-1695), which states that he was buried on 4 March 1664 as "Osmund, John, an old man".

WIFE - Elizabethe Bery

The burial of Elizabeth (Osman) is listed in the parish register of Burford (FHL Microfiche # 6142017, Part 4 of 6, Burials for the period 1630-1695), which states that she was buried on 5 Mar 1667 as "Osman, Eliz. wid. aged.".

The christening is listed in the IGI (via the LDS Extraction Program).

CHILD 1 - Ann Osmonde

The christening of Ann Osmonde is listed in the parish register of Burford (FHL Microfiche # 6142017, Part 1 of 6, Baptisms for the period 1612-1660), which states that she was christened on 30 September 1628 as "Osmonde, Ann d. o. John".

CHILD 2 - Frances Osman

The christening of Ann Osmonde is listed in the parish register of Burford (FHL Microfiche # 6142017, Part 1 of 6, Baptisms for the period 1612-1660), which states that he was christened on 24 January 1629 as "Osman, Francis s. o. John". However, the IGI lists Frances Osman as being christened on 24 January 1630.

The burial of Francis Osman is listed in the parish register of Burford (FHL Microfiche # 6142017, Part 4 of 6, Burials for the period 1630-1695), which states that he was buried on 30 December 1655 as "Osman, Francis".

CHILD 3 - Elizabeth Osman

The burial of Elizabeth Osman is listed in the parish register of Burford (FHL Microfiche # 6142017, Part 3 of 6, Burials for the period 1614-1630), which states that she was buried on 28 March 1630 as "Osman, Elizabeth d. o. John".

Family Group Record

Husband **John Osmund**

Wife **Elizabethe Bery**

Notes

CHILD 4 - Jane Osman

The christening of Jane Osman is listed in the parish register of Burford (FHL Microfiche # 6142017, Part 1 of 6, Baptisms for the period 1612-1660), which states that she was christened on 21 February 1631 as "Osman, Jane and Margery dd. o. John O".

The burial of Jane Osman is listed in the parish register of Burford (FHL Microfiche # 6142017, Part 4 of 6, Burials for the period 1630-1695), which states that she was buried on 22 February 1631 as "Osman, Jane and Margery dd. o. John".

CHILD 5 - Margery Osman

The christening of Margery Osman is listed in the parish register of Burford (FHL Microfiche # 6142017, Part 1 of 6, Baptisms for the period 1612-1660), which states that she was christened on 21 February 1631 as "Osman, Jane and Margery dd. o. John O".

The burial of Margery Osman is listed in the parish register of Burford (FHL Microfiche # 6142017, Part 4 of 6, Burials for the period 1630-1695), which states that she was buried on 22 February 1631 as "Osman, Jane and Margery dd. o. John".

CHILD 6 - Jane Osmund

The christening of Jane Osmund is listed in the parish register of Burford (FHL Microfiche # 6142017, Part 1 of 6, Baptisms for the period 1612-1660), which states that she was christened on 26 May 1633 as "Osmund, Jane, d. o. John".

The burial of Jane Osmun is listed in the parish register of Burford (FHL Microfiche # 6142017, Part 4 of 6, Burials for the period 1630-1695), which states that she was buried on 23 May 1695 as "Osmun, Jane, an aged maid".

CHILD 7 - John Osmund

The christening of John Osmund is listed in the parish register of Burford (FHL Microfiche # 6142017, Part 1 of 6, Baptisms for the period 1612-1660), which states that he was christened on 14 February 1635 as "Osmund, John, s. o. John".

John Osmund's occupation was that of a "Slatter", and he was called a "jun" (or junior) in one of the christenings of his two sons.

CHILD 8 - Robert Osmund

The christening of Robert Osmund is listed in the parish register of Burford (FHL Microfiche # 6142017, Part 1 of 6, Baptisms for the period 1612-1660), which states that he was christened on 2 September 1638 as "Osmund, Robert s. o. John".

Family Group Record

Husband John Osmund

	Date	Place	LDS ordinance dates		Temple
Born	Abt 1575	of Burford, Oxfordshire, England			
Chr.			Baptized	9 Jan 1993	PORTL
Died			Endowed	12 Jun 1993	PORTL
Buried	5 Oct 1633	Burford, Oxfordshire, England	SealPar		
Married	Abt 1598	of Burford, Oxfordshire, England	SealSp	16 Jul 2010	MTIMP
Husband's father					
Husband's mother					

Wife Alice

	Date	Place	LDS ordinance dates		Temple
Born	Abt 1577	of Burford, Oxfordshire, England			
Chr.			Baptized	17 Jul 2010	MTIMP
Died			Endowed	20 Jul 2010	MTIMP
Buried	1 May 1654	Burford, Oxfordshire, England	SealPar		
Wife's father					
Wife's mother					

Children List each child in order of birth.

1 F **Elizabeth Osmande**

	Date	Place	LDS ordinance dates		Temple
Born	Abt 1599	of Burford, Oxfordshire, England	Baptized	16 Jul 2010	MTIMP
Chr.			Endowed	20 Jul 2010	MTIMP
Died			SealPar	20 Jul 2010	MTIMP
Buried					
Spouse	John Baker				
Married	20 Jul 1620	Burford, Oxfordshire, England	SealSp	24 Apr 1973	LOGAN

2 F **Priscilla Osmand**

	Date	Place	LDS ordinance dates		Temple
Born	Abt 1602	of Burford, Oxfordshire, England	Baptized	16 Jul 2010	MTIMP
Chr.			Endowed	20 Jul 2010	MTIMP
Died			SealPar	20 Jul 2010	MTIMP
Buried					
Spouse	Alselme Blanche				
Married	19 Jan 1628	Burford, Oxfordshire, England	SealSp	16 Jul 2010	MTIMP

3 M **John Osmund**

	Date	Place	LDS ordinance dates		Temple
Born	Abt 1604	of Burford, Oxfordshire, England	Baptized	9 Jan 1993	PORTL
Chr.			Endowed	9 Jan 1993	PORTL
Died			SealPar	18 Mar 1993	PORTL
Buried	4 Mar 1664/1665	Burford, Oxfordshire, England			
Spouse	Elizabethe Bery				
Married	14 Oct 1629	Burford, Oxfordshire, England	SealSp	24 Apr 1973	SLAKE

4 M **Thomas Osmund**

	Date	Place	LDS ordinance dates		Temple
Born	Abt 1606	of Burford, Oxfordshire, England	Baptized	9 Jan 1993	PORTL
Chr.			Endowed	9 Jan 1993	PORTL
Died			SealPar	18 Mar 1993	PORTL
Buried	30 Sep 1675	Burford, Oxfordshire, England			
Spouse	Mrs. Thomas Osmund				
Married	Abt 1628	of Burford, Oxfordshire, England	SealSp	16 Jul 2010	MTIMP

5 F **Alice Osman**

	Date	Place	LDS ordinance dates		Temple
Born	Abt 1608	of Burford, Oxfordshire, England	Baptized	16 Jul 2010	MTIMP
Chr.			Endowed	20 Jul 2010	MTIMP
Died			SealPar	20 Jul 2010	MTIMP
Buried					
Spouse	Zacharie Jellyman				
Married	25 Jun 1639	Burford, Oxfordshire, England	SealSp	14 May 1973	SLAKE

6 F **Susan Osman**

	Date	Place	LDS ordinance dates		Temple
Born	Abt 1610	of Burford, Oxfordshire, England	Baptized	16 Jul 2010	MTIMP
Chr.			Endowed	20 Jul 2010	MTIMP
Died			SealPar	20 Jul 2010	MTIMP
Buried					
Spouse	Thomas Daniel				
Married	3 May 1640	Burford, Oxfordshire, England	SealSp	5 Jul 1973	LOGAN

Notes

HUSBAND - John Osmund

The burial of John Osmund is listed in the parish register of Burford (FHL Microfiche # 6142017, Part 4 of 6, Burials for the period 1630-1695), which states that he was buried on 5 October 1633 as "Osmund, John O., Sen., a very poore man".

Family Group Record

Husband **John Osmund**

Wife **Alice**

Notes

WIFE - Alice

The burial of Alice (Osmund) is listed in the parish register of Burford (FHL Microfiche # 6142017, Part 4 of 6, Burials for the period 1630-1695), which states that she was buried on 1 May 1654 as "Osman, Alice, wid [widow]".

CHILD 1 - Elizabeth Osmande

Christening records for Burford begin in 1612. However, the early parish records of Burford (FHL Microfiche # 6142017, Parts 1 through 6) and the patronymics (or naming patterns) of Osmond descendants were used in determining the possible parentage and approximate birth year of Elizabeth Osmande.

CHILD 2 - Priscilla Osmand

Christening records for Burford begin in 1612. However, the early parish records of Burford (FHL Microfiche # 6142017, Parts 1 through 6) and the patronymics (or naming patterns) of Osmond descendants were used in determining the possible parentage and approximate birth year of Priscilla Osmand.

CHILD 3 - John Osmund

Christening records for Burford begin in 1612. However, the early parish records of Burford (FHL Microfiche # 6142017, Parts 1 through 6) and the patronymics (or naming patterns) of Osmond descendants were used in determining the possible parentage and approximate birth year of John Osmund.

The burial of John Osmund is listed in the parish register of Burford (FHL Microfiche # 6142017, Part 4 of 6, Burials for the period 1630-1695), which states that he was buried on 4 March 1664 as "Osmund, John, an old man".

CHILD 4 - Thomas Osmund

Christening records for Burford begin in 1612. However, the early parish records of Burford (FHL Microfiche # 6142017, Parts 1 through 6) and the patronymics (or naming patterns) of Osmond descendants were used in determining the possible parentage and approximate birth year of Thomas Osmund.

The order of children christened in the early-to-mid-1600's in Burford, Oxfordshire, suggests that Thomas Osmund may have been the younger brother of John Osmund (b.abt.1604)--who married Elizabethe Bery in 1629 in Burford and whose father was John Osmund (b.abt.1575).

The burial of Thomas Osman is listed in the parish register of Burford (FHL Microfiche # 6142017, Part 4 of 6, Burials for the period 1630-1695), which states that he was buried on 30 September 1675 as "Osman, Thomas, Mason, very aged".

CHILD 5 - Alice Osman

Christening records for Burford begin in 1612. However, the early parish records of Burford (FHL Microfiche # 6142017, Parts 1 through 6) and the patronymics (or naming patterns) of Osmond descendants were used in determining the possible parentage and approximate birth year of Alice Osman.

CHILD 6 - Susan Osman

Christening records for Burford begin in 1612. However, the early parish records of Burford (FHL Microfiche # 6142017, Parts 1 through 6) and the patronymics (or naming patterns) of Osmond descendants were used in determining the possible parentage and approximate birth year of Susan Osman.

Osmond Descendants of Burford, Oxfordshire, England

The ancestry of the Osmonds of Utah extend back to the Osmonds of Burford, Oxfordshire, England.

The following pages on the *Descendants of John Osmund* shows over 400 years of Osmond-related descendants.

Descendants of John Osmund

1. **John Osmund (b.1575-of Burford,Oxfordshire,England;b.1633)**
sp: Alice (b.1577-of Burford,Oxfordshire,England;m.1598;b.1654)
- 2. Elizabeth Osmande (b.1599-of Burford,Oxfordshire,England)
  sp: John Baker (b.1599-of Burford,Oxfordshire,England;m.1620)
- 2. Priscilla Osmand (b.1602-of Burford,Oxfordshire,England)
  sp: Alselme Blanche (b.1605-of Burford,Oxfordshire,England;m.1628)
- 2. John Osmund (b.1604-of Burford,Oxfordshire,England;b.1664)
  sp: Elizabethe Bery (c.1598-Brize Norton,Oxford,England;m.1629;b.1667)
  - 3. Ann Osmonde (c.1628-Burford,Oxfordshire,England)
    sp: Simon Hayter (b.1629-of Burford,Oxfordshire,England;m.1658)
  - 3. Frances Osman (c.1629-Burford,Oxfordshire,England;b.1655)
    sp: Joane Freeman (b.1631-of Burford,Oxfordshire,England;m.1653)
    - 4. Anne Osman (c.1654-Burford,Oxfordshire,England)
    - 4. Francis Osman (c.1655-Burford,Oxfordshire,England;b.1660)
  - 3. Elizabeth Osman (b.1630-of Burford,Oxfordshire,England;b.1630)
  - 3. Jane Osman (c.1631-Burford,Oxfordshire,England;b.1631)
  - 3. Margery Osman (c.1631-Burford,Oxfordshire,England;b.1631)
  - 3. Jane Osmund (c.1633-Burford,Oxfordshire,England;b.1695)
  - 3. John Osmund (c.1635-Burford,Oxfordshire,England)
    sp: Joane Wicks (b.1638-of Burford,Oxfordshire,England;m.1660)
    - 4. George Osmund (c.1663-Burford,Oxfordshire,England;b.1694)
      sp: Mary King (c.1665-Burford,Oxfordshire,England;m.1691)
      - 5. John Osmund (c.1692-Burford,Oxfordshire,England;d.1767)
        sp: Sarah Bly (c.1688-Piddington,Oxfordshire,England;m.1715;b.1722)
        - 6. George Osmond (c.1716-Bicester,Oxfordshire,England;d.1754)
          sp: Mary Allen (c.1721-Bicester,Oxfordshire,England;m.1742)
          - 7. John Osmond (c.1743-Bicester,Oxfordshire,England;b.1805)
            sp: Elizabeth Phillips (b.1740-of Blockley,Worcester,England;m.1766;b.1787)
            - 8. John Osmond (b.1786-of Chipping Norton,Oxfordshire,England)
              sp: Ann Tidmas (b.1763-of Wincott,Oxfordshire,England;m.1799;d.1853)
          - 7. George Osmond (c.1745-Bicester,Oxfordshire,England;d.1821)
            sp: Anne Phillips (c.1779-Stoke Lyne,Oxfordshire,England;m.1807;d.1842)
            - 8. George (Sr.) Osmond (c.1808-Bicester,Oxfordshire,England;d.1860)
              sp: Nancy Ann Canham (b.1805-of Blackheath,London,England;d.1876)
              - 9. George (Jr.) Osmond (b.1836-Hackney,London,England;d.1913)
                sp: Mary Georgina (Georgiana) Huckvale (c.1835-Chipping Norton,O,England;m.1855;d.1922)
                - 10. Clara Georginia Osmond (b.1856-Bountiful,Davis,Utah;d.1936)
                  sp: Adam Pugh Welker (b.1853-Alpine,Utah Co.,Utah;m.1879;d.1926)
                  - 11. Roy Anson Welker (b.1878-Bloomington,Bear Lake,Idaho;d.1973)
                    sp: Elizabeth (Lizzie) Hoge (b.1879-Paris,Bear Lake,Idaho;m.1906;d.1971)
                  - 11. Raymond Welker (b.1880-Bloomington,Bear Lake,Idaho;d.1928)
                    sp: Elizabeth (Libbie) Wright (b.1883-Bennington,Bear Lake,Idaho;m.1904;d.1950)
                  - 11. Georgena (Gena) Welker (b.1883-Bloomington,Bear Lake,Idaho;d.1972)
                    sp: Milton John Floyd (b.1879-St. Charles,Bear Lake,Idaho;m.1906;d.1938)
                  - 11. Rose Welker (b.1886-Bloomington,Bear Lake,Idaho;d.1963)
                    sp: Melvin Welker (b.1885-Bloomington,Beak Lake,Idaho;d.1906)
                    sp: Frank Edward Floyd (b.1884-St. Charles,Beasr Lake,Idaho;m.1915;d.1933)
                  - 11. George Adam Welker (b.1888-Bloomington,Bear Lake,Idaho;d.1899)
                  - 11. Nina Welker (b.1891-Bloomington,Bear Lake,Idaho;d.1914)
                  - 11. Pearl Welker (b.1896-Bloomington,Bear Lake,Idaho;d.1994)
                    sp: Harold Lambert Shaw (b.1893-Salt Lake City,Salt Lake Co.,Utah;m.1918;d.1953)
                  - 11. Clara Gladys Welker (b.1903-Bloomington,Bear Lake,Idaho;d.1980)

sp: John William (m.1936)

10. George Anson Osmond (b.1858-Bountiful,Davis,Utah;d.1904)

sp: Alice Catharine Hart (b.1864-Salt Lake City,Salt Lake Co.,Utah;m.1883;d.1942)

11. Alice Maude Osmond (b.1884-Bloomington,Bear Lake,Idaho;d.1971)

sp: Alonzo Laker Cook (b.1882-Garden City,Rich,Utah;m.1907;d.1963)

11. Effie Eugenie Osmond (b.1886-Bloomington,Bear Lake,Idaho;d.1970)

sp: Andrew Thomas Burnham (b.1887-Draper,Salt Lake Co.,Utah;m.1925;d.1948)

11. James George Osmond (b.1889-Bloomington,Bear Lake,Idaho;d.1969)

sp: Dorothy

11. Charles Anson Osmond (b.1893-Bloomington,Bear Lake,Idaho;d.1985)

sp: Delilah LaVoyle Peterson (b.1895-Amalga,Cache,Utah;m.1918;d.1984)

11. Ruby Hermoine Osmond (b.1895-Bloomington,Bear Lake,Idaho;d.1998)

sp: Merrill Jex Brockbank (b.1896-Spanish Fork,Utah Co.,Utah;m.1924;d.1954)

11. Ivie Fern Osmond (b.1899-Bloomington,Bear Lake,Idaho;d.1988)

sp: Bringham H. Robinson (b.1899-Grantsville,Tooele,Utah;m.1927;d.1967)

11. Iona Sabina Osmond (b.1904-Bloomington,Bear Lake,Idaho;d.2002)

sp: Horton Christensen Miller (b.1900-Farmington,Davis,Utah;m.1931;d.1987)

10. Alfred Osmond (b.1861-Willard,Box Elder,Utah;d.1938)

sp: Josephine Frances Nelson (b.1869-Bloomington,Bear Lake,Idaho;m.1887;d.1888)

11. Pearl Osmond (b.1888-Willard,Box Elder,Utah;d.1889)

sp: Annie Elizabeth Lloyd (b.1869-Wellsville,Cache,Utah;m.1897;d.1961)

11. Alfred Wendell Osmond (b.1898-Paris,Bear Lake,Idaho;d.1986)

sp: Erma Christensen (b.1899-Richfield,Sevier,Utah;m.1930)

11. Harvard Reginald Osmond (b.1903-Cambridge,Middlesex,Massachusetts)

sp: Melba Condie (b.1902-Springville,Utah Co.,Utah)

11. Waldo Lloyd Osmond (b.1905-Provo,Utah Co.,Utah;d.1944)

sp: Miriam Lillywhite

11. Constance Georgina Osmond

sp: Merrill John Bunnell (b.1899-Lakeview,Utah Co.,Utah)

11. Mary Irene Osmond (b.1907;d.1997)

sp: William Everett Spears (b.1894-Spring Lake,Simpson,Kentucky)

11. Nan (Annie Hermese) Osmond

sp: Harry Grass (b.1894-Salt Lake City,Salt Lake Co.,Utah)

11. Martha Bliss Osmond (b.1912-Provo,Utah Co.,Utah)

sp: John Rogers Bourne (b.1911-Salt Lake City,Salt Lake Co.,Utah)

10. Rosebell (Rose) Osmond (b.1864-Willard,Box Elder,Utah;d.1949)

sp: Benjamin Erastus Rich (b.1855-Salt Lake City,Salt Lake Co.,Utah;m.1885;d.1913)

sp: William John Starkey (b.1863-,,Illinois;m.1888)

11. Leonard Jay Starkey (b.1889-Salt Lake City,Salt Lake Co.,Utah;d.1973)

sp: Edna M. Buran (b.1908-Thief River Falls,Pennington,Minnesota;m.1914)

11. Blaine Osmond Starkey (b.1893-Salt Lake City,Salt Lake Co.,Utah;d.1976)

sp: Margaret Charlotte Roberts (b.1895-Falcon,,Colorado;m.1916;d.1990)

11. Martha Irene Starkey (b.1895-Bloomington,Bear Lake,Idaho;d.1974)

sp: Moyne Charles Robb (b.1891;m.1917;d.1979)

11. Alice Starkey (b.1898-Long Valley,Caribou,Idaho;d.1900)

11. Harold Starkey (b.1904-Bloomington,Bear Lake,Idaho;d.1925)

10. Ira Osmond (b.1866-Bloomington,Bear Lake,Idaho;d.1946)

10. Ida Ann Osmond (b.1869-Bloomington,Bear Lake,Idaho;d.1943)

sp: Oliver Cowdery Dunford (b.1863-St. Louis,St. Louis Co.,Missouri;m.1889;d.1943)

11. Rao Bingham Dunford (b.1891-Nuhaka,Hawke-Bay,New Zealand;d.1969)

sp: Venice Blanche Smith (b.1900-Georgetown,Bear Lake,Idaho;m.1921;d.1993)

11. William Stanley Dunford (b.1893-Bloomington,Bear Lake,Idaho;d.1955)

sp: Zina Adelia Patterson (b.1897-Bloomington,Bear Lake,Idaho;m.1917;d.1993)
11. Hazel Dunford (b.1895-Bloomington,Bear Lake,Idaho;d.1970)
sp: Don Carlos Haddock (b.1892-Bloomington,Bear Lake,Idaho;m.1917;d.1971)
11. Alma Teller Dunford (b.1897-Bloomington,Bear Lake,Idaho;d.1958)
sp: Thelma Evalyn Tueller (b.1900-Paris,Bear Lake,Idaho;m.1919;d.1976)
11. Ralph Osmond Dunford (b.1900-Bloomington,Bear Lake,Idaho;d.1966)
sp: Edna Mae Neil (b.1905-Maitland,Huerfano,Colorado;m.1926;d.1975)
11. Mabel Dunford (b.1901-Bloomington,Bear Lake,Idaho;d.1978)
sp: Charles Wesley Woolley (b.1897-Norfolk,Madison,Nebraska;m.1919;d.1942)
sp: Harold James Lyle (b.1904;m.1947;d.1996)
11. Della Maud Dunford (b.1903-Bloomington,Bear Lake,Idaho;d.1988)
sp: Joy Edward Briscoe (b.1905-Bloomington,Bear Lake,Idaho;m.1926;d.1966)
11. George Osmond Dunford (b.1905-Bloomington,Bear Lake,Idaho;d.1975)
sp: Venna Luette Patterson (b.1906-Bloomington,Bear Lake,Idaho;m.1928;d.1987)
11. Isaac Dunford (b.1908-Bloomington,Bear Lake,Idaho;d.1956)
sp: Lela Violet Christensen (b.1908-Bloomington,Bear Lake,Idaho;m.1929;d.2004)
11. Ida Georgina Dunford (b.1912-Bloomington,Bear Lake,Idaho;d.1986)
sp: Donald Augustus O'Brien (b.1909-,,Oregon;m.1934;d.1958)
sp: Liddell
11. Oliver Wendell Dunford (b.1912-Bloomington,Bear Lake,Idaho;d.1913)
10. Ella Osmond (b.1872-Bloomington,Bear Lake,Idaho;d.1938)
sp: Louis Charles Newman (m.1893)
10. Nellie Osmond (b.1874-Bloomington,Bear Lake,Idaho;d.1968)
sp: Eugene Scheib Hart (b.1867-Bloomington,Bear Lake,Idaho;m.1897;d.1950)
11. Mary Larue (Lou) Hart (b.1918-Salt Lake City,Salt Lake Co.,Utah;d.1967)
sp: Howard David Elliott (b.1921-Fallen,Churchhill,Nevada;m.1946;d.2006)
10. Georgina Osmond (b.1877-Bloomington,Bear Lake,Idaho;d.1877)
10. Alice Maud Osmond (b.1879-Bloomington,Bear Lake,Idaho;d.1947)
sp: Forrest Eldridge Reed (b.1879-,Wirt Co.,West Virginia;m.1908;d.1968)
11. Jeanne Osmond Reed (b.1909-Salt Lake City,Salt Lake Co.,Utah;d.2004)
sp: Emmett Theodore (Sr.) Myers (b.1904-Windom,Mcpherson,Kansas;d.1979)
11. Virginia E. Reed (b.1912-Bloomington,Bear Lake,Idaho;d.2002)
sp: Cox
11. Rosamond Reed (b.1917-Salt Lake City,Salt Lake Co.,Utah;d.1955)
sp: James Ellsworth McClintock (b.1913-,Ventura Co.,California;d.1980)
sp: Christena (Christiana) Serina (Lovina) Amelia Jacobsen (b.1862-BC,BE,Utah;m.1881;d.1946)
10. James Arthur Osmond (b.1882-Bloomington,Bear Lake,Idaho;d.1965)
sp: Lucy Isabel Call (b.1883-Chesterfield,Bingham,Idaho;m.1901;d.1979)
11. Lenna Cleo Osmond (b.1903-Afton,Uinta Co.,Wyoming;d.1998)
sp: Wallace Rolland Wimmer (b.1909-Vernal,Uintah Co.,Uah;m.1934;d.1998)
11. George Arthur Osmond (b.1905-Afton,Uinta Co.,Wyoming;d.1993)
sp: Lavon Harmon (b.1909-Fairview,Uinta Co.,Wyoming;m.1928;d.1994)
11. Grace Afton Osmond (b.1909-Afton,Lincoln,Wyoming)
sp: Ronald James Bute (b.1910-,Illinois;d.1996)
sp: Howard Spencer
11. Joseph Call Osmond (b.1912-Afton,Lincoln,Wyoming;d.1977)
sp: Cleone Rogers (b.1916-Logan,Cache,Utah;m.1937;d.1985)
11. Barlow Frederick Osmond (b.1915-Grover,Lincoln,Wyoming;d.1917)
11. Lowell Call Osmond (b.1919-Afton,Lincoln,Wyoming;d.1975)
sp: Dorothy Vona Gerber (b.1927-Murray,Salt Lake Co.,Utah;m.1943;d.1981)
10. William Archer Osmond (b.1884-Bloomington,Bear Lake,Idaho;d.1907)
sp: Amy Lucille Hale (b.1884-Grantsville,Tooele Co.,Utah;m.1907;d.1937)

11. William A. Osmond (b.1907-Afton,Uinta,Wyoming;d.1998)
sp: Jennett Steenblik (b.1907-Salt Lake City,Salt Lake Co.,Utah;m.1931;d.2005)
10. Vasco Osmond (b.1889-Bloomington,Bear Lake,Idaho;d.1971)
sp: Mary Anna Moser (b.1892-Bedford,Uinta Co.,Wyoming;m.1912;d.1980)
11. Arlo Vasco Osmond (b.1916-Bedford,Uinta Co.,Wyoming;d.1981)
sp: Josephine (b.1911-,,Pennsylvania;d.1969)
sp: Irene Z. Olson (m.1970)
11. John (Jack) Darwin Osmond (b.1918-,,Wyoming)
sp: Martha (Mart) Jensen (b.1916-Afton,Lincoln,Wyoming;d.1983)
sp: Wyoma R. (b.1925)
11. Loa Mae Osmond (b.1923-,,Idaho;d.2007)
sp: John Harris Edgren (b.1919-Kaysville,Davis,Utah;m.1940;d.1979)
sp: Larry R. Billings (m.1981)
sp: Richard M. Engelbert (m.1984)
10. Rulon Osmond (b.1893-Afton,Uinta Co.,Wyoming;d.1917)
sp: Agnes LaVerna Van Noy (b.1892-Thayne,Uinta,Wyoming;m.1913;d.1975)
11. Rulon Van Noy Osmond (b.1914-Thayne,Lincoln,Wyoming;d.2001)
sp: Norma Kennington (b.1913-Fairview,Lincoln,Wyoming;m.1937;d.2003)
11. Ralph Jacobson Osmond (b.1915-Afton,Lincoln,Wyoming;d.1977)
sp: Lydia Tullis (b.1917-Veyo,Washington,Utah;m.1938;d.1981)
11. George Virl Osmond (b.1917-Etna,Lincoln,Wyoming;d.2007)
sp: Olive May Davis (b.1925-Samaria,Oneida,Idaho;m.1944;d.2004)
11. Cora (Bell) Elizabeth Neyman Osmond (b.1925-San Diego City,San Diego Co.,California)
sp: Harold Edgar Womack (b.1918-Mancas,Montezuma,Colorado;m.1943;d.2002)
sp: Adelbert (Del) Francis Thinnes (b.1927-Ogden,Weber,Utah;m.1953)
10. Elizabeth Mary Osmond (b.1896-Afton,Unita Co.,Wyoming;d.1974)
sp: Darwin Joshua Willis (b.1894-Cannonville,Garfield,Utah;m.1921;d.1986)
11. Darwa Osmond Willis (b.1922)
sp: Keith Seymour Mendenhall (b.1920-Hazelton,Jerome,Idaho;d.1985)
11. Scharlene Willis (b.1924)
sp: Wayne Maxwell Tippets (b.1926-Cowley,Big Horn,Wyoming;d.1987)
11. Lemuel Josiah Willis (b.1934)
sp: Dixie Gladys Hansen (b.1936;m.1955)
10. Leona Osmond (b.1899-Afton,Unita Co.,Wyoming;d.1990)
sp: Guy Leonard Umscheid (b.1898-Beaver City,Furnas,Nebraska;m.1937;d.1990)
10. Wesley Osmond (b.1901-Afton,Unita Co.,Wyoming;d.1971)
sp: Vera Leona Dray (b.1905-Smoot,Uinta,Wyoming;m.1922(Div);d.1971)
11. Eugene D. Osmond (b.1922-Smoot,Lincoln,Wyoming;d.1922)
11. James Duane Osmond (b.1925-Smoot,Lincoln,Wyoming;d.1994)
sp: Virginia Woodbury (b.1922-St. George,Washington,Utah;m.1948(Div);d.2007)
sp: Ruby Josephine Nelson (b.1908-Bloomington,Bear Lake Co.,Utah;m.1934;d.1974)
11. Rex Wesley Osmond (b.1940)
sp: Judith (Judy) Parker
11. Leona Ruby Osmond (b.1944)
sp: Roland Bickmore Stander (b.1938;m.1961(Div))
sp: Nicholas (Nick) Amar Valentine
9. John Osmond (b.1836-Hackney,London,England;d.1843)
8. Ann (Anne) Osmond (c.1809-Bicester,Oxfordshire,England;d.1864)
sp: George Osmond (c.1793-Holy Trinity,Coventry,Warwick,England;m.1832;d.1837)
sp: Wellington Ellis (b.1813-Pwlldu,Llantillio,Monms.,England;m.1840;d.1893)
8. John Osmond (c.1811-Bicester,Oxfordshire,England;d.1848)
8. William Osmond (b.1814-Bicester,Oxfordshire,England;d.1855)

sp: Elizabeth Jarvis (b.1817-of Woodstock,Oxfordshire,England;m.1837)
9. George Henry Osmond (b.1839-Market End,Bicester,Oxfordshire,England;d.1894)
sp: Florence Emily Watts (b.1844-Banbury,Oxfordshire,England;m.1864;d.1878)
sp: Ann (Annie) Jarvis (b.1855-Warlingham,Godstone district,Surrey,England;m.1878;d.1935)
10. Henry Cecil Osmond (b.1882-118 St. Aldale Street,St. Martin,Oxford,Oxford, England;d.1970)
sp: Mary Jane Levett (b.1884-Mayfield,Tunbridge Wells,Kent,England;m.1911;d.1972)
11. Reginald Kenneth (Ken) Osmond
11. Dorothy Margaret Osmond
sp: Noel Waters
11. Joyce Agnes Osmond (b.1918-,,New Zealand;d.1921)
11. Madge Ethel Osmond (b.1918-,,New Zealand)
sp: Farquhar
11. Ronald (ron) Thomas Osmond (b.1922-Kaikoura,South Island,New Zealand)
sp: UNKNOWN
10. Ronald George Osmond (b.1884-118 St. Aldale Street,St. Martin,O,Oxford, England;d.1947)
sp: Maud Mary Heath (b.1884-Aldershot,Surrey,Southampton,England;m.1913;d.1964)
11. Hubert Ronald George Osmond (b.1914-West Ashford district,Kent,England;d.1996)
sp: Isabel Chisholm Mains (b.1919-Gateshead,County Durham,England;m.1943;d.1986)
10. Reginald Herbert Osmond (b.1886-118 St. Aldale Street,St. Martin,O,Oxford, England;d.1891)
10. Frederick William Osmond (b.1888-118 St. Aldale Street,St. Martin,O,Oxford, England;d.1973)
7. Sarah Osmond (c.1748-Bicester,Oxfordshire,England)
7. William Osmond (c.1750-Bicester,Oxfordshire,England;b.1832)
7. Thomas Osmond (c.1753-Bicester,Oxfordshire,England)
sp: Mary (b.1758-of Oxfordshire or Warwickshire,England;m.1788)
8. Mary Ann Osmond (c.1789-Holy Trinity,Coventry,Warwickshire,England)
sp: John Watts (m.1826)
8. John Osmond (c.1791-Holy Trinity,Coventry,Warwickshire,England;d.1810)
8. George Osmond (c.1793-Holy Trinity,Coventry,Warwick,England;d.1837)
sp: Ann (Anne) Osmond (c.1809-Bicester,Oxfordshire,England;m.1832;d.1864)
8. Julia Osmond (c.1799-Holy Trinity,Coventry,Warwickshire,England)
8. Thomas Osmond (c.1800-Holy Trinity,Coventry,Warwickshire,England)
sp: Mary Court (c.1809-Meriden,Warwickshire,England;m.1830)
9. George Osmond (c.1831-Berkswell,Warwickshire,England)
sp: Ann Kelsall (c.1818-Hanley,Staffordshire,England;m.1861)
9. Caroline Amelia Osmond (c.1834-Berkswell,Warwickshire,England)
9. Thomas Osmond (c.1835-Berkswell,Warwickshire,England;d.1906)
sp: Priscilla Christabel (Christable) Packer (Parker) (b.1847-Bristol,K,W,England;m.1884;d.1896)
10. Thomas Osmond (b.1885-36 Belgrave Road,Edgbaston,Birmingham,Warwickshire, England)
sp: Elizabeth Annie Fern (b.1878-Stoke upon Trent,Staffordshire,England;m.1906)
9. John Osmond (b.1838-Berkswell,Warwickshire,England;d.1864)
9. William Osmond (c.1838-Berkswell,Warwickshire,England;d.1894)
9. Louisa Theresa Osmond (b.1840-Berkswell,Warwickshire,England)
9. Julia Augusta Osmond (c.1842-Berkswell,Warwickshire,England)
9. Mary Osmond (b.1845-Berkswell,Warwickshire,England)
9. Arthur Osmond (b.1851-Berkswell,Meriden district,Warwickshire,England)
sp: Emily Bottely (b.1851-Birmingham,Warwickshire,England;m.1874(Div);d.1889)
10. Emily Lucy Osmond (b.1875-Willenhall,Wolverhampton district,Staffordshire,England)
10. Florence Amelia (Louisa or C.) Osmond (b.1882-Birmingham,Warwickshire,England)
10. Thomas William Osmond (b.1884-Birmingham,Aston district,Warwickshire,England)
10. Ethel Osmond (b.1886-Birmingham,Ashton district,Warwickshire,England)
sp: Florence Farley (b.1857-Woodstock,Woodstock district,Oxfordshire,England;m.1889)
10. Mabel Osmond (b.1890-Birmingham,King's Norton district,Warwickshire,England)

10. Hilda Osmond (b.1893-Birmingham,King's Norton district,Warwickshire,England)
8. Emma Osmond (c.1803-Holy Trinity,Coventry,Warwickshire,England)
8. Lucy Osmond (c.1805-Holy Trinity,Coventry,Warwickshire,England)
6. John Osmond (c.1718-Bicester,Oxfordshire,England;b.1720)
6. William Osmond (c.1719-Bicester,Oxfordshire,England;b.1719)
6. Sarah Osmond (c.1721-Bicester,Oxfordshire,England;b.1753)
sp: Elizabeth Harding Cross (b.1710-of Bicester,Oxfordshire,England;m.1730;b.1755)
5. George Osmund (c.1694-Burford,Oxfordshire,England;b.1694)
4. John Osmond (c.1666-Burford,Oxfordshire,England)
sp: Katharine Pattin (b.1680-of Burford,Oxfordshire,England;m.1714)
3. Robert Osmund (c.1638-Burford,Oxfordshire,England)
2. Thomas Osmund (b.1606-of Burford,Oxfordshire,England;b.1675)
sp: Mrs. Thomas Osmund (b.1607-of Burford,Oxfordshire,England;m.1628;b.1679)
3. Elizabeth Osman (c.1629-Burford,Oxfordshire,England)
3. Thomas Osman (c.1631-Burford,Oxfordshire,England)
sp: Alice Cooke (b.1635-of Burford,Oxfordshire,England;m.1659)
4. Stephen Osman (c.1660-Burford,Oxfordshire,England)
4. Margaret Osman (c.1663-Burford,Oxfordshire,England)
3. William Osmond (c.1633-Burford,Oxfordshire,England)
sp: Phebis (b.1637-of Burford,Oxfordshire,England;m.1658;b.1708)
4. William Osman (c.1659-Burford,Oxfordshire,England)
sp: Mrs. William Osman (b.1660-of Burford,Oxfordshire,England;m.1681)
5. Richard Osman (b.1682-of Burford,Oxfordshire,England;b.1689)
5. William Osmun (c.1684-Burford,Oxfordshire,England)
5. Thomas Osmun (c.1686-Burford,Oxfordshire,England)
sp: Mrs. Thomas Osmun (b.1687-of Burford,Oxfordshire,England;m.1708)
6. Margarett Osmond (c.1709-Burford,Oxfordshire,England)
5. Mary Osmun (c.1692-Burford,Oxfordshire,England;b.1714)
4. Johnathon Osmund (c.1660-Burford,Oxfordshire,England)
sp: Margaret Fowler (b.1663-of Gloucestershire and Oxfordshire,England;m.1694;b.1701)
5. Jonathan Osmun (c.1695-Burford,Oxfordshire,England)
5. Mary Osmund (c.1696-Burford,Oxfordshire,England)
5. Dennis Osmund (c.1698-Burford,Oxfordshire,England)
5. Joseph Osmund (c.1699-Burford,Oxfordshire,England)
5. Margaret Osmun (c.1701-Burford,Oxfordshire,England;b.1701)
sp: Mary Hayter (b.1671-of Burford,Oxfordshire,England;m.1702)
5. Robert Osmund (c.1703-Burford,Oxfordshire,England)
5. Joan Osmund (c.1705-Burford,Oxfordshire,England)
4. Phebe Osman (c.1663-Burford,Oxfordshire,England)
sp: Jonathan Grove (b.1660-of Burford,Oxfordshire,England;m.1691)
4. Joseph Osman (c.1666-Burford,Oxfordshire,England)
4. Benjamin Osman (c.1666-Burford,Oxfordshire,England;b.1666)
4. Jeremiah Osman (c.1668-Burford,Oxfordshire,England;b.1669)
4. Richard Osman (c.1668-Burford,Oxfordshire,England)
sp: Elizabeth Jordan (b.1672-of Burford,Oxfordshire,England;m.1695)
5. William Osmun (c.1695-Burford,Oxfordshire,England)
5. Jane Osmund (c.1697-Burford,Oxfordshire,England)
5. Joseph Osmund (c.1700-Burford,Oxfordshire,England)
5. Richard Osmund (c.1703-Burford,Oxfordshire,England)
5. Thomas Osman (c.1706-Burford,Oxfordshire,England)
5. Betty Osmond (c.1708-Burford,Oxfordshire,England)
4. Mary Osman (c.1671-Burford,Oxfordshire,England)

sp: James Moncke (b.1669-of Burford,Oxfordshire,England;m.1694)
3. John Osmund (c.1634-Burford,Oxfordshire,England;b.1650)
3. Richard Osmund (c.1636-Burford,Oxfordshire,England)
3. Symon Osman (c.1639-Burford,Oxfordshire,England;b.1643)
3. Mary Osman (c.1641-Burford,Oxfordshire,England;b.1643)
3. Zacharie Osman (c.1642-Burford,Oxfordshire,England;b.1643)
3. Anne Osman (b.1643-of Burford,Oxfordshire,England;b.1643)
3. Mary Osman (c.1645-Burford,Oxfordshire,England)
sp: Thomas Prestidge (b.1638-of Burford,Oxfordshire,England;m.1669)
3. Symon Osman (c.1648-Burford,Oxfordshire,England)
2. Alice Osman (b.1608-of Burford,Oxfordshire,England)
sp: Zacharie Jellyman (b.1608-of Burford,Oxfordshire,England;m.1639)
2. Susan Osman (b.1610-of Burford,Oxfordshire,England)
sp: Thomas Daniel (b.1609-of Burford,Oxfordshire,England;m.1640)

Osmond Extraction Project

In 2009-2010, the Osmond Family Organization (OFO) of Utah financially supported an *Osmond Extraction Project*--which enabled the purchase of dozens of historical birth, marriage and death certificates of selected Osmond individuals who had resided in England and New Zealand during the 1800's and early 1900's. This project resulted in the identification and extension of many Osmond-related families in England and New Zealand--some of whom are listed on the following Descendant charts.

Descendants of Francis John Osmond

1. Francis John Osmond (b.1861-Bath,Somerset,England)

sp: Emily (b.1869-Dudley,Worcestershire,England;m.1889)

- 2. Hilda Emmeline Osmond (b.1889-,,India)
- 2. Ernest F. Osmond (b.1892-,,India)
- 2. Frank Osmond (b.1894-,,India)
- 2. Arnold N. Osmond (b.1896-,,India)
- 2. Cyril Osmond (b.1901-Altrincham,Cheshire,England)
  - sp: Dulcie Enid Randall (b.1903-Andover district,Hampshire or Wiltshire,England;m.1927)
    - 3. Anthony Michael John Osmond (b.1934-Warren Hospital,Abingdon,Berkshire,England)

Descendants of Michael Osmond

1. **Michael Osmond**
   sp: UNKNOWN
   - 2. Michael Kingham Osmond (b.1847-Andover district,Hampshire or Wiltshire,England)
     sp: Ida Effie Newton (b.1844-of Newbury,Berkshire,England;m.1869)
     - 3. Ida Elizabeth Osmond (b.1871-Grange Farm,Shaw-cum-Donnington,Speen,Berkshire, England)
       sp: Edward Lidderdale (m.1905)
     - 3. Newton Kingham Osmond (b.1872-Grange Farm,Shaw-cum-Donnington,Speen,Berkshire, England)
     - 3. Michael John Osmand (Osmond) (b.1874-Grange Farm,Shaw-cum-Donnington,Speen,Berkshire, England)
       sp: Lilian Louisa Susan King (b.1874-Abingdon district,Berkshire,England;m.1912)
     - 3. Robert Stanley Osmond (b.1876-Grange Farm,Shaw-cum-Donnington,Speen,Berkshire, England)
     - 3. Agnes Maud Osmond (b.1878-Grange Farm,Shaw-cum-Donnington,Speen,Berkshire, England)
       sp: Thomas Litten (b.1870-Faringdon district,Berkshire,England;m.1900)
     - 3. George Cyril Osmond (b.1884-Manor Farm,Stanford Dingley,Berkshire,England)
     - 3. Richard Mathews Osmond (b.1886-Manor Farm,Stanford Dingley,Berkshire,England)

Descendants of Richard Osmond

1. Richard Osmond (b.1624-of Exeter,Devonshire,England)
sp: Mary Trueman (Trheman) (b.1628-of Exeter,Devonshire,England;m.1649)
2. William Osmond (c.1659-Stoke Canon,Devonshire,England)
2. Richard Osmond (c.1660-Stoke Canon,Devonshire,England)
2. Edward Osmond (c.1664-Stoke Canon,Devonshire,England)
sp: Sarah Fish (c.1671-Newton St. Cyres,Devonshire,England;m.1700)
3. Mary Osmond (c.1701-Saint David,Exeter,Devonshire,England)
3. Martha Osmond (c.1703-Saint David,Exeter,Devonshire,England;d.1703)
3. Joan Osmond (c.1708-Saint David,Exeter,Devonshire,England)
3. Elizabeth Osmond (c.1710-Saint David,Exeter,Devonshire,England)
3. Sarah Osmond (c.1713-Saint David,Exeter,Devonshire,England)
3. Hanah Osmond (c.1717-Saint David,Exeter,Devonshire,England)
3. Gregory Osmond (c.1719-Saint David,Exeter,Devonshire,England)
sp: Ann Bradford (c.1719-Rewe By Exeter,Devonshire,England;m.1758)
4. Elizabeth Osman (c.1759-Newton St. Cyres,Devonshire,England)
4. Anne Osmond (c.1761-Newton St. Cyres,Devonshire,England)
sp: William Henry Knight (c.1763-of Yeowton,Somerset,England;m.1787;d.1826)
5. George Knight (b.1790-of Yeowton,Somerset,England)
5. John Knight (b.1792-West Camel,Somerset,England;d.1825)
5. Charles Knight (b.1797-Yeowton,Somerset,England;d.1797)
5. Phobe Knight (b.1798-Yeowton,Somerset,England;d.1798)
5. Thomas Knight (b.1799-Yeowton,Somerset,England)
5. Patience Knight (b.1808-Yeowton,Somerset,England;d.1808)
4. Edward Osmond (c.1765-Newton St. Cyres,Devonshire,England)
sp: Betty Hunt (b.1773-of Upton Pyne,Devonshire,England;m.1796)
5. Edward Osmond (c.1797-Upton Pyne,Devonshire,England)
sp: Sarah Rew (c.1798-Netherexe,Devonshire,England;m.1820;d.1854)
6. Mary Ann Elizabeth Osmond (c.1823-Upton Pyne,Devonshire,England)
6. Sarah Ann Osmond (c.1824-Upton Pyne,Devonshire,England)
6. Edward Osmond (c.1826-Upton Pyne,Devonshire,England;d.1905)
sp: Charlotte Coles (b.1830-Stoke Cannon,Devonshire,England;m.1853;d.1899)
7. Emily Coles Osmond (b.1854-Brampford Speke,Devonshire,England)
7. Ellen Osmond (b.1856-Brampford Speke,Devonshire,England)
7. Edward Osmond (b.1858-Brampford Speke,Devonshire,England)
7. Charles Coles Osmond (b.1860-Brampford Speke,Devonshire,England)
sp: Eliza Hunt (m.1891)
7. John Osmond (b.1861-Brampford Speke,Devonshire,England)
7. Gregory Osmond (b.1862-Brampford Speke,Devonshire,England)
7. Arthur Osmond (b.1865-Brampford Speke,Devonshire,England)
7. Henry Osmond (b.1868-Brampford Speke,Devonshire,England)
7. Florence Osmond (b.1869-Brampford Speke,Devonshire,England)
7. Bertha Osmond (b.1872-Brampford Speke,Devonshire,England)
6. John Osmond (c.1827-Newton St. Cyres,Devonshire,England)
6. John Gregory Osmond (c.1829-Newton St. Cyres,Devonshire,England;d.1888)
sp: Emma Norris (b.1833-Broad Clyst,Devonshire,England;m.1854;d.1862)
sp: Harriet (Harriett) Poole (b.1843-of Bampton,Devonshire,England;m.1864;d.1871)
7. George P. Osmond (b.1865-Newton St. Cyres,Devonshire,England;d.1889)
7. John Gregory Osmond (b.1866-Hayne Barton,Newton St. Cyres,Devonshire,England)
7. Lucy Osmond (b.1868-Hayne Barton,Newton St. Cyres,Devonshire,England)
7. Charles Osmond (b.1870)
sp: Amy Benmore Pentecost (b.1849-Harcroft,Kenton,Devonshire,England;m.1872;d.1920)
7. Gregory Benmore Osmond (b.1873-Hayne Barton Newton St. Cyres,Exeter,Devonshire,England;d.1956)

sp: Margaret Adam Sims (b.1870-North Shore,Auckland,North Island,New Zealand;m.1896)
8. Phillip Gregory Osmond. (b.1898-Russell Street,Ponsonby,Auckland,North Island, New Zealand)
sp: Esther Ruth Samuel (b.1896-Tauranga,North Island,New Zealand;m.1924)
8. Douglas Stuart Osmond (b.1902-Ponsonby,Auckland,North Island,New Zealand)
8. Elsie Doreen Osmond (b.1905-Russell Street,Ponsonby,Auckland,North Island, New Zealand;d.1905)
7. Ernest Alfred Osmond (b.1874-Hayne Barton,Newton St. Cyres,Devonshire,England)
sp: Lottie Maslin (m.1903)
8. Raymond Ernest Osmond (b.1904-,,New Zealand)
8. Rita Osmond (b.1906-,,New Zealand)
8. Mary Osmond (b.1907-,,New Zealand)
8. Amy Osmond (b.1909-,,New Zealand)
7. Mary Edith Osmond (b.1877-Spestos Grange,Bow,Devonshire,England)
sp: Walter James Piggot (m.1904)
7. James Ingram Osmond (b.1879-Exeter district,Devonshire,England;d.1931)
sp: Eva Gertrude (b.1882;d.1969)
8. Roie Osmond (b.1911-Auckland,North Island,New Zealand)
7. Herbert John Osmond (b.1881-Park Cottage,Ponsonby,Auckland,North Island, New Zealand;d.1945)
sp: Mary Anne (Wereane) Wairingiringi Wilkinson (b.1882-PT,NI,New Zealand;m.1908;d.1966)
8. Mollie Rau Kamoe (Raukamori) Osmond (b.1910-Otorohanga,North Island,New Zealand;d.1932)
8. Ringi May Osmond (b.1911-Otorohanga,North Island,New Zealand;d.2000)
8. Gladys Lorna Osmond (b.1914-,,New Zealand;d.1976)
8. Constance Benmore Osmond (b.1917-,,New Zealand;d.2000)
7. Harold Percival Osmond (b.1886-Rata Street Ponsonby,Auckland,North Island,New Zealand;d.1887)
6. Emma Osmond (c.1830-Newton St. Cyres,Devonshire,England)
6. Henry Osmond (c.1831-Newton St. Cyres,Devonshire,England)
6. James Francis Osmond (c.1833-Newton St. Cyres,Devonshire,England)
sp: Elizabeth Frean (c.1829-How Street Baptist,Plymouth,Devonshire,England;m.1856)
7. Charles Henry Osmond (b.1859-Exeter district,Devonshire,England;d.1937)
sp: Phoebe Jessie Jervis (b.1857-Auckland,North Island,New Zealand;m.1882(Div))
8. Gordon Osmond (b.1885-Epsom,North Island,New Zealand)
8. Charles Clifton Osmond (b.1886-Epsom,North Island,New Zealand)
8. Kathleen Osmond (b.1890-Bradford Street,Parnell,Auckland,North Island, New Zealand)
sp: Ethel Maslin (b.1878;m.1926)
6. Caroline Osmond (b.1840-Newton St. Cyres,Devonshire,England)
5. John Osmond (c.1798-Upton Pyne,Devonshire,England)
2. John Osmond (c.1666-Stoke Canon,Devonshire,England)
2. Sarah Osmond (c.1670-Stoke Canon,Devonshire,England)
2. Henry Osmond (c.1673-Stoke Canon,Devonshire,England)
2. Charles Osmond (c.1676-Stoke Canon,Devonshire,England)
2. Samuel Osmond (c.1678-Stoke Canon,Devonshire,England)

Descendants of Richard Osmond

1. Richard Osmond

sp: UNKNOWN

└ 2. Richard Osmond (b.1847-Linkenholt,Hampshire,England)

sp: Anna Maria Humphries (b.1849-Wootten Bassett,Wiltshire,England;m.1871)

├ 3. Alice Maria Osmond (b.1872-East Ilsley,Berkshire,England)

├ 3. Gertrude Jane Osmond (b.1874-East Ilsley,Berkshire,England)

├ 3. Willie Osmond (b.1877-East Ilsley,Berkshire,England)

└ 3. Louise Humphries Osmond (b.1881-East Ilsley,Berkshire,England)

Descendants of Thomas Osmond (Osement)

1. Thomas Osmond (Osement) (b.1754-of Tisbury,Wiltshire,England)
sp: Betty (Bety or Elizabeth) Kellow (b.1756-of Tisbury,Wiltshire,England;m.1779;b.1802)
- 2. John Osmond (c.1779-Tisbury,Wiltshire,England)
- 2. Mary Ozment (c.1782-Tisbury,Wiltshire,England)
- 2. James Osement (c.1784-Tisbury,Wiltshire,England)
- 2. Thomas Osement (c.1787-Tisbury,Wiltshire,England)
- 2. William Osmond (c.1790-Tisbury,Wiltshire,England;d.1875)
  sp: Charity Marsh (c.1799-St. Sidwell,Exeter,Devonshire,England;m.1820;d.1851)
  - 3. William Osmond (b.1821-Salisbury,Wiltshire,England;d.1890)
    sp: Sarah Brown Pike (c.1831-Semley,Wiltshire,England;m.1851)
    - 4. Gertrude Osmond (c.1864-Salisbury,Wiltshire,England)
    - 4. Sidney Osmond (c.1868-Salisbury,Wiltshire,England)
    - 4. Clement Osmond (c.1871-Salisbury,Wiltshire,England)
  - 3. Louisa (Elizh Susan) Osmond (b.1823-Salisbury,Wiltshire,England;d.1873)
  - 3. Alfred Osmond (c.1824-Salisbury,Wiltshire,England;d.1826)
  - 3. Emma Charity Osmond (c.1826-Salisbury,Wiltshire,England)
  - 3. Arthur Osmond (c.1827-Salisbury,Wiltshire,England)
  - 3. Alfred Thomas Osmond (c.1828-Salisbury,Wiltshire,England)
  - 3. Henry James Osmond (c.1831-Salisbury,Wiltshire,England)
  - 3. Charles Marsh Osmond (b.1832-Salisbury,Wiltshire,England)
  - 3. Herbert Osmond (b.1833-Salisbury,Wiltshire,England)
  - 3. Lucy Jane Osmond (c.1834-Salisbury,Wiltshire,England;d.1850)
  - 3. Edward Osmond (c.1836-Salisbury,Wiltshire,England;d.1856)
  - 3. Agnes Peirce Osmond (b.1838-Salisbury,Wiltshire,England)
  - 3. Ellen Osmond (b.1839-Salisbury,Wiltshire,England)
  - 3. Walter Marsh Osmond (b.1840-Salisbury,Wiltshire,England)
  - 3. Gertrude Osmond (c.1842-Salisbury,Wiltshire,England;d.1856)
- 2. Elizabeth Osmond (c.1794-Tisbury,Wiltshire,England)
- 2. George Osmond (c.1796-Tisbury,Wiltshire,England)
- 2. Edward Osmond (c.1798-Tisbury,Wiltshire,England;b.1803)

Descendants of Thomas Osmond

1. Thomas Osmond

sp: UNKNOWN

└ 2. Uriah Osmond (b.1850-Wincanton district,Dorset or Somerset,England)

sp: Eliza Coombs (b.1852-Chucklington,Somerset,England;m.1870)

├ 3. Edith Osmond (b.1877-Gould's Grove,Bendington,Wallingford,Oxfordshire, England)

├ 3. Gertrude Dora Osmond (b.1880-The Lodge,Theale,Berkshire,England)

└ 3. William George Osmond (b.1882-Lotteridge,Wycombe,Buckinghamshire,England)

Descendants of Thomas Osmond

1. Thomas Osmond

sp: UNKNOWN

- 2. Walter Osmond (b.1863-Mile End Old Town district,London and Middlesex,England)
  - sp: Sarah Agnes Holdham (b.1871-Aylesbury district,Buckinghamshire,England;m.1892)
    - 3. Walter Osmond (b.1898-7 Marlborough Road,St. Aldate,Oxford,England)
    - 3. Gladys Muriel Osmond (b.1899-7 Marlborough Road,St. Aldate,Oxford,England)
    - 3. Doris May Osmond (b.1903-7 Marlborough Road,St. Aldate,Oxford,England)

Descendants of William Osmond

1. William Osmond

sp: UNKNOWN

- 2. Joseph Osmond (b.1843-Huddersfield,Yorkshire,England;d.1910)

  sp: Jane Caddie (Cuddie) (b.1853-Maybole,Ayrshire,Scotland;m.1873)

  - 3. Emma Osmond (b.1875-Forbury Near Dunedin,South Island,New Zealand)
  - 3. Joseph Osmond (b.1877-,South Island,New Zealand)
  - 3. David Osmond (b.1879-,South Island,New Zealand)
  - 3. John Osmond (b.1880-Dunedin,Otago,South Island,New Zealand)
  - 3. William Henry Osmond (b.1882-South Dunedin,South Island,New Zealand)
  - 3. Matilda Jane Osmond (b.1884-South Dunedin,South Island,New Zealand)
  - 3. Margaret Osmond (b.1886-South Dunedin,South Island,New Zealand)
  - 3. Charles Osmond (b.1888-South Dunedin,South Island,New Zealand)
  - 3. William Osmond (b.1889-South Dunedin,South Island,New Zealand)
  - 3. Ellen Jane Osmond (b.1891-South Dunedin,South Island,New Zealand)
  - 3. Hannah Elizabeth Osmond (b.1894-South Dunedin,South Island,New Zealand)
  - 3. Elizabeth Osmond (b.1895-South Dunedin,South Island,New Zealand)

Osmond Research: 1950's to the 1990's

Olive May Davis Osmond: Family Genealogist "Extraordinaire"

by R. Clayton Brough, Geographer, M.S., July 2010

Olive May Davis Osmond (1925-2004) was one of the greatest--and perhaps the most famous--"family genealogist's" of the 1900's. In 1954, at the age of 29, Olive accepted the responsibility of researching and documenting her husband's ancestry and that of her own lineage in the United States and the British Isles.

As the wife of George Virl Osmond (1917-2007) and the mother of the famous Osmond singers of Utah, she was constantly on-the-go. But wherever she went she was continually answering and sending family history letters, compiling and directing genealogical research work, devising and suggesting new ways to enter family data into computer programs, and constantly encouraged relatives and her worldwide audience to become more involved in genealogy and family history.

From the 1950's to the 1990's, Olive and George spent countless hours and thousands of dollars on genealogical research and family history projects and activities. With the support of her husband's relatives--who formed the George Osmond Family Organization, and through three decades of expert guidance and research help from a good friend and professional genealogist--David E. Gardner, Olive was able to do more research and produce more Osmond-related genealogies than anyone else has ever done. Truly, Olive Osmond, was a family genealogist "extraordinaire"; and although she passed away in 2004, her extensive genealogical information and dedication to family history still lives on--through her children's love of family and genealogy.

The following documents (found on pages 81-131) date from the 1950's to the 1990's, and are only a small sample of Olive's otherwise large collection of genealogy and family history materials.

ESTABLISHED 1864

PEARL ASSURANCE COMPANY LIMITED

INCORPORATED IN ENGLAND

PACIFIC DEPARTMENT

DAVID A. BARRY, MANAGER

369 PINE STREET, SAN FRANCISCO 6

GEORGE V. OSMOND, Agent
FIVE POINTS AGENCY
229 WASHINGTON BOULEVARD
OGDEN, UTAH
PHONE: 28661

March 28, 1954

W. E. C. Cotton
31 Royal Avenue
London S. W. 3, England

Dear Sir:

I have this date visited with Mrs. Vera Hunsaker of Garland, Utah and her mother, Mrs. A. L. Cook of Tremonton, Utah, with whom I understand you have been corresponding regarding the Osmond line.

They have asked me to take over this line as they are very busy and will be working on some of their other lines. Mrs. Hunsaker said she would write to you soon and verify this.

They mentioned that they wish they knew more about Rosabelle Flight, half-sister of our Grandfather George Osmond, (born 23 May 1836) and when I mentioned that (George) I knew her last name, they suggested that I send it to you right away. In a Salt Lake newspaper, Sept. 15, 1919 she advertised for information concerning Grandfather. Her address was given: Mrs. Rosabella Croker, 132 High Road, London N 15, England. The notation by the name in the book I have says: "She is the last heard from of Grandfather George Osmond's family in England." - so I presume this must be the Rosabelle we are interested in.

Another possible clue concerning Grandfather's birth: While visiting some relatives recently they had his birthplace listed as Hackney, London, England. I don't know too much about locations, etc. but it may mean something to you.

We are in the process of organizing the family now for family reunions, donations, etc. and plan to really go into this genealogy. We are grateful to know you take such an interest in the line and if things turn out as we plan, we will be able to make it well worth your time.

I am enclosing a ~~$5~~ $10 bill. I understand you can change the money over there. Please advise me if the money orders are better, or if you would rather have them.

I will be looking forward to your letters. May God bless you in this work!

Sincerely,

Please use this address:........................ Mrs. George V. Osmond (Olive)
228 North Washington Blvd.
Ogden, Utah
U.S.A.

LETTER NO. 1

June 17, 1955

Dear Osmond Kinsfolk:

As a member of our Osmond Family Genealogical Committee, I thought now might be a good time to write to you and perhaps get you thinking along these lines before our family reunion(scheduled for August, I believe.)

Also, I have some very good news from our researcher in England. Perhaps a little explanation is necessary to most of you as to what our problem has been, what has been done, etc. This researcher has been trying to find a clue to the mystry on the Osmond line for ten years or more now. (And , by the way, I think credit should go where it belongs--to Maude Cook and her daughter, Vera Hubsaker of Tremonton--,also other members of their family--for their tireless efforts and funds they have put out for this work.) We are quite certain now that he has finally located information about our grandfather, George Osmond. One letter not too long ago stated:

"The censes search of the Greenwich area of Kent has now been completed and I am enclosing a second instalment of entries of your names which have been found. You will find on the third page a youth named George Flight, aged 14, living in the household of William White. It seems to me that this must be the person afterwards known as George Osmond. He was of just the right age and occupation and it interests me to find that his birth place is given as Ha as Hackney which agrees with the information in your possession. Do you think it possible that he can have been baptised under the surname Flight? I was under the impression that his mother did not marry Hansen Flight until some time after George's birth. It may be, however, that the marriage took place earlier than I had supposed. This would account for our being unable to find any reference to it in the indexes at Somerset House. These indexes begin in July 1837. A search has also been made in the census of 1851 in the town of Bicester Oxfordshire where George Osmond, Senior, was in practice as a solicitor but no reference whatever was found of the name in the whole town and I presume that he did not set up in practice there until fairly late in life. This is a minor disappointment but a solicitor should be easy enough to trace at any point in his career."

The most recent letter was as follows:

"I believe I have at last found the baptism of George Osmond. The following is an entry in the register of St. Matthew, Bethnal Green, in North East London:

> 14 June 1837, George son of George and Ann Osmond, Howards Place, Gentleman, born 23 May 1837

This entry satisfies all the known conditions, except that George Flight, as he was then known, in the censes of 1851 was said to be 14 years old. The censes took place on the night of 30 March and this George would then have been nearly two months short of his forteenth birthday. I understand that the family have ~~kxx~~ always believed that his father was a solicitor and in those days, and in fact today, a solicitor in England is always officially styled a gentleman. Those who practice as barristers are similarly officially styled esquire. Young George Flight gave his birthplace as Hackney and Hackney adjoins Be Bethnal Green to the North. On this occasion as on many others the child was baptised in a different parish from that in which he was born and that is why the search has taken so long. Before lighting on this entry in the Bethnal Green register, I had in turn tried the registers of three then existing churches in Hackney itself."

I am sure you will all relize the importance of this wonderful work and want to keep it going now that we are finally on the right track. It is going to take a lot of funds--the fee is approximately $1.50 per hour. I think we would all enjoy doing our part by contributing whatever we can no matter how small. As I recall, Joe Osmond was appointed Secretary last year. (If I am mistakenon this, please forgive me)--therefore, you may send your contributions to him, or, if you so desire, you may send them to the Genealogy Committee and we will send you a receipt and forward the money to the researcher in England. I hope this meets with everyon's approval until we can make better arrangements at our reunion. Names and addresses of the Secretary and Committee are as follows:

Joe Osmond	Vera C. Hunsaker	Lydia T. Osmond	Olive D. Osmond
1197 Orchard Drive	Tremonton, Utah	3525 Quincy Ave.	228 N. Washington Blvd.
Bountiful, Utah		Ogden, Utah	Ogden, Utah

Now, for another favor-- I am still trying to get records compiled for our Book of Remembrance. I would like this to be something really worth looking at by the time we hold the reunion, but I need your help in getting the information. I am enclosing a family group sheet for those whose records I need. I would appreciate pictures of any kind. If you have some you don't want to part with, perhaps your photographer would make a copy of some of them for you. Kindly mail them to me a 228 N. Washington Blvd., Ogden, Utah

I do hope to hear from all of you. I plan on writing more of these letters to keep you informed of any new developments, interesting bits of family news, etc., so if you would all take the part of reporters, it would make them more interesting. I would like to write to as many mambers of the family as possible so would appreciate more names and addresses.

Sincerely,

Olive D. Osmond (14-3W) *

* 14-3W is my number. It shows that I am the wife of George V. Osmond (3rd child), son of Rulon Osmond (14th child), son of George Osmond. I am assigning everyone in the family a number, but I will tell you more about that in my next letter. I am even sending you a list of the family members if I can get the records complete. I need your cooperation in sending me the needed information.

GEORGE V. OSMOND
227 WASHINGTON
OGDEN, UTAH

SAFECO
INSURANCE
COMPANY OF AMERICA
SEATTLE

228 N. Washington Blvd.
Ogden, Utah
February 23, 1959

David E. Gardener
Genealogical Society
80 N. Main St.
Salt Lake City, Utah

Dear Brother Gardener:

I have been reviewing the correspondence which you sent me and which has been microfilmed for our files down there.

There is one letter dated 23 March 1956 from Oxfordshire County Council, 10 New Road Oxford which lists the death of George Osmond, a Solicitor, who died at the age of 52, on 1st Dec. 1860, in Bicester. I really feel confident that this man is the father of our Grandfather George Osmond inasmuch as Grandfather had on some of his own papers in his own handwriting "George Osmond, born in 1808, died in Bicester Oxford 1860--my father".

Letter #32 appears to be on the right line too and I feel that the records from Bicester are most important. I agree with your letter of 19 November that the registers of Bicester should be thoroughly searched.

I believe we should accept the above mentioned George Osmond as our ancestor and proceed to trace his ancestry.

Mrs. George V. Osmond

6 Dec 1974

DAVID ENSIGN GARDNER, FS[illegible]

Fellow of the Society of Genealogists, London.
Member of the Historical Association, London.
Member of the Heraldry Society, London.
Member of the Devon and Cornwall Record Society.
Member of the Scottish Genealogical Society, Edinburgh
Director of BYU Travel Study groups (ancestral research) to Britain in 1960, 1967, 1968, 1971, 1974.
Instructor in Religion and Genealogy, B.Y.U. since 1957.

Specialist in modern and ancient ancestral research, evaluation of evidence and systems analyst for over 40 years.

Accredited Genealogist, The Genealogical Society of the Church.

Staff member, Systems Department, The Genealogical Society

Author of accepted text-books:

- Genealogical Research in England and Wales, vols. 1,2,3.
- Genealogical Atlas of England and Wales
- Genealogical Atlas of Scotland
- Genealogical Atlas of Ireland
- A Basic Course in Genealogy
- The Lambies First One Hundred Years in New Zealand (an ancestral study and family history)

City of London College and Clark's College, London.

Member Utah Genealogical Association

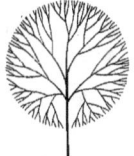

DAVID E. GARDNER
Systems Analyst

Phone (801) 531-2376

THE GENEALOGICAL SOCIETY
of The Church of Jesus Christ of Latter-day Saints
50 East North Temple Street • Salt Lake City, Utah 84150

6 December 1974

Dear Brethren:

The sources used in the research reported under date 6 December 1974 included the records listed below. Those marked with a * were records in the Library of the Genealogical Society.

1. Early LDS Church records * (British Mission, TIB, Logan Temple records).

2. Diary (Journal) of George Osmond the Utah pioneer.

3. 1841 and 1851 Census Records,* England.

4. Civil Registration records (since July 1837) of births, marriages and deaths kept in London, with indexes* on microfilm.

5. Principal Probate Registry, London, records in England, the index is on microfilm*.

6. London Directories kept in London, some on microfilm*.

7. Official LAW LIST kept in London.

8. Parish Registers in London area, most <u>not</u> on microfilm.

9. Marriage Indexes (Pallot and Co., and Boyds*). Also the Oxfordshire Marriage Index.*

10. The CFI (Computer File Index) was used in the Library including the Parish (alphabetical) print-outs. The records found there-in had either been placed there by temple work generated by the family or through controlled extraction. Some of the controlled extraction was based on incomplete BT's. The parish registers are not on film and require searching (this is being done).

11. Apprenticeship Records (Inland Revenue Series*) checked, but additional work is required in the non-indexed* portion.

12. Local probate jurisdictions, Archdeaconry and Bishop's courts, plus the Prerogative Court of Canterbury, London. Research in Library microfilms* and transcriptions from originals in England.

Other services involved are:

1. Preparation and submission of Entry Forms and Marriage Entry forms to the Genealogical Society for clearing for temple work.

2. Preparation and editing for publication information on the pedigree.

3. Advising the family on the organizing of a Family Association for reunions and involvement in genealogical research and temple work.

4. Preparation and submission of direct line family group records for the Priesthood Continuing Program - four generation program.

5. Preparation of the reported material, correct analysis of it in demonstrating connected ancestral work, and recommendations for continued research. This involves giving precise and correct instructions to record searchers (or genealogists) in the locality of the ancestral research in England or through use of record searchers using the resources in the Library of the Genealogical Society.

   Unless the analysis and preparation are well done the resulting reports may not locate the records required for finding trace of the pedigree and the compilation of records that are complete and correct.

6. By request of members of the family indicating how to use the DCC (card catalogue) of the Genealogical Society and the extremely valuable Registers (typescripts) detailing valuable source material. The family members are involved in research at the Library of the Genealogical Society.

Sincerely,

David E. Gardner
Systems Analyst

DEG:sjw

6 December 1974

Memorandum

The purpose of this memorandum is to demonstrate the finding trace of ancestral connections for the following:

2. George Osmond

George OSMOND
Born 23 May 1836
Hackney, London, England
Convert to the LDS Church
and baptized 27 November 1851
in Woolwich LDS Branch, London
Conference, British Mission
Changed his name from George
Flight to George Osmond

3. NANCY CANHAM
She also married Hanson Flight of London

Woolwich L.D.S. Branch Records, British Mission disclosed:
Baptized; 27 Nov 1851 George Flight, born 23 May 1836 at Hackney

1851 Census, Charlton (Ecclesiastical dist. of St. Thomas near Woolwich)

19 New Charlotte) Street)	Visitor:	George Flight, age 14, shipwrights) apprentice)	Bom at Hackney, Middlx.

Diary of George Osmond (in possession of family)
Date: 23 May 1886: "I am fifty years old today."

Genealogical Society Correspondence.

1952. Mrs. Alice M. Osmond Cook wrote to the Genealogical Society and stated:

> "I have a number of papers sent to me by my father's sister, Nellie Osmond Hart. Among them is a list of Osmond . . . names in my grandfather, George Osmond's own handwriting. In that list is this entry:
>
> "George Osmond, born 1808, died Bicester, Oxford, 1860, my father".
>
> "Nancy Canham, born 1807, Blackheath, Kent, died Brighton 1876, my mother."

Death records, Registrar General, Somerset House, London, England

1837-1860. The only death record fitting the identity of Geoige Osmond shows:

> Died 1 Dec 1860 at Sheep Street, Bicester, Oxfordshire.
> GEORGE OSMOND, age 52 years, solicitor.
> Informant: Sarah Shrowesbury, Sheep Street.

A solicitor is a lawyer (attorney) who can conduct litigation in a court.

1851 Census of Bicester, Oxfordshire:

No entry for the OSMOND family. George Osmond was a lawyer (solicitor) who was absent from his residence in 1851, but the following was at home:

Sheep Street: Martha Scarsbrook, solicitors housekeeper.

1841 Census of Bicester, Oxfordshire:

Causeway & Churchway, Bicester: (Bundle 885)	ANN OSMOND	61	Ind.	Y
	GEO. db.	30	attorney	Y
	Elizabeth TRIPP	65	Ind.	Y
	Martha Scarsbrook	25	FS	Y

This apparently is the solicitor (attorney) residing with a person who is probably his mother, Ann. Y means Yes born in county. Ind. means of independent means. FS means female servant. Ages are usually within five years of true age.

Principal Probate Registry, London.

Probate granted in the estate of GEORGE OSMOND, Bicester, Oxford, attorney at law. Will dated 15 Mar 1860. Left all property to Martha Scarsbrook, his housekeeper, whom he appointed sole executrix.
Proved at London 29 Dec 1860 by Martha Scarsbrook, spinster.

London Directory 1838:

> OSMOND, George, solicitor, Threadneedle Street [London].

Law List, 1852:

> OSMOND, George, Bicester, master extra-ordinary and commissioner for affidavits.

Searches for the christening (birth entry) of George Osmond.

According to records left by George Osmond, he was born 23 May 1836 in Hackney, one of the London boroughs, almost adjoining the city of London. Other records left by him, including his journal and papers, indicate that his mother was Nancy (or Ann) Canham. That his mother had also married a Hanson Flight of London, and that George Osmond had some half-brothers and a half sister, they having the surnames of Canham and Flight. George Osmond also recorded that he was sent down to the dockyards of the British Navy at Woolwich to be apprenticed as a shipwright.

This marriage of his mother to Mr. Hansom Flight appears to be the reason why George Osmond is recorded in the 1851 Census as a shipwright's apprentice living near Woolwich under the name of GEORGE FLIGHT, age 14 years.

It also helps to explain his record of joining the Church in Woolwich, (London Conference, British Mission) under thename of George FLIGHT.

Searches for his birth (christening record) took place in the parish of Hackney (St. John) without success. The adjoining parishes were searched, including St. Leonard, Shoreditch; St. Mary Whitechapel, Stepney; Christ Church, Spitalfields, Stepney; Christ Church Watney Street, Stepney; and St. Matthew Bethnal Green; and various other London locality parishes.

The two following birth records were found which are of direct importance:

1. Parish Register, St. Matthew, Bethnal Green, Middlesex, a suburb of London and adjoining HACKNEY: -

   Christened 14 June 1837) George, son of George and Ann Osmond,
   Born 23 May) of Howards Place, gentleman.

2. Parish Register of Church, Watney Street (Commercial Road, Stepney,) London:

   Christened 20 September 1843) George Canham son of Hanson and Ann Flight, of Jane
   Born 23 May 1836) Street, Coal merchant, born at Hackney.

Other records found by research include: -

1. Parish Register, St. Mary, Whitechapel, Middlesex (London):

   Chr. 19 May 1844) Sarah Jane, dau. Hanson and Martha Flight, of Gloucester Stre.
   Born 24 Apr 1844) collector. (See page 20 of Mr. Cotton's material).

   i. The certificate of birth from the Registrar General records on 24 April 1844, at No. 26 Gloster Street, Mile End Old Town, Stepney, the following birth:

      Jane, daughter of) Hanson Flight, clerk to a coal merchant and Martha Flight
) formerly Hopkinson.

      Informant signed: Hanson Flight, Father, 26 Gloster Street.

2. Marriage entry, 19 August 1858, St. Philip, Bethnal Green.
   Hanson Flight) age 51, Widower, Collector, 15 Upper King Street,
) son of Joseph Flight, miller

   to

   Martha Hopkinson) age 39, spinster, of 15 Upper King Street,
) dau. of Joseph Hopkinson, Sawmaker

3. Death entry, 29 Oct 1858, at 15 Upper King Street, St. George in East: -

   HANSON FLIGHT, age 50, collecting clerk to a draper.
   Died of cancer of neck, 8 months.

   Informant: Elizabeth Masters, 1 New Street, Kingsland, Middlesex.

4. Death entry, 5 Nov 1876, at 17, Marlborough Place, Brighton, Sussex.

   Nancy Flight, age 69, widow of Hanson Flight, general clerk.
   Informant: Robert H.C. Flight, son, same address.

   This is the mother of George OSMOND. It is also noted that Robert H. C. FLIGHT is his half-brother.

5. Pallot and Co. Marriage Index. This consists of marriages from certain London parishes between 1789 and 1837. This disclosed:

   Ref: 1827. FLIGHT, Hanson to Nancy CANHAM, St. Michael Crooked Lane,
   City of London.

6. Marriage register of St. Michael, Crooked Lane, City of London:

   10 June 1827.
   HANSON FLIGHT, Bachelor, minor, this parish
   NANCY CANHAM spinster, of Greenwich, Kent.
   Consent of Jane Flight, widow, his mother.

COMMENTS:

A. Ann Canham (also known as Nancy) had only one husband, Hanson Flight, to whom she was married in 1827 in London. He died in 1858 and she died as his widow in 1876.

B. Her son, George, was born 23 May 1836. He was christened twice, first in 1837 as son of George Osmond, gentlemen. He was later christened in 1843 (when he was seven years of age) and described as the son of Hanson Flight.

a. The christening entry of 1837 infers that George was the legitimate son of George Osmond and Ann. We cannot tell who took the child to the parish church to secure a birth registration and a christening, but he was undoubtedly the son of George Osmond by Mrs. Ann (Canham) Flight.

b. The christening entry of 1843 infers that George was the legitimate son of Hanson Flight and Ann. Undoubtedly his mother was Mrs. Ann Flight.

c. The only legal name that Ann Canham had from the time of her marriage in 1827 until her death in 1876 was "Mrs. ANN (or NANCY) FLIGHT." Probably she decided in 1843 that there was no legal recording for her son George's birth and so she had him registered (and christened) under the family name which she, Mrs. Flight, held legally. The officiating clergyman would not bother to ask her whether or not her husband, Hanson Flight, was the father of her child! Again, we do not know who took the child to the parish church in 1843.

d. According to the journal and history written by George Osmond (born 1836) he had a brother John who died during a house fire in London about 1842 or 1843. The upset of the house fire and death of a child may have shaken the family and created the need for a registration and christening entry under the surname of Flight (the legal surname of George Osmond's mother).

C. Hanson Flight certainly was living with Martha Hopkinson by 1843-44, and registered the birth of their child in 1844. He committed BIGAMY by marrying (during the lifetime of Ann Canham to who he was married in 1827) in 1858.

D. George Osmond, the attorney, born 1808 died 1860, apparently never married. He is described by George Osmond (born 1836) as "George Osmond, born 1808 died Bicester, Oxford, 1860, my father."

E. At this stage of British divorce law, it would be probably impossible for (Mrs.) Ann (Canham) Flight to get a divorce. No doubt Hanson Flight had deserted her and they remained separated. (Even the divorce act of Parliament, 1852, would not help them). Searches for records of birth of her other children have been made in the records of Somerset House (Registrar General) without success, under surnames of Canham, Flight and Osmond.

F. The descendants of George Osmond (born 1836) will, according to the rulings covering sealings of wives to husbands, have a sealing line of Hanson Flight and Ann Canham, who were married in 1827 in London. They will have a blood ancestral line of George Osmond.

G. On the 6 May 1939 at the Logan Temple, proxy sealing took place for ANN or NANCY CANHAM (born 1805) to GEORGE OSMOND (born 1808). Their son, George Osmond (born 1836) was sealed to them by proxy on 5 July 1941. The twin brother, John Osmond, was sealed on the same day.

No record of temple work has been found for sealing of the half-sister, Rosabelle Flight, to her parents.

On 2 Oct 1959, the two half-brothers, Henry Canham and James Canham, were sealed by proxy to Ann or Nancy Canham and George Osmond (the attorney).

Next steps in the research:

George Osmond, attorney, died 1860 age 52, by calculation was born 1807-1808. His record was not found in the 1851 census, but in the 1841 census of Bicester, Oxon, he was age 30-34, born in the county of Oxford, and residing with ANN OSMOND, age 61, probably his mother.

BICESTER, Oxon.

The parish registers are not in the Library of the Genealogical Society, but the Bishops Transcripts (BT's) are available on microfilm. There are many missing years. The period covers 1680-1834, with christenings 1813-1834 in the Controlled Extraction program. The period 1765-1812 in the chr. marrs, burs, have been searched, plus 1813-1834. The microfilm is difficult to read in parts but the following items are of importance:

chr [1808] (?George] son of George and Ann Osmond
chr 7 May 1809 Ann dau of George and Ann Osmond
chr 1 Sept bn 31 Aug 1814 William s. George and Ann Osmond

married [1807] George Osmond and Ann Phillips.

buried 9 Oct 1805 John Osmond, no age shown in BT's.

buried 16 Oct 1821 George Osmond age 75 (by calculation born 1745-1746).

The BT's have a gap 1720-1765 and some of the years are very difficult to read. They also end in 1834 making it difficult to make a full study and analysis.

The original parish registers in Bicester will be searched for additional facts.

Apprenticeship Records for lawyers.

Men in this profession had to serve five years as clerks under articles (bond). The documents are in the Public Record Office, London, and there are about eight divisions, such as Queen's (King's) Bench; Common Pleas; Exchequer; Chancery; etc. The microfilm index to the Court of Common Pleas 1725-1838,(Class CP 5), is at the Genealogical Society, but this did not disclose George Osmond's articles of clerkship. The other courts' records could be searched, if required, at a later date.

Death Record of George Osmond's mother:

The 1841 census showed George Osmond (attorney) residing with Ann Osmond. They were not found in the 1851 census. A search was made for the death record of Ann Osmond, and the record found by the Superintendent Registrar, and shows:

REGISTRATION DISTRICT: Bicester
Death in sub-district: Bicester, Co Oxford.
No. 267 Book 2
Died 26 Feb 1842 at Bicester Market End

ANN OSMOND, age 64 years, widow of George Osmond, draper.

Informant: Martha Scarsbrook, Bicester Market End.

The above does not show that George Osmond, the attorney, is son of Ann, but her probate record does show that, therefore George Osmond, the attorney, turns out to be the son of George Osmond, a draper, and Ann. The christening in 1808 is therefore acceptable.

Probate Records: Consistory Court of Oxford, Letters of Administration.

1. ANN OSMOND of Bicester, grant made 30 March 1842.

   Bondsmen: George Osmond, Bicester, gentleman
   Wellington Ellis, Cheltenham, surgeon

   Sworn testimony: George Osmond, eldest and lawful son. . . of Ann Osmond, late of Bicester, widow, interstate died 26 Feb 1842. Value under £200.

2. The calendar (index) to the Oxford probate court, the Archdeaconry Court of Oxford was searched 1766-1858, and five additional probate records were noted. Of these the following is of importance:

   ARCHDEACONRY OF OXFORD, Will dated 30 May 1848 proved 8 Mar 1854. (Abstract enclosed).

   ANN OSMOND, of 30 Peers Row, Oxford, widow.

   Executor and principal beneficiary: GEORGE OSMOND, Bicester, Oxfords, gentleman
   Others mentioned: WELLINGTON ELLIS, ANN his wife and sister of George Osmond, attorney; WILLIAM OSMOND brother of George.
   Oath to the executor: George Osmond, Bicester, solicitor [i.e. a lawyer].

   SPECIAL NOTE: Nothing stated or implied as to relationship between the deceased, (Mrs.) Ann Osmond, and her executor, George Osmond, solicitor of Bicester.

   She might be his grandmother, or perhaps his "step"-grandmother, that is a possible second wife of her late husband. (see next item below).

Death Certificate. Obtained from evidence of death in the above Will:

REGISTRATION DISTRICT OF HEADINGTON
death in sub dist. of SAINT CLEMENT, OXFORD
No 308 Book 10:
Died: 4 Dec 1853 at 30, St. Giles Road, Saint Giles, Oxford

ANN OSMOND, age 90 years, widow of JOHN OSMOND, farmer
died of old age.
Informant: SUSAN BARGUS, present at death Tredwell's Yard, St. Michaels, Oxford.

[no indication given that she is the mother of No. 2 GEORGE OSMOND, the draper]

1851 census of City of Oxford: St. Clements sub-district

No. 30, Peers Row, entry no 157 of district:
Head: ANN PEARSON age 72, widow annuitant born OXFORD, Oxon
followed by entry no. 158 of district:

Head: ANN OSMOND age 86, widow, fund holder born WORCESTER, Wincott.

(The whole of the City of Oxford, 1851 census, checked for [Dr.] Wellington Ellis and Ann his wife; Susan Bargus present at death above; and Osmond families. None found belonging to this family connection.)

The above information now supplies the name of the husband of (MRS) ANN OSMOND, who is believed to be either a grandmother or "step" grandmother of George Osmond, the attorney.

The Oxford probate courts did not disclose any probate record for JOHN OSMOND therefore the search was extended to the P.C.C. (new item below).

Prerogative Court of Canterbury, London, probate court, records at PRO and also on microfilm:

Calendars and Indexes searched 1800-1853, over eighty references found for OSMOND or similar surname. Six of these were read and abstracts made. Among them was the desired record, as follows:

1806 PITT, April, folio 423:

JOHN OSMOND,will made 20 April 1799, will proved PCC 15 April 1806 by sole extrix.

JOHN OSMOND of STANTON ST. JOHNS, OXFORDS.

To be buried: BICESTER as near my first wife as possible.

wife: ANN OSMOND, sole executrix, all property both real and personal.

wits. ELIZTH CROWTHER, REBECCA BOWLEY, ROBERT SPENDLOVE.

Oxfordshire Marriage Index:

This covers about 138 parishes in the county (or about 55% of the county) for varying periods. This is on microfilm at the Genealogical Society.

No JOHN OSMOND to a first wife listed
No JOHN OSMOND to a second wife, ANN, before 1799, listed.

Pallot Marriage Index:

This was also checked, but the search was inconclusive and not known if completely covered.

Boyds Marriage Index:

This has yet to be searched for appropriate areas.

Wellington Ellis and his wife Ann Osmond (sister of George Osmond, attorney).

Attempts were made to find this family in Cheltenham, Gloucestershire. This was not successful. Old directories were used and the 1851 census of the locality was searched.

The records of probate were searched, the P.C.C. down to 1858, and the Principal Probate Registry index, down to 1900 were searched. This involved searching a considerable number of microfilms.

The Will of Wellington Ellis was located and a copy obtained. This showed that Wellington Ellis died 30 Dec 1893 at Ashcombe Lodge, Weston Super Mare, Somerset and he made his will 17 Dec 1891 at that address. It was proved at Wells district court on 30 March 1894.

He mentions his only child: AUGUSTA HOPE ELLIS and his wife ELIZABETH ELLIS.

This indicates that (Mrs.) Ann Ellis (nee Osmond) probably died and he married second to Elizabeth.

His death record was found by searching the records at Somerset House, London, and reads:

Registration District: Ashbridge.
30 Dec 1893 at Ashcombe Lodge, Weston super Mare, USD.

WELLINGTON ELLIS, age 79 years, M.D. London

Informant: Thos. R. Evans, Ashcombe Lodge

During the course of this research a death record was found for:

REGISTRATION DISTRICT, ABERGAVENNY, sub-district ABERGAVENNY.
No. 320. 14 May 1857 at TWY DEE PARK, LLANTILLIO PERTHOLEY.

WILLIAM OSMOND ELLIS age 23 months son of Leopold Ellis, Esquire.

An effort is being made to find this child's birth and more about his connection with the Osmond family.

Additional research will be made to find more about Wellington Ellis's first wife, Ann Osmond, and if she was the mother of above Augusta Hope Ellis.

TO:

Research is continuing in the following records:

1. Records available in the Library, Genealogical Society.

   i. Probate court records (continuation of previous work)
   ii. Marriage indexes, including Boyd's and Oxfordshire
   iii. The Computer File Index (CFI) the next edition (probably January 1975) The previous edition (August 1973) has already been checked
   iv. Other records as required by the complexities of this case
   v. Certain temple (LDS Church) records

2. Sources available in England by the use of competent record searchers.

   i. In Oxfordshire the parish registers of Bicester, Burford, Chipping Norton, and Stanton St. John
   ii. An Osmond family of Chipping Norton, Oxon., needs to be investigated as there is a Baptist Church connection with this branch of the Osmonds.
   iii. The marriage bonds and allegations of certain marriages that took place "by license" need to be found.
   iv. Tombstone inscriptions, especially in Bicester and City of Oxford need to be located.
   v. The burial entry at Bicester, 9 Oct 1805, for John Osmond, needs further checking. This is probably the ancestor, and his age at death will be helpful. Also the burial of his 1st wife, as she is probably the ancestress. (The will of John Osmond indicates that he was married to a first wife (unnamed) and a second wife named Ann).
   vi. Librarians in the City of Oxford and at Weston Super Mare
   vii. The county archivist for Worcestershire with regard to the recorded birthplace of (Mrs.) Ann Osmond in the 1851 census of Oxford.
   viii. The 1891 and 1881 census records of Wellington Ellis family. This will be edited and continued from time to time.

3. The narrative account of the OSMOND research, for editing for publication in the OSMOND WORLD magazine, has been prepared. This will be edited and continued from time to time.

4. The family has requested services to help organize a worth-while family association to take care of the history and genealogy of the living descendants of George Osmond (born 1836) who emigrated to Utah after joining the LDS Church in Woolwich, England.

5. Temple work: There have been submitted for clearing for temple work some records. When the present searching, now in progress, comes to hand, it is expected that additional records will be available. These will be placed on the acceptable Entry and Marriage Entry forms and sent for clearing for temple ordinances.

6. Family group records on the Priesthood Continuing Program, that is, the Four Generation program, need to be typed and filed in the Archives of the Library.

(This is a NARRATIVE version of Report, for PUBLICATION in "OSMOND WORLD")

THE BRITISH OSMONDS. (From notes by David E. Gardner, FSG)

No. 1

The OSMONDS are a mixture of English and Welsh. Have you ever thought about your 4th great-grandparents? Well that is, your great-great-great-great-grandparents. Here are the OSMONDS 4th gg.parents:-

JOHN OSMOND, who lived in Oxfordshire in the 1700's, was a farmer in the countryside between BICESTER & BURFORD. He died a long time ago. He made his will of 20 April 1799 at Stanton St. Johns in Oxfordshire, and was buried at Bicester in October 1805. His first wife had died at an even earlier date, as he wrote in his will that he wished "to be buried at Bicester, Oxfordshire, as near to my first wife as possible", and he appointed his second wife, Ann, to be his sole exectutrix. She proved the will in the Prerogative Court in London on 15 April 1806. His widow, Mrs. Ann Osmond, lived until she was 90 years of age!

In 1848, when she was 87 years old, she made a will and signed her name, and that old will is at the Bodleian Library of Oxford University among the records of the Archdeaconry of Oxford probate court.

She resided at No. 30, Peers Row, adjoining St. Giles parish in the City of Oxford. In her will she appointed her step-grandson, George Osmond, Jr., as her trustee and executor. He was an attorney in the nearby town of Bicester, and was the son of George Osmond, Senr., a draper in Bicester, Burford and Oxford, but George Osmond, Senr., had died some years earlier. In her will, Mrs. Ann Osmond bequeathed to George Osmond, Jr.,"her household goods and furniture and implements of household, plate, china, linen and woollen and wearing apparel." She also forgave George his indebtedness and left him £500 plus other property. Mention was also made of George's sister Mrs. Ann Ellis, wife of Wellington Ellis a physician, and of his brother William Osmond and also William's son George Henry Osmond. After she made her will in 1848 she resided in Oxford for another five years and passed away at the age of 90 on 4 Dec 1853 at 30, St. Giles Road, Oxford. It is believed that some of the Osmond family of Oxford became jewellers.

Perhaps some of the folks living around Oxford might be interested in finding if Mrs. Ann Osmond who died in St. Giles, Oxford, locality in 1853 was buried in Oxford or Bicester and find some old OSMOND tombstones and copy the inscriptions that are visible.

Here is a facsimile of her signature when she was 85 years old:

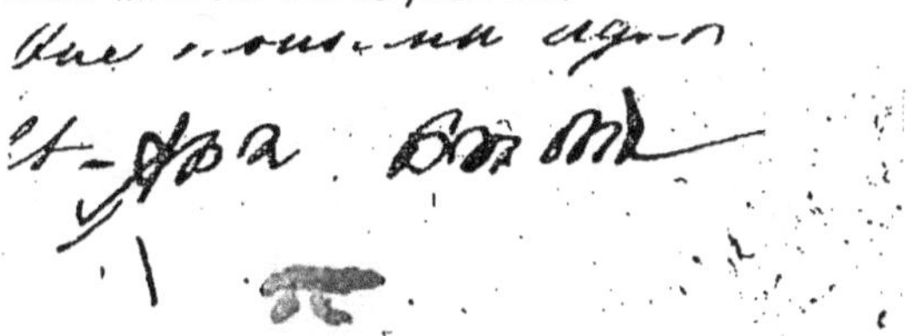

THE BRITISH OSMONDS.

No. 2

The topic of the OSMOND ancestry was left with the 4th g.g.parents, perhaps we should now mention the 3rd g.g.parents (that is, the great-great-great-grandparents of the OSMONDS).

Well, they were GEORGE OSMOND, Senr., who became a draper in Bicester, Burford and the City of Oxford, and ANN PHILLIPS. They were married at Bicester, after obtaining a license, in 1807. Their son, George Osmond, Junr., was born in 1808, and became an articled clerk, then a solicitor and finally an attorney in the town of Bicester. His father, George OSMOND, Senr., died fairly young, but his mother, as a widow, survived until 25 Feb 1842, at the age of 64 years. She died at Market End, in Bicester. She left some property but she had not bothered to make a will, so her son, George Osmond, the attorney, had to attend the Consistory Court of the Bishop of Oxford in order to obtain Letters of Administration. The details of the documents made at the time which are now in the Bodleian Library at Oxford University, are of interest and give the following information:

> GEORGE OSMOND of Bicester, gentleman, and WELLINGTON ELLIS of Cheltenham, surgeon, attended the court on 30 March 1842. George Osmond made oath that he is the eldest and lawful son of the deceased (his mother, Mrs. Ann Osmond).

George Osmond, the attorney, after he made the form of oath as the administrator, would then lay his hand on the Bible, and with the words SO HELP ME GOD, kiss the Bible and sign his name. The following is a facsimile of his signature:

When his mother resided in Market End, Bicester, she had a companion that looked after her during her last illness. Her name was Martha Scarsbrook. It is assumed that Mrs. Ann Osmond was buried in Bicester churchyard in early March 1842. Perhaps someone might find if she and her family has a tombstone with an interesting inscription.

THE BRITISH OSMONDS.

No. 3

Previously we have mentioned the OSMOND ancestry in the time of the 4th and the 3rd g.g.parents. Perhaps we should now deal with the great-great-grandparents (that is, 2 g.g.parents).

GEORGE OSMOND, Junr., was an attorney in London and in Bicester. He was born in 1808 in Bicester, Oxfordshire, the son of George Osmond (a draper) by his wife Ann Phillips.

When GEORGE OSMOND, Junr., was residing in London, he met NANCY CANHAM in 1835.

Nancy Canham was the daughter of George Canham and his wife Elizabeth White, of Woolwich, Kent. She had married, 10 June 1827, at St. Michael, Crooked Lane in the City of London, to her first husband, Hanson Flight, the son of Joseph Flight of West Ham, Essex (now London). Her second husband was George Osmond, the attorney, and their son was also named George Osmond. Here is the birth and baptism record as recorded in the parish church registers for St. Matthew, Bethnal Green, London:

Born 23 May [1836]) George son of George and Ann Osmond
Chr 14 June 1837) of Howards Place, gentleman

In the London Directory for 1838 the father is described as George Osmond, a Solicitor (a lawyer who can conduct litigation in a court) with his offices in Threadneedle Street, City of London. He is described as an attorney when he died at his residence on Sheep Street, Bicester, Oxfordshire, on 1 December 1860 at the age of 52 years. His will is filed in the Principal Probate Registry, Somerset House, London, dated 15 March 1860 and proved 29 Dec 1860.

We should now look at the first of this family who emigrated to America, that is the great grandfather of the OSMONDS, George Osmond born in London in 1836. When he was 14 years of age he was sent to Woolwich and became a shipwright's apprentice in Her Majesty's (Queen Victoria) Dockyard. At that time he was residing with friends of his mother's family, William and Mary White at 19, New Charlotte Street, Charlton near Woolwich, Kent (now London). In connection with his apprenticeship he attended school and he did well in the classics and mathematics and was well advanced in trigonometry. It was also at this time that George Osmond, in his 16th year, began his quest along the road of "Man's Search for Happiness" to find for himself the true religion that would elevate him and bring him solutions of "why we are here" on earth.

How To Trace Your Roots

AND WHY

By OLIVE D. OSMOND

How To Trace Your Roots AND WHY

By OLIVE D. OSMOND

Date: After 1974

A. Gather Your Supplies

You will need the following:

1. Large pedigree chart with numbering system (see center fold for one example) Fig. 1
2. Index cards, 5"x 8" (For personal history of each relative) (I use pink for female direct ancestors, blue for male direct ancestors and white for all others) See Fig. 2 for illustration.
3. A to Z, 5"x 8" index tabs for above cards.
4. File box, 5"x 8" for above cards.
5. File folders, legal or letter size. (I prefer legal because so many available genealogical records are legal size.)
6. A to Z index tabs, legal or letter size. (Again, I prefer legal size.)
7. File box for above folders.
8. Family group sheets, 8½"x 11", 3-ring (Fig. 3)
9. Family group sheets, 8½"x 14" (Fig. 4)
10. Notebook, 8½"x 11", 3-ring.

Your filing system may be as elaborate or as simple as you care to make it. The important things are to be well-organized and consistent.

B. Become Familiar With the Numbering System

I have tried several methods over the years of keeping track of my relatives. After "trial and error," I firmly believe that assigning an identifying number to each one is the very best way. Once again, study the centerfold pedigree chart for the Osmonds and you'll see how it works. Then, apply it to your own family tree like this:

You are #1
Your FATHER is #2
Your MOTHER is #3
Your FATHER'S FATHER (paternal grandfather) is #4
Your FATHER'S MOTHER (paternal grandmother) is #5
Your MOTHER'S FATHER (maternal grandfather) is #6
Your MOTHER'S MOTHER (maternal grandmother) is #7
Your FATHER'S FATHER'S FATHER is #8
Your FATHER'S FATHER'S MOTHER is #9
Your FATHER'S MOTHER'S FATHER is #10
Your FATHER'S MOTHER'S MOTHER is #11
Your MOTHER'S FATHER'S FATHER is #12
Your MOTHER'S FATHER'S MOTHER is #13
Your MOTHER'S MOTHER'S FATHER is #14
Your MOTHER'S MOTHER'S MOTHER is #15

Notice that all men have even numbers and all women have odd numbers on the Pedigree Chart.

Study the above until you become familiar with the numbers. When you record the names of your ancestors on the chart according to this numbering system, you will understand it better. Notice that if you take the number of any person on the chart and **double** it, you will be able to trace the paternal line immediately. For instance, take #2 (Father) and double it--that's #4 (Father's Father), double it--that's #8 (Father's Father's Father). Take any odd number (#3 for example), double it--that's #6, double it--#12, double it--#24, and you have traced your Mother's paternal line. Easy, isn't it?

C. Record Names, Birthdates and Places On Your Chart

You are now ready to proceed with your own pedigree chart. Write your own name as #1, your father's name as #2, your mother's name as #3 and so on. (See previous instructions) When recording a birthdate always write it in this order: The day of the month, the month and then the year, for example: 4 May 1925. Practice this way of writing dates on everything until it becomes a habit.

D. Make A Search For Additional Information

There are countless places where you might pick up information about your ancestors. Here are some of them:

1. Family Bibles (It has been quite traditional for families to record family statistics such as births, marriages and deaths into family Bibles). They are an excellent source. They may be on a dusty shelf, in a basement or attic, but they are priceless when found.
2. Visit relatives and ask questions about other members of the family. Don't be too aggressive, just show genuine interest in your "roots" and you'll find your relatives most helpful. They will probably even have pictures to show you.

3. Write to relatives. If you are unable to make a personal visit, letters can be a great source of information. Be sure to send a self-addressed, stamped envelope (SASE) when you write. This is a matter of courtesy as well as convenience. Make it easy for them to help you. It often speeds up the work. Don't ask for original records or pictures either. People treasure these things and no matter how careful you may be you could lose them or they could get damaged or destroyed. It is much better to ask for "copies" of things and pay for any costs involved. Always keep a copy of the correspondence you write as well as that you receive. File them in folders alphabetically, so they will be easy to refer to.
4. Search in libraries or wherever records are kept for information. It is amazing what you can find. Here are some places to look:

   a. Diaries
   b. Biographies
   c. Wills
   d. Deeds
   e. Birth Certificates
   f. Marriage Certificates
   g. Death Certificates
   h. Cemeteries
   i. Obituaries
   j. Old newspapers
   k. Immigration papers
   l. Citizenship papers
   m. Divorce records
   n. Probate records
   o. Census records
   p. Tax files
   q. Pension files
   r. Ship passenger lists
   s. Church registers
   t. Military service records
   u. Other - the list could go on and on. You must become a good detective.

5. Write for information wherever it can be found. Here are some interesting pamphlets now available:

   a. HE 20 6202: B53/976 - "Where to Write for Birth and Death Records"
   b. HE 20 6202: M34/976 - "Where to Write for Marriage Records"
   c. HE 20 6202: D64/976 - "Where to Write for Divorce Records"

   Write to: U.S. Government Printing Office
   Washington, D.C. 20402

E. Write Your Own History

While collecting all this genealogical information, take time to write your own history so details of your life will be available for your posterity. You may think you can't do it because you are not a writer. Well, that's really no excuse. A friend once told me, "To be a writer you just write." So, try putting a few thoughts down on paper. Soon it will become easy.

If you have an organized system for your "life's story" it will be much easier. I have a 3-ring loose leaf notebook with a tab for each year of my life. When I think of some interesting incident that has happened, I write it on a sheet of paper and file it back of the appropriate year. I also have an A-Z index in this notebook for my "philosophy" on various subjects. Some day maybe my posterity will be interested in finding out what my opinions were on various subjects. A little philosophy makes a story more interesting if and when you decide to write your story in book form.

F. File Your Information Properly

When you begin to collect information it is important to keep it filed properly so you can refer to it as often and as quickly as you want to. Here are some suggestions:

1. Use a separate folder for every direct ancestor. (I use pink (or red) for the direct female ancestors blue for the direct male ancestors.) For all others I use plain manila folders. Actually, the colored folders are optional--but helpful.
2. Number each folder using the same number as the pedigree chart followed by the person's name and birthdate. This will identify him accurately. File the folders in numerical order.
3. Into the folders, put such things as pictures, news clippings, birth certificates, marriage certificates, histories, military discharge papers, etc.--anything that may pertain to the individual. Since I belong to the Church of Jesus Christ of Latter Day Saints (Mormon), I would include patriarchal blessings, ordinations, temple marriage certificates, mission calls, church awards, etc.

G. Create the Card File

1. Use a 5"x 8" card for each person. I use pink for female direct ancestors, blue for male direct ancestors, white for all others. Again, color coding is optional but helpful.
2. Type or write the person's name in the upper, left-hand corner. Always put last names (surnames) first so cards can be arranged in alphabetical order. Try to get into the habit of using last names first on all genealogical forms.
3. On each card put the following information: Birthdate, birthplace, father's name, mother's name, who married, when married, place married, names and birthdates of children and any other pertinent data such as divorces or other marriages. Detailed information will make it easier to link families together properly in later reasearch.

H. Assign Numbers To Relatives

1. Assign numbers to relatives just the same way they are recorded on your pedigree chart. (These will be pink and blue cards.)
2. Assign numbers to other relatives (white cards) **as you prove the relationship.** By now you have discovered that there are a lot of relatives whose names do not appear on the pedigree chart. Yet, to be a true genealogist, you should keep track of all your relatives. Each one should have a card filed in an alphabetically indexed file and as soon as you can tie them in to the family tree, they should also have a number assigned.

Before proceeding further, be sure you understand the numbering system thus far because now we are going to get a little more complicated. Does it make sense to you that each person on the pedigree chart has two numbers--one as a parent and one as a child? Let me explain by an example. Take #8 (your great-grandfather). Suppose he had five children. Only one of them #4 (your grandfather), is shown on the pedigree chart. In numbering your great grandfather's children, however you do it this way: 8-1, 8-2, 8-3, 8-4, 8-5. If your grandfather was his third child, his number would be 8-3. But since he is also #4 on your pedigree chart, he now has two numbers #4 and #8-3. The #4 is the most important but #8-3 should also be shown on his card so you can double check relationships if necessary.

Let's take another example--your great-grandfather's first child #8-1. Let's assume we are four generations down from his by now and we have a card with this number on it: 8-1-3-5-7. That number tells us that the person identified is the 7th child of the 5th child of the 3rd child of the 1st child of #8 on the pedigree chart. It is simple. Just study it for awhile.

3. Number the in-law spouses. How do you do that? By using "W" for Wife and "H" for Husband along with the relative's number. For example, John Doe #6-5. His wife would be numbered #6-5W. If he had a second wife, her number would be #6-5WB. A third wife would be #6-5WC, etc. Just for a check now look at that last number (#6-5WC). It tells you that this is the third wife of the fifth child of #6 on the pedigree chart. It wouldn't matter if they were divorced or separated by death, their number would remain.
4. Number all children starting with the father's number (Don't use the "H" however). Use a dash between each number. All numbers should have as a **first** number the closest ancestor on the pedigree chart. For example, you want to index a cousin--say the first child of your father's brother. Your father is #6 on the pedigree chart. You are #3. Your father's other number (as a child) was #12-1, his brother would probably be #12-2. His brother's first child would be #12-2-1. By finding the closest ancestor on the pedigree chart you are able to obtain the first number. From then on it's very easy.

I. Start A Family Organization

1. Get your relatives involved. Contact them and tell them what you are doing. Ask if they would be interested in helping. Some of them might be doing the same thing you are.

A united family organization could eliminate much duplicated effort by establishing a common "clearing house" for information. Definite assignments for research could be made to various interested relatives such as searching through certain books or microfilms. Don't try to do all the work yourself. There is too much to be done. Do you realize that every time you go back just one generation, you have doubled the number of your ancestral lines?

2. Appoint someone to be responsible for collecting data. Yourself? Why not? You are the one that is really interested or you wouldn't be reading this right now. Perhaps, though, someone in your family is extremely talented or trained as a secretary. If they can type or do accounting it would be especially helpful. Get them involved.
3. Plan a family reunion. Keep your family close to one another by having a party once in awhile. It doesn't have to be an elaborate affair nor an expensive one. Have everyone bring something for a good old-fashioned "pot-luck" dinner. Make some charts, read some histories, honor the older members with a little gift and some words of appreciation for the things they have done. You will be surprised how interested they will all become in tracing their "roots".
4. Write a newsletter periodically and report to the relatives any progress you have made. Include newsy items about different members of the family. You might add such things as pictures, poetry, diaries, news clippings--just anything that would be interesting.

K. Compile a Book of Rememberance.

Once you have gone this far in your research, you will no doubt want to compile a "Book of Remembrance." Loose-leaf binders are wonderful for this purpose. Family group sheets (I have designed a special one for a loose-leaf binder, 3-ring, 8½"x 11" (See Fig. 6) are to be placed therein **numerically** along with pictures and documents of various kinds you have collected thus far in the individual folders. They fit beautifully on book shelves and are very handy to refer to. Just think how entertaining it will be some day when you are visited by a distant relative. You find that your common acestor was #32 on the pedigree chart for example. You simply go to your "Book of Remembrance," turn to Section 32 and you will find everything about #32 and his family all together in one place. I promise you it will be one of the most fascinating hobbies you can possibly select.

If you happen to be a member of the Church of Jesus Christ of Latter-day Saints (Mormon), you are already aware of the importance that is placed on seeking your genealogy and compiling it into the legal size Book of Remembrance books where the temple ordinances are recorded.

If you are not a member, let me explain briefly why Mormons place such importance on this particular work. Mormons believe that there is really no such thing as "death". Yes, there is a separation of the spirit and the body but we believe that the spirit lives on in the Spirit World. We also believe there are certain ordinances that are necessary for our progress in the next phase of life and if they haven't been done when our ancestors were living, we may do them in their behalf (vicariously) in our temples. These are "baptism", "endowment" and "sealing" ordinances.

Baptism: We believe if a child "dies" before the age of accountability (eight years of age), he is taken back into the presence of God. No ordinances have to be performed for the child in his "saved" condition. For those who have "passed away" after the age of eight and have not been baptized (by one having the authority--and you will need a visit from a Mormon missionary to fully understand this), then someone, usually a young person, actually is baptized in a baptismal font in one of our temples, taking upon him the name of the person who has "gone on" to the spirit world.

Endowment: This is a simple but beautiful ceremony wherein a person makes some sacred vows that will perfect his life to a great degree. This is done for the living as well as for the dead. If it is for the dead, a living person "stands in" for him.

Sealings: Marriages are performed for the living as well as the dead. Wives are sealed to their husbands and children are sealed to their parents by those having the authority to perform such an ordinance. Families are "sealed" together for time and all eternity in the temples. Accurate records are kept in the temples.

Please consider the following Biblical passages:

"Else what shall they do which are baptized for the dead, if the dead rise not at all? Why are they then baptized for the dead?" (I Corin. 15:29)

Baptism for the dead was practiced in ancient times. Another truth has been restored in these latter days.

"And I saw the dead, small and great, stand before God; and the books were opened: and another book was opened, which is the book of life: and the dead were judged out of those things which were written in the books, according to their works. And the sea gave up the dead which were in it; and death and hell delivered up the dead which were in them; and they were judged every man according to their works." (Revelation 20: 12, 13)

"For this cause was the gospel preached also to them that are dead, that they might be judged according to men in the flesh, but live according to God in the spirit." (I Peter 4:6)

How could the dead be preached to and be judged if they didn't have the capacity of hearing and responding? Yes, they are very much alive and waiting in that spiritual realm for the resurrection. Think of the justice and mercy of God allowing them to repent, change, grow and develop even after "death" and then providing a way for the important ordinances to be done for them by their posterity.

"For as in Adam all die, even so in Christ shall all be made alive." (I Corinthians 15:22)

Notice that word "all". That means everyone--no exceptions. Jesus Christ is the Savior for all mankind. Because of His glorious atonement, everyone who has ever lived upon this earth will be partakers of a resurrected body. To me this is what is meant by being "saved by grace."

"There are also celestial bodies, and bodies terrestrial; but the glory of the celestial is one, and the glory of the terrestrial is another. There is one glory of the sun, and another glory of the moon, and another glory of the stars; for one star differeth from another star in glory. So also is the resurrection of the dead..." (I Corinthians 15:40-42)

The above passage tells us that there will be different types of bodies in the resurrection. Read it again carefully. Could our works have something to do with our status in the hereafter? I think so.

We would not be saved at all without the atonement of Jesus Christ. He broke the bands of death and provided immortality for all. But he expects us to put forth effort, too. He has provided the ladder but we must climb it and to the degree we climb we shall be rewarded. School might be a good comparison. To the extent we put forth effort in studying we are rewarded with good grades. Life is similar. It is important to keep God's commandments. He has given us laws through His divine wisdom and the more we can keep, the higher we can climb. We can live on a celestial, terrestrial or telestial plane--all based on our own free agency and initiative.

We believe this is God's plan and it is as old as the world itself. Adam and Eve were married by God in the Garden of Eden. The "fall of Adam" (taking on a mortal body) was part of "The Plan" a wise Father in Heaven had developed for us. It was a necessary step in our eternal progress to have this mortal experience. We are not "depraved" and "sinful" as some ministers would have us believe. We are God's offspring. He has great plans for us. Just as we love to see our children grow and become like us and have the experiences we have had, so He in His infinite wisdom and love is preparing us for something greater, too. We are "Gods in embryo" being tested with the trials, temptations and hazards as well as the happy wonderful experiences of mortality. Let's read a few more Biblical passages along these lines:

"I have said, Ye are gods; and all of you are children of the most High." (Psalm 82:6)

"For in him we live, and move, and have our being; as certain also of your own poets have said, For we are also his offspring. For as much then as we are the offspring of God, we ought not to think that the Godhead is like unto gold, or silver, or stone, graven by art and man's device." (Acts 17:29, 30)

"The Spirit itself beareth withness with our spirit, that we are the children of God:" (Romans 8:16)

The main reason I have explained the foregoing doctrine to you is because you will now be able to choose which forms you will want to use for your Book of Remembrance.

1. There is a standard form used by most members of the Church of Jesus Christ of Latter-day Saints called the Family Group Sheet. On these sheets you record family units together and have spaces on the right-hand side for temple ordinance data. (See Fig. 8) Lovely binders are available for this form. (See Fig. 7)

2. Another form is now available in case you want to compile a Book of Remembrance loose-leaf style. It is quite simple and self-explanatory as you can see. (See Fig. 5) No temple ordinance data is recorded on this sheet although you may put it on the reverse side.

Either of the above forms makes a wonderful Book of Remembrance. Merely place numbers in the upper right-hand corner of the sheets and file them in numerical order. Be sure they correspond with the large circular pedigree chart. Then when you want to find some information about a certain person on your family tree, you can quickly find them by looking at the pedigree chart for their number or by checking the card file and then referring to the Book of Remembrance for details.

You may want to make this Book of Remembrance into a real family treasure, not just a book containing records of births, marriages, and deaths. If so, you can turn to your file folders where you have been collecting pictures, documents, etc., mount them onto plain, loose-leaf paper and file them back of the proper numbered tab.

If you are planning to index your family tree, Figure 4 shows the information you need. These forms are available too.

L. Listen to the Prophets

"7. Surely the Lord God will do nothing, but he revealeth his secret unto his servants the prophets." (Amos 3:7)
Let's hear what His latter-day prophets have to say about genealogy:

JOSEPH SMITH: "Therefore, renounce war and proclaim peace, and seek diligently to turn the hearts of the children to their fathers..."
(Doctrine and Covenants 98:16 - August 6, 1833)

"Those Saints who neglect it in behalf of their deceased relatives, do it at the perils of their own salvation." (History of the Church, 4:426, April 3, 1841)

"The greatest responsibility in this world that God has laid upon us is to seek after our dead." (History of the Church 6:313, April 7, 1844)

BRIGHAM YOUNG: "To accomplish this work there will have to be not only one temple but thousands of them." (Journal of Discourses, 3:372, June 22, 1856)

"We have a work to do just as important in its sphere as the Savior's work was in its sphere. Our fathers cannot be made perfect without us; we cannot be made perfect without them. They have done their work and now sleep. We are now called upon to do ours which is to be the greatest work man ever performed on the earth..." J.D. 18:213

JOHN TAYLOR: "God is looking upon us and has called us to be saviors upon Mount Zion. And what does a savior mean? It means a person who saves somebody...Would we be saviors if we did not save somebody? I think not. Could we save anybody if we did not build Temples? No, we could not; for God would not accept our offerings and sacrifices." (Journal of Discourses, 22:308, August 28, 1881)

WILFORD WOODRUFF: "When the Savior comes, a thousand years will be devoted to this work..." (Journal of Discourses, 18:230, September 16, 1877)

LORENZO SNOW: "This entire continent is the land of Zion, and the time will come when there will be temples established over every portion of the land and we will go into these temples and work for our kindred dead night and day, that the work of the Lord may be speedily accomplished, that Jesus may come and present the kingdom to his father." (Millennial Star, 61:546, May 8, 1899)

JOSEPH F. SMITH: "The same gospel prevails today, and the same ordinances are administered today, both for the living and for the dead, that were administered by the prophet himself, and delivered by him to the church...

We realize that one of the greatest responsibilities that rests upon the people of God today is that their hearts shall be turned unto their fathers, and that they shall do the work that is necessary to be done for them...

I perceived that the Lord went not in person among the wicked and the disobedient who had rejected the truth, to teach them; but behold, from among the righteous he organized his forces and appointed messengers, clothed with power and authority and commissioned them to go forth...

And thus was the gospel preached to the dead." (Gospel Doctrine, pp. 471, 474, October 1900)

HEBER J. GRANT: "I am deeply interested in this work. I am anxious to encourage the people to press on in securing their genealogies and after doing so in laboring in our temples...Up to the first day of April I had endowments to my credit of more than two a week for this year.

We can generally do that which we wish to do. A young man can find an immense amount of time to spend with his sweetheart. He can arrange affairs to do that. We can arrange our affairs to get exercise in the shape of golf and otherwise. We can arrange our affairs to have amusements. And if we make up our minds to do so we can arrange our affairs to do temple work.

Millions of dollars have been invested in the Salt Lake Temple. Month after month, as a boy, I contributed one dollar a month. As my wages increased I contributed two dollars a month, and later three dollars, four dollars, five dollars, and finally gave several thousands of dollars toward the completion of that temple. Why? Because the Lord God Almighty had given me a knowledge that the hearts of the children have been turned to their fathers; that the keys held by Elijah the prophet were in very deed delivered to Joseph Smith and Oliver Cowdery. The very granite bears witness to the faith, the knowledge, and the testimony that God has given to the Latter-day Saints. (Gospel Standards, pp. 33-34, April , 1928)

GEORGE ALBERT SMITH: "May it be pleasing to thy people to search out the genealogy of their forbears, that they may become saviors on Mount Zion by officiating in the temples for their kindred dead. We pray thee also that the spirit of Elijah may rest mightily upon all peoples everywhere that they may be moved upon to gather and make available the genealogy of their ancestors; and on behalf of the dead all ordinances pertaining to their eternal exaltation." (Temples of the Most High, pp. 189-190, September 23, 1945)

DAVID O. MCKAY: "One of the most important phases of gospel activity is associated with the temples. Upon intelligent, constant genealogical research, vicarious temple work is wholly dependent.

Genealogical reasearch is not only a function of the priesthood, but also a responsibility of every family.

When conscientiously performed it contributes to unity in the home and permits us to catch the vision of the divine nature.

Therefore, let us as a church and as a people labor with all our might to qualify as saviors on Mount Zion."

JOSEPH FIELDING SMITH: "Many there are, it is true, who comprehend this great work and are faithfully discharging their duties in the temples of the Lord. This is a good sign, showing the willingness and activity of the Saints. But this does not relieve the inactive, dilatory members who are doing nothing for their dead. These persons cannot expect to receive credit for what others may be doing; the responsibility rests with equal force on all, according to our individual ability and opportunities.

It matters not what else we have been called to do or what position we may occupy or how faithfully in other ways we have labored in the church; none are exempt from this great obligation. It is required of the apostle as well as the humblest elder. Place, distinction, or long service in the cause of Zion, in the mission field, the stakes of Zion, or elsewhere will not entitle one to disregard the salvation of one's dead.

Some may feel that if they pay their tithing, attend their regular meetings and other duties, give of their substance to the poor, or perchance spend one, two, or more years preaching in the world, they are absolved from further duty. But the greatest and grandest duty of all is to labor for the dead.

We may and should do all these other things, for which reward will be given, but if we neglect the weightier privilege and commandment, notwithstanding all other good works, we shall find ourselves under severe condemnation.

And why such condemnation? Because 'the greatest responsibility in this world that God has laid upon us, is to seek after our dead." Because we cannot be saved without them, 'it is necessary that those who have gone before and those who come after us should have salvation in common with us, and thus hath God made it obligatory to man,' says the Prophet Joseph Smith. From this, then, we see that while it is necessary to preach the gospel in the nations of the earth and to do all other good works in the church, yet the greatest commandment given us, and made obligatory, is temple work in our own behalf and in behalf of our dead." (The Ensign, February 1971, p. 2)

HAROLD B. LEE: "Temple work is the most unselfish work a member of the church can do in the kingdom of God and no earthly remuneration or glory can equal the satisfaction that comes from doing work for the dead...

'When a young couple has a civil ceremony so relatives can witness the wedding and then go into the temple after, they are not married in the temple. They are sealed, and therefore miss the blessing of having their marriage ceremony performed in the house of the Lord where it should be,' President Lee said.

He added that temple marriage is the Lord's way and a sealing ceremony shouldn't be second to a temple marriage...

He told the congregation that the temple is the place the savior will come to when he comes again.

'The temple is a place of instruction for the saints. For the perfecting in the doctrine and for the learning of the ordinances hidden from the world. Temple work is the most sacred work to be given to anyone,' (Church News, November 14, 1970, pp. 3 & 5)

And, now, let's really catch the vision of this great work from our beloved living prophet, President of the Church of Jesus Christ of Latter-day Saints, Spencer W. Kimball. He wrote this message shortly after our temple in the Washington, D.C. area was constructed.

SPENCER W. KIMBALL: One of the purposes of this temple, and all temples of the Church, is to bring families closer together, to strengthen the home, and to help the individual realize his or her importance and potential in the divine plan. Through ordinances performed in the temple, ties between parents and children are established so that they may endure in love not only in this earth life but beyond into eternity. We believe that no institution in society is more important than the family. The strength of the community and of the nation begins in the home. That is where integrity begins and is nurtured. In the home come the first lessons in unselfishness and caring about others. Learning begins with the family, too, and so does self esteem. The home is where a child should first discover his divine relationship to his heavenly Father, that he is truly a child of God as well as of his earthly parents.

The Washington Temple becomes the sixteenth in use today by Latter-day Saints, or Mormons, as some call us. Other temples are situated in various parts of the United States, in Canada, Great Britain, Switzerland and New Zealand.

But temples are not new. The Bible records how sacred ordinances were performed by ancient Israel while they traveled in the wilderness. They had a portable tabernacle, which sheltered the Ark of the Covenant. Later, Solomon replaced the tabernacle with a beautiful temple. Other temples followed.

Through the Prophet Joseph Smith, the fullness of the gospel of Jesus Christ was restored to earth in the nineteenth century. Under the Prophet Joseph Smith's inspired leadership, two temples were erected. Others since then have been constructed and put into use.

Temples are not public houses of worship. Our regular meetings are not held within their walls. As we have said, temples are for sacred ordinances. One of them is that of the marriage ceremony. But our temple marriages are different. Here the couple is not joined "until death do you part." In the temple man and woman are joined in a marriage covenant which extends beyond the grave into eternity. If man and woman continue after death, as indeed they do, why should death separate them? Why should death end their companionship, their love? In this temple ceremony, a union is formed, too, between the couple and the children which will come to them as parents. That union with their children also continues after death.

Can you see how the family is strengthened through a temple marriage ceremony?

Other ordinances performed in our temples are baptisms on behalf of ancestors and others who have left this life.

We believe, as all Christians should believe, in the words of Jesus in reply to Nicodemus:

"Except a man be born of the water and of the Spirit, he cannot enter into the kingdom of God." (John 3:2-5)

Every person must indeed be baptized to enter into the kingdom of God. "But," you may ask, "what about those who have lived without having the opportunity to accept the gospel of Jesus Christ or to be baptized?"

In our Washington Temple, as well as in our other temples, provision is made for baptisms to be performed in behalf of the deceased. Thus, Latter-day Saints are encouraged to seek out the records of their ancestors, so that temple ordinances can be performed for them.

The Apostle Paul anciently spoke of this practice of performing baptisms for the deceased when he said:

"Else what shall they do which are baptized for the dead, if the dead rise not at all? Why are they then baptized for the dead?" (1 Corinthians 15-29)

Can you see how our temples bring us closer together, not only as families here today, but as members of families extending back through generations?

We might explain also, that temple marriage ceremonies may also be performed on behalf of others who have not had this privilege during this earth life. Temple marriages may also be performed with couples who have previously had their marriage ceremony performed outside the temple, provided, of course, that they subsequently meet the requirements for this sacred temple ordinance.

Another temple ordinance is that of the sacred endowment, which has been described as "pertaining to man's eternal journey and limitless possibilities and progress which a just and loving (Heavenly) Father has provided for the children whom he made in his own image — for the whole human family."

An ancient prophet declared: "Men are that they might have joy." (2 Nephi 2:25)

What greater joy can come to a man or woman than to feel the strength of strong family ties?

President Spencer W. Kimball

M. Keep a Proper Attitude - My Personal Testimony

I sincerely believe that tracing your "roots" (genealogical research) and doing the temple work that goes along with it, is the great work of the Lord in this era of the world's history.

When we find someone interested in tracing his ancestry we often say he has the "spirit of Elijah," referring, of course, to this Biblical passage:

"Behold, I will send you Elijah the prophet before the coming of the great and dreadful day of the Lord. And he shall turn the heart of the fathers to the children, and the heart of the children to their fathers, lest I come and smite the earth with a curse." (Malachi 4:5, 6)

We believe that Elijah the prophet has already visited the earth and that the Lord's coming is nigh at hand. Can you thing of anything that turns the hearts of children to their fathers or hearts of fathers to their children as much as genealogical research?

Tracing "roots" as a hobby has gone from #3 position to #1 position just this year. People are fascinated. They have been touched by the "spirit of Elijah."

Whatever you do, once you embark upon this glorious work, don't become discouraged! If you get blocked on one line, try another. They are all important. Besides being diligent, be prayerful and you will receive help from "beyond." I have been guided many times in my own research.

Someone once said, "There is no limit to the amount of good you can do if you don't care who gets the credit." I love that thought. Let's help everyone who needs or wants our help and let's get this good work moving along!

Sincerely,

Olive D. Osmond

Olive D. Osmond

P.S. Hopefully our relatives will write and send their pedigree charts, family group sheets or any other pertinent information to us. We're putting all this information into a computer. Someday soon we should have "print-outs" available which should save countless hours of time for those doing research on these lines. Eventually (as soon as we have tested the program ourselves), we hope to have this service available for other families, too. If you are interested, please let us know.

Our address (for genealogical purposes only):

The Osmonds
c/o C/O "Osmondology"
Provo, Utah 84601

Anthony Wood

The Osmond who is buried at Bicester

Oxford Times newspaper
Article written 22 April 1975
by Anthony Wood (Conway)

Two young Osmond fans searching for the tombs of their idols' ancestors in Bicester Churchyard. Picture by Athar Chaudhry.

THE OSMONDS (I thought I'd mention the name stright away to capture the attention of my younger readers).

I suppose everyone will have heard of this astonishingly successful American pop group. For the benefit of anyone who has been on a three year trip to Siberia let me explain: they are five (six if you count youngest brother, Jimmy) well-groomed youngsters whose following fans rivals, nay even exceed, that of the Beatles in their heyday.

Well, it now appears that the Osmonds' ancestors lived in the Oxford area. And that information has been enough to send bevies of young ladies — teenyboppers is the somewhat unkind description, I gather — scuttling around Oxfordshire looking for their graves.

It began with a short article about the group's ancestors in the latest edition of Osmonds World, the official magazine of their fans. Presumably the information was furnished by the Osmonds themselves, who doubtless share with many Americans a boundless curiosity about their forbears.

The furthest back the magazine goes is to the mid-18th century and the Osmonds' great-great-great-great grandfather, a certain John Osmond, a farmer between Bicester and Burford who was buried in Bicester in October 1805.

Thanks to the efforts of my good friends Shirley Barnes, of the county records office, and Malcolm Graham, who looks after the local history section of the city library, I have managed to dig up some information about even earlier Osmonds.

I ought to say here that I cannot state categorically that these are *definitely* the direct ancestors of John and hence the later Osmonds. But a coincidence of Christian names — all are called either John or George, as are later Osmonds — and the fact that these are the only Osmonds in the records who lived in this area — these two things make the supposition almost irresitible.

Ale house

Malcolm Graham managed to find a marriage bond, dated 1742, dealing with a marriage of one George Osmond, a 25-year-old Bicester butcher, and Mary Alan, 21, also of Bicester. Miss Barnes also found reference to a George Osmond in a document of 1753; he was described as a churchwarden or overseer of Bicester Market End. Was this John's father?

But it is in the records of the county quarter sessions that the name Osmond crops up most frequently — and in rather surprising ways.

In 1735 and 1744 a John Osmond (the father of the above George?) applied for licences for his ale house in Bicester Market End. I don't suppose the present day Osmonds would be too keen to acknowledge this man as an ancestor — they are Mormons and hence complete abstainers from liquor.

Then in 1713, 1723 and 1725, another John Osmond, this time of Burford and perhaps the publican's father, appeared before the court charged with riotous assembly. In view of the period, it is possible that John's appearances, as a result of which he entered into recognisances to be of good behaviour, had something to do with opposition to enclosures.

Firmer ground

In 1687 and 1690, George Osmond, a slater of nearby Fulbrook (John's father?), also made two court appearances. The first time, he was found not guilty of riotous assembly, involving the destruction of a wall, and of insulting behaviour; in 1690 he was fined 6s 8d for insulting behaviour and ordered to keep the peace towards one Joan Ellis, wife of James Ellis.

That's just about as far back as we can go with the Osmonds. Returning to farmer John in the mid-18th century, we are on rather firmer ground.

His son George, whom the Osmonds' magazine describes as a draper in Bicester, Burford and Oxford, also appears to have been a funeral director, providing an almost total service with the exception of the coffin.

In 1811, the executors of the late Josiah Jones paid him nearly £32 for funeral equipment, a hefty sum in those days. It included 14 silk hatbands at a total of nine guineas, the use of the best velvet pall (10s), a winding sheet for the body (14s), even the hire of eight underbearers, £1 8s 6d.

George's son was George Herbert Osmond, a solicitor of Sheep Street, Bicester, whose name appears in many legal documents, wills and directories in the mid-19th century.

His brother, William, was a coachbuilder in New Buildings, Bicester, so Mr Graham has discovered; and William's son, George Henry Osmond, seems likely to have been the jeweller George H. Osmond who crops up in the 1871 census and in the 1894 Oxford directory as having premises at 118 St Aldate's, Oxford, the present site of the Southern Gas Board offices.

All these men are mentioned in the will of Mrs Ann Osmond (except George the draper, who died before her).

She was the second wife of John the farmer, and died on December 4, 1853, at the ripe old age of 88 in Peers Row (now vanished), St Giles, Oxford.

Mrs Ann Osmond's tomb is the main object of the local fans' search among the graveyards. My own researches have thrown no light on its whereabouts, so I should be interested to learn if anybody does locate it.

Bad name

Incidentally, I do hope those youngsters involved in the hunt will be on their best behaviour in the graveyards, and that means keeping to the paths and not tramping over graves. I would be sorry to see Osmonds' fans getting a bad name.

Just one more thing: you are probably wondering when the first Osmond set sail for America — I am too. Unfortunately it has been impossible for me to discover the date; but the Osmonds' magazine has promised another article on the subject, so I'll keep you posted.

flat 3, 15, View Road,
Mt. Eden.
Auckland. 3.
New Zealand.

2nd. July. 1975.

Mrs. Olive Osmond,
c/- Osmond Brothers' Fan Club,
P. O. Box 5000,
Provo.
Utah 84601, U.S.A.

Dear Mrs Osmond,

re the missing links for your Family tree.

As you will see by my name I am also an "Osmond", and have always been interested in your family, after seeing them on the Andy Williams show about 11 years ago. Osmond is not a very common name. My grandparents came from Devonshire, England.

I very much enjoyed the Concert at Eden Park on 18/3/75, it was great, and I have the lovely souvenir book sold at this evening, and I hope you all enjoyed your brief stay in New Zealand.

Your magazine "Osmonds World" is now being sold here and I have the issues from May 1974 (No 7) to April 1975 (No 18). They are most interesting, and I note that you and Mr. Viril Osmond are working on a family tree.

I am not directly related, as my immediate relations are all in New Zealand, but there might be a link from my grandfather or his brothers – we only have bits and pieces of information from notings in the family Bible, held by my cousin, and I set these out as they appear.

Great great grandmother was Sarah Osmond – the date shown 1854.

My grandfather John Gregory Osmond 1829 – 1888 was married twice. His first wife was named Emma Osmond. There were several children of this marriage – the eldest son, G. P. Osmond died in Exeter on 16/3/1889. The younger son named Charles Osmond, came some years later to New Zealand and saw my father, but returned to England and died there, date unknown, we think he would have been then about 35 years old. My father thought that some members of this first family travelled to America, but their names are unknown to me.

Returning to my grandfather, John Gregory Osmond above, – he had a brother, Edward Osmond who lived in Union Road, Exeter, there were 8 children – 4 boys and 4 girls, and Edward died on 30/6/1905. One of these children – Charles Osmond married a Doctor Hunts' daughter. He was the manager of a Bank near Manchester about 1891.

When Emma Osmond died – date unknown – my grandfather John Gregory Osmond, of Alyne, Devonshire, married Amy Benmore Penticost on

21/2/1872 in the Anglican Church of Littleham Exmouth. They lived at "Spestos Grange", Grange Place, near Crediton, Devonshire. This was a country home, he was a farmer, and he bred pedigree hunting horses. My cousin visited this home in 1961 and took some photographs.

It appears that John Gregory Osmond lived in the districts of Hayne, Newton St Cyres, Bow and near Crediton. There were 5 children of this second marriage and my grandparents and their 5 children came to New Zealand – 1890/1891, when my father was about 2 years old, and settled in Auckland. John Gregory Osmond died in Auckland on 19/8/1888 aged 59. Amy Benmore Osmond died in Auckland on 13/6/1920 aged 72.

My father James Ingram Osmond grew up in Auckland and went to the Boer War and returned and married, and he died on 17/5/1931 aged 52.

My mother Eva Gertrude Osmond died on 27/1/1969 aged 86½.

I am 64 years of age and was born in Auckland – I was an only child and never married and my closest living relations are my cousins.

When your family release new records or appear on T.V., my telephone rings – the young people look up the 'phone book, see "Osmond" and ring me to talk to Donny!!! I have been averaging about 4 calls a month for the past 2 years. You have a lot of friends here.

4.

It has been a pleasure to write to you and I send my best wishes for your family's continued success.

Yours very sincerely,
(Miss) Rose Osmond.

Letter from New Zealand about the Osmonds of Devonshire, England
July 2, 1975

2 July 1975

From:
Miss Roie Osmond
Flat 3, 15, View Road
Mt. Eden, Auckland. 3.
New Zealand

To:
Mrs. Olive Osmond
c/o Osmond Brother's Fan Club
P.O. Box 5000
Provo, Utah, 84601, USA

Dear Mrs. Osmond,

Regarding the missing links for your Family Tree:

As you will see by my name I am also an "Osmond", and have always been interested in your family, after seeing them on the Andy Williams show about 11 years ago. Osmond is not a very common name. My grandparents came from Devonshire, England.

I very much enjoyed the Concert at Eden Park on 18 March 1975; it was great, and I have the lovely souvenir book sold at this evening, and I hope you all enjoyed your brief stay in New Zealand.

Your magazine "Osmonds World" is now being sold here and I have the issues from May 1974 (N.7) to April 1975 (No.18). They are most interesting, and I note that you and Mr. Virl Osmond are working on a family tree.

I am not directly related, as my immediate relations are all in New Zealand, but there might be a link from my grandfather or his brothers--we only have bits and pieces of information from notings in the family Bible, held by my cousin, and I set these out as they appear.

Great-great-grandmother was Sarah Osmond - the date shown 1854.

My grandfather John Gregory Osmond, 1829-1888, was married twice. His first wife was named Emma Osmond [Emma Norris]. There were several children of this marriage--the eldest son, G. P. Osmond died in Exeter on 16 March 1889. The younger son named Charles Osmond, came some years later to New Zealand and saw my father, but returned to England and died there, date unknown. We think he would have been then about 35 years old. My father thought that some members of this first family traveled to America, but their names are unknown to me.

Returning to my grandfather, John Gregory Osmond above - he had a brother Edward Osmond who lived in Union Road, Exeter, there were 8 children - 4 boys and 4 girls, and Edward died on 30 June 1905. One of these children - Charles Osmond married a Doctor Hunts' daughter. He was the manager of a bank near Manchester about 1891.

When Emma Osmond died - date unknown - my grandfather John Gregory Osmond of Hayne, Devonshire, married Amy Benmore Penticost on 21 February 1872 in the Anglican Church of Littleham, Exmouth [Devonshire]. They lived at "Spestos Grange", Grange Place, near Crediton, Devonshire. This was a country home, he was a farmer, and he bred pedigree hunting horses. My cousin visited this home in 1961 and took some photographs.

It appears that John Gregory Osmond lived in the districts of Hayne [Devonshire], Newton St. Cyres [in Exeter, Devonshire], Bow [in Crediton, Devonshire] and near Crediton [Devonshire]. There were 5 children of this second marriage and my grandparents and their 5 children came to New Zealand - 1890/1891, when my father was about 2 years old, and settled in Auckland. John Gregory Osmond died in Auckland on 19 July 1888 [but his death certificate states that he died on 10 August 1888], aged 59. Amy Benmore Osmond died in Auckland on 13 June 1920 aged 72.

My father James Ingram Osmond grew up in Auckland and went to the [Second] Boer War [that took place during 1899-1902 in South Africa] and returned and married, and he died on 17 May 1931 aged 52.

My mother Eva Gertrude Osmond died on 27 January 1969 aged 86½.

I am 64 years of age and was born in Auckland - I was an only child and never married and my closest living relations are my cousins.

When your family releases new records or appear on T.V., my telephone rings - the young people look up the phone book, see "Osmond", and ring me to talk to Donny! I have been averaging about 4 calls a month for the past 2 years. You have a lot of friends here.

It has been a pleasure to write to you, and I send my best wishes for your family's continued success.

Yours very sincerely,

(Miss) Roie Osmond

22 July 1975

Mrs. George V. Osmond
1505 North Canyon Road
Provo, UT 84601

Dear Sister Osmond:

Research has been continuing since the last report sent to you about the Osmond and allied lines.

Ralph D. Osmond, a cousin, has been searching in the Genealogical Society Library and has carried out assignments, including the following:

1. Boyd's Miscellaneous Marriage Index, 1600-1837. A xerox copy of the findings has been placed in the research files. This is a valuable aid, as it will be used from time to time as research proceeds. This is for Osmond and Flight entries.

2. Gibson's Oxfordshire Marriage Index, 1538-1837, covering parts of 132 parishes out of around 210 parishes in the county of Oxford. This is for Osmond and Phillips entries. This is in the research files of the family under Oxfordshire and is proving helpful as research proceeds.

3. Probate Records. A search of these has been made and the will of Wellington Ellis, (who married Ann Osmond) uncle of George Osmond, has been found. A check has also been commenced by Ralph Osmond in the Oxfordshire probate court records and other probate records. These will be used as research proceeds.

Vera C Hunsaker, a cousin, has been meeting with David E. Gardner and discussing the previous research (by Sister Hunsaker and others) and has searched some records in the Genealogical Society Library by request.

A complete set of family group records has also been made by Sister Hunsaker, and these are in the research files.

Russell L. Osmond. Brother Osmond is a chaplain in the Armed Services and has consulted with Brother David E. Gardner about the ancestral research, pedigree development and the organizing of the George Osmond Family.

In addition to voluntary work by members of the family, research has been conducted by Brother David E. Gardner who has also assigned research to the noted genealogist, Richard L. Millett, of Salt Lake City and to researchers or registrars and librarians in England. Funding for all the paid research has been by Brother George V. Osmond and Sister Olive

D. Osmond, parents of the Osmond Brothers. Since June 1971 this has amounted to deposits of working funds with Brother Gardner of $600.00. Earlier reports have been made, and the following is, the final report to date:

<u>Miss Barbara Crooks</u>, record searcher and genealogist of Woodstock, Oxford, England.

As the records of the Genealogical Society Library have been exhausted on the direct line of GEORGE OSMOND, the attorney of Bicester, Oxfordshire, it was necessary to have a reputable record searcher visit the parishes of Oxfordshire and make searches on the following ancestry:

GEORGE OSMOND (attorney) born about 1808 probably Bicester, Oxfordshire He had a sister, ANN OSMOND and a brother WILLIAM OSMOND	GEORGE OSMOND (draper) born about ? married 1807, Bicester died ?	Probable OSMOND buried Bicester Will dated proved
		Probable ANN born about died 4 Dec. St. of Oxford
	ANN PHILLIPS born about 1777 died 26 Feb 1842, age 64 Market End, Nicester Probate record in 1842	

Of major consideration is above pedigree of Osmond and Phillips ancestry, and identity of Ann Osmond (sister of George, the attorney) who married Wellington Ellis, and of William Osmond, a brother in the family, and perhaps others.

On microfilm at the Genealogical Society is an incomplete and badly faded copy of Bicester parish registers known as Bishops Transcripts. These had already been searched, but the poor condition of the record plus missing records of certain years, it was necessary to check the original parish registers in England.

In addition to the surnames of Osmond and Phillips, and the Ellis connection, there are two marriages at Bicester that were thought to be ancestral:

Married in 1730	John Osmond to Eliz Cross
Married in 1742	George Osmond to Mary Allen

For research purposes the surnames of Cross and Allen will also be taken into consideration. The record searcher has made several reports, but research is still continuing. The reported material includes:

<u>BICESTER PARISH REGISTERS</u> (originals):

1st	Christenings 1700-1812	burials 1700-1812	
	Marriages 1700-1803		
2nd	Christenings 1813-1900	burials 1813-1900	
	Marriages 1799-1900		

STANTON ST. JOHN REGISTERS

These were searched because the John Osmond who died in 1805, buried in Bicester, left a will. In the will, dated 1799, proved 1806 in London, he is described as a resident (in 1799) of Stanton St. John parish. Stanton St. John registers did not disclose anything about the family.

JACKSON'S OXFORD JOURNAL, the newspaper published in the City of Oxford starting in 1753 is available in Oxford, and we have had it checked for information (on certain selected dates and by a partial index.) The information is quite useful and in one instance of great value. Work on information from this Journal is to continue.

An analysis of the material on hand shows the following ancestral connections:

2nd gg father of GEORGE OSMOND of Utah, Idaho and Wyoming.

JOHN OSMOND, (the elder, of Market End, Bicester, Oxfordshire.) He may be from Caversfield, Bucks, born around 1692. (He had a sister Mary, married to Mr. Brown of Burford, Oxfordshire.)

He died 10 March 1767, age 74, at Bicester Market End, buried 13 March 1767, Bicester.

His will is dated 3 September 1766 and proved at Oxford 20 March 1767. He was an eminent butcher and greatly esteemed for his honesty, and an obituary appears in the City of Oxford newspaper, The Oxford Journal, in which he was stated to be age 74 years.

He married, 1st - 1715/6 at Piddington, Oxford to Sarah Bly (the ancestress.) Sarah Bly was born around 1693, the record of her birth (chr.) has yet to be found. It might be at Piddington (where the records prior to 1792 are poor) or at Bicester, or Caversfield, Bucks.

Their children are recorded at Bicester:

1. George, christened 25 December 1716, buried 16 July 1754, married 26 June 1742 to Mary Allen.

2. John, christened 31 March 1718, buried 25 May 1720, a child.

3. William, christened 3 October 1719, buried 13 March 1719/20, a child.

4. Sarah, christened 21 September 1721, buried 22 April 1753, probably unmarried.

Great-grandfather:

GEORGE OSMOND, butcher.

Christened 25 December 1716 at Bicester. He was a butcher, but died before his father died. No will found, but this reseach is still in progress.

Buried 16 July 1754 at Bicester (An obituary will be searched for.)

Marriage, 26 June 1742 at Bicester, by license,

Marriage license, issued 26 June 1742 for George Osmond of Burcester, butcher, with Richard Raymond, Burcester, yeoman, as bondsman. George Osmond is shown as age 25, married Mary Allen, of Burcester, age 21. She was probably married 2nd - 12 August 1759 to William White.

Their children are recorded at Bicester:

1. John, christened 3 December 1743, buried 9 October 1805, married 1st - Elizabeth (she died 1787,) married 2nd - Ann (she died 1853, age 90.)

2. George (a draper), christened 15 October 1745, buried 16 October 1821 age 75, married 1807 - Ann Phillips. (He is the ancestor.)

3. Sarah, christened 8 August 1748 "under age 22 in grandfather's will of 1766."

4. William, christened 30 July 1750, buried 7 February 1832, age 82, from "Wandsworth Surrey," "under 22 in grandfather's will of 1766."

5. Thomas, christened 8 February 1753, "under 22 in grandfather's will of 1766."

   (All above children are mentioned as grandchildren in will of 1766.)

Step-great-grandfather:

WILLIAM WHITE of Bicester, a bachelor, married 12 August 1759 by license to (Mrs.) Mary Osmond, described in the marriage license allegation as Mary Osmund, widow of Bicester, 11 August 1759. No doubt she is Mary Allen, widow of George Osmond.

Their children are recorded at Bicester. No record is shown in Bicester registers of further children, marriages, or burials of this family after 1763:

1. James White, christened 5 May 1760.

2. Mary White, christened 15 August 1763.

Grandfather of GEORGE OSMOND of Utah, Idaho and Wyoming:

GEORGE OSMOND, draper of Bicester.

Christened 15 October 1745. He was a draper according to christening of his son, William (1814) and on death record of his widow (Mrs. Ann Osmond (1842). No will found, but this is still being searched for as also an obituary.

Buried 16 October 1821, age 75, at Bicester, so was born 1745/6. He would be age 62 and is described as a bachelor when he married.

Married 25 November 1807 at Bicester, by license (no marriage bond found) to Ann Phillips, (described as a spinster,) born around 1776 (christening not yet found) of Bicester. She was buried 4 March 1842 age 65 (death certificate, died 26 February 1842, age 64). Letters of admon. for her, Consistory Court of Oxford.

Their children are recorded at Bicester:

1. George (the attorney) christened 6 March 1808, died 1 December 1860 and buried 6 December 1860, Bicester. Married (Mrs.) Ann (Canham) Flight. (No record.)

2. Ann, christened 7 May 1809, died 15 July 1864, Weston super Mare, Somerset, Married - 1st, Mr. Osmond (not yet found.) Married - 2nd, 12 September 1840 to Wellington Ellis, surgeon.

3. John, christened 4 July 1811, buried 30 March 1848, age 36, Bicester.

4. William, christened 1 September 1814, alive in 1848 (mentioned in will dated 1848 of his uncle's widow.) Married Elizabeth ...

Father of GEORGE OSMOND of Utah, Idaho and Wyoming:

GEORGE OSMOND, attorney of London and Bicester, christened 6 March 1808 at Bicester. Described in the official Law List of 1852 as "Master Extra-ordinary and Commissioner for Affidavits" at Bicester, Oxfordshire. The London directory of 1838 states his office was on Threadneedle Street, London. No marriage record has been found for George Osmond to Ann(e) or Nancy, daughter of George Canham and she married 1st - 10th June 1827 at St. Michael, Crooked Lane, City of London to Hanson Flight.

Died 1 December 1860, buried 6 December 1860, Bicester. Will proved in Principal Probate Registry, London.

Children:

1. George, born 23 May 1836, christened 14 June 1837, "son of George and Ann Osmond, of Howards Place, gentleman" recorded at St. Matthew, Bethnal Green, (Middlesex) London, a suburb adjoining Hackney.

2. John, born 23 May 1836, a twin brother mentioned by George Osmond in his personal records.

(And other children of Ann or Nancy Canham (Mrs. Flight.))

GEORGE OSMOND, Mormon Pioneer, bishop in Bloomington Ward, counselor in Bear Lake Stake Presidency, Probate Judge in Bear Lake County, State Senator in Wyoming State Legislature, missionary, president of Star Valley Stake. He was also known as George Flight but changed his name to George Osmond. Apprenticed at Her Majesty's Dockyard.

He was born 23 May (1836) and christened 14 June 1837, St. Matthew Bethnal Green, (suburb adjoining London and Hackney.) (See also, born 23 May 1836, christened 20 September 1843 at Christ Church, Watney Street, Stepney (suburb near London, Bethnal Green and Hackney.)

Converted and baptized into the LDS Church 27 November 1851 at Charlton (near Woolwich) London Conference, record states, "George Flight born 23 May 1836 at Hackney (Bethnel) Middlesex (London.) Ordained Priest at Eltham; ordained Elder at Eltham, 8 March 1852 and active in missionary duties."

Emigrated to St. Louis, Missouri, enroute to Utah. Left Liverpool, England, on Monday, 27 November 1854 on the ship "Clara Wheeler," with 422 saints on board. Arrived in New Orleans 11 January 1855.

Died 25 March 1913, Afton, Wyoming; buried 29 March 1913, Bloomington, Idaho.

Married 1st - in 1855 at St. Louis, Missouri, Mary Georgina Huckvale.
Married 2nd - 8 September 1880. Amelia Jacobson.

WILLIAM OSMOND, currier, of Oxfordshire (brother to the George Osmond, attorney of Bicester.) Christened 1 September 1814 at Bicester - living in 1848. Married Elizabeth ...

Children:

1. George Henry Osmond, christened 31 July 1839, Bicester (Jeweller of City of Oxford,) died 23 December 1894, age 54, St. Aldate Street, Oxford.

   Married 1st - Florence Emily, born 1843-4, died 11 March 1878, age 34, St. Aldate Street, Oxford. Married 2nd - Ann, born 1855-6, died 11 March 1935, age 79, Oxford City. One known child: Reginald Herbert Osmond, born 1855-6, died 11 April 1891, age 5, Oxford.

   Other Children:

   1. F. W. Osmond, living in 1935 at 39 Lauderdale Street, Preston.

Other research involving the Osmond family is as follows:

1. (Mrs.) Ann Osmond, (widow of John Osmond 1743-1805) is recorded in the 1851 census of the City of Oxford as age 86, born Wincott, Worcestershire. This place is not identified.

   The Senior Assistant Archivist for Worcestershire was contacted, but after a considerable amount of gratis research, no identification or trace of this place name and the Osmond family was found.

2. The Osmond family members were buried in the churchyard at Bicester, Oxfordshire. A letter was sent to the Oxfordshire county branch librarian, Bicester Branch Library, requesting information on copies of the inscriptions on tombstones in the churchyard.

   In reply the librarian stated that no copies had been made, but an attempt would be made to go around the churchyard and copy Osmond stones, if any could be found.

3. A similar letter was sent to the Central Library in the City of Oxford, concerning tombstones in Bicester, Burford, Stanton St. John and Chipping Norton, also concerning Jackson's Oxford Journal. A reply indicated that nothing was known about tombstones, but that the index to the Oxford Journal did give information on the Osmond family.

4. Mrs. Vera Hunsaker and Brother Ralph Osmond have cooperated in volunteer research work and with their help in searching library records, some additional items on descent have been found. This is because it would be helpful if we could find living cousins in England on the Osmond family lines.

   a. The marriage record of Wellington Ellis, a surgeon, to Ann Osmond, sister to George Osmond (the attorney) and daughter of George Osmond (gentleman, who was a draper prior to his decease,) 12 September 1840 at Bicester.

   b. The death record of Dr. Wellington Ellis, M.D., of London, but who died 30 December 1893 at his residence, Ashcombe Lodge, Weston super Mare, Somersetshire, age 79 years.

   c. The 1871 census of Ashcombe Lodge, Weston super Mare, Somersetshire shows:

      Head - Wellington Ellis, age 56, retired surgeon, born Llantillio, Monmouthshire. (There were 3 visitors and 2 servants at this address also.)

   d. The will of Wellington Ellis was also found, made 17 December 1891 and proved at Wells, Somerset, 30 March 1894.

   e. The will of his widow, but apparently his second wife (and not Ann Osmond) was found, and a copy made. She was Mrs. Elizabeth Ellis, age 73, died 26 June 1919 at Weston super Mare. Her will names various relatives, some could be connected with the Osmonds, but a careful analysis is being made of the will.

   f. The librarian of Woodspring Central Library, Weston super Mare was contacted and he furnished some helpful details on the Ellis family.

   g. The cemetaries office at Weston super Mare, also furnished helpful details on the Ellis and allied families. Of importance, however, was the burial entry for Ann Osmond.

under the name of (Mrs.) Anne Ellis, age 52, buried 21 July 1864, the sister of George Osmond, the attorney.

The birth record of Augusta Hope Ellis, records she was born 3 October 1874 at Ashcombe Lodge, daughter of (Dr.) Wellington Ellis and Elizabeth, formerly Evans.

The death record of Ann Osmond, recorded as (Mrs.) Anne Ellis, age 52 years, wife of (Dr.) Wellington Ellis, shows she died 15 July 1864 at Chandos Villa, Weston super Mare.

h. During the course of research, Sister Vera Hunsaker found reference to a child named William Osmond Ellis. The death record was obtained as follows:

WILLIAM OSMOND ELLIS, age 23 months, son of Leopold Ellis, 14 May 1857, Twy Dee Park, Llantillio Pertholy, Monmouthshire.

The birth record of this child has not been found. The middle given name of Osmond undoubtedly comes from the association of Wellington Ellis who married Ann Osmond. Leopold Ellis was born 15 April 1815 at Twy Dee Park, Llantillio Pertholy, Monmouthshire, and died 17 May 1881 at Weston super Mare and is buried in the grave next to (Dr.) Wellington Ellis who married Ann Osmond.

This is the report to date.

Sincerely,

David E.

David E. Gardner, FSG., AG.

P.S. A genealogical tree illustrating this report has been made and will be of interest to all Osmonds.

DEG:bb

George Osmond's Family Organization NEWSLETTER

Number 3 September 1976

George Osmond's Family Organization NEWSLETTER

Volume II. Number 1 March 1977

THE PRESIDENT'S PEN

First, a thank you to Virl Osmond for the fine work he does on each edition of our Newsletter. He spends untold hours in the layout and printing of each edition. Without Virl's donated time and skill, we simply would not have this document. Hats off to Virl!!!

Some more good news on genealogy. Dennis Osmond has agreed to accept the responsibility for overseeing all of the original genealogical research. He will be working hand in hand with David Gardner and making work assignments to those who wish them. Already he has begun a thorough review of work to date and he is meeting with David Gardner, our professional genealogist, as needed.

You may be interested to know that David Gardner has thus far compiled some 10 large notebooks full of research pertaining to George Osmond and related lines. I was in Salt Lake recently and providentially met one of the researchers that has been working our lines under David Gardner's direction--Ralph Millett. I was most impressed with his thoroughness and competence. If you would like a research assignment to help him out, and thus help our GOFO money go further, PLEASE WRITE ME NOW!

Some special treats inside: a poem by George Osmond; a 5 generation picture; a Perpetual Family History proposal; the GOFO Officers and Governing Board; and a reminder of the August 6, 1977 Reunion!!! Please read and heed!

Russell L. Osmond
President,
George Osmond Family Organization

George Osmond Family Organization
24612 Patricia Court
Hayward, CA. 94541

17 Stansell Ave.
Nelson.
New Zealand.
19th Dec 1980.

Dear Mr. Gardner,

Thank you for your letter enclosing such comprehensive information on the Osmond family and I must apologise for the delay in replying. We've had so much to do to catch up on everything since our visit to America that its only in the past few days we have had a chance to study the material properly. My wife is delighted to have such a fine record of her ancestry dating back to the 17th century. Her father Henry Cecil Osmond was one of two other sons of George Henry Osmond Jeweller and Ann Jarvis, of which you have no record. The other son was Ronald Osmond who died in 1947 He married ~~Isobelt Chisholm Faison~~ Maud Mary Heath and they had a son Hubert R.G. Osmond who lives at Herne Bay Kent England.

My wifes father was born on 18th Dec 1881 or 1882 – (I'll have to confirm which year with my wife's sister). He married Mary Jane Levett at the Church of St. Marks, Broadwater Down, Sussex, England on Dec 12th 1912 & they emigrated to Kaikoura New Zealand in 1913. They had 5 children 4 of whom are alive My wife's twin sister Joyce was drowned in 1921 aged 3. The two eldest are also twins Reginald Ken Osmond of Christchurch N.Z. married with 2 married daughters. Dorothy Margaret Osmond married to Noel Waters ~~who~~ of Blenheim N.Z. 2 married daughters, and an unmarried son in Adelaide Australia My wife Madge Ethel Osmond. born on 7th April 1918 & we have 2 married daughters, and the youngest Ronald Thomas Osmond of Cambridge N.Z. who is married & has 2 married sons and an unmarried son & daughter. When I have gathered all the relevant information I'll prepare a descent chart for you giving birth dates etc & include the present younger generation of grand-children. My wife's father died on 28th Dec 1970 aged 88 or 89 & was buried at Blenheim New Zealand. His wife Mary Jane was born on 23rd March 1884 at Mayfield near Tunbridge Wells Kent England and died on 26th Sept 1972 aged 88 and was also buried in Blenheim. Would I be correct in the assumption that my wife and her brothers & sister are third cousins of George ~~Osmond~~ Veil Osmond, Rulon Van Noy Osmond, Ralph J. and Cora Elizabeth Osmond?

Thank you also for sending a copy of the President's newsletter and other interesting leaflets and these we are keeping on a file together with all other Osmond information we are gathering. Its only in recent years I have taken an interest in family "trees" & I had been researching the Farquhars. I was born in Scotland & was most interested in being able to trace back to my great great great grandfather in Barrhead Scotland in 1776 and am certain I could have gone back further had we had more time in Salt Lake City at the excellent genealogical library ... the l... Mrs Hunsaker and will write to her too.

Osmond Family Relatives of New Zealand

October-December, 1980

In October 1980, a Mr. Farquhar of New Zealand visited the LDS Church Office building in Salt Lake City, while on a tour of the United States. According to David E. Gardner, a genealogist for the George Osmond Family Organization of Utah, Mr. Farquhar "did not know about the Utah Osmonds but made an inquiry or two to see if there were any" Osmonds in Utah. "His wife was...born Madge Osmond in New Zealand, the daughter of Henry Cecil Osmond who was born in the 1880's in Oxford." Also, "Mrs. Farquhar has a brother, Ronald Thomas Osmond, an attorney in Cambridge, New Zealand. "Mr. Farquhar was a representative of the Linen & Merchant company in New Zealand, and he and his wife have two daughters, five grandsons and one grand-daughter."

Below is a letter from Mr. Farquhar of New Zealand, dated 19 December 1980, which was addressed to David Gardner--and which he then sent on to Rulon Osmond and Olive Osmond of the George Osmond Family Organization:

----

19 December 1980

From:
17 Stansell Avenue
Nelson, New Zealand

Dear Mr. Gardner,

Thank you for your letter enclosing such comprehensive information on the Osmond family and I must apologize for the delay in replying. We've had so much to do to catch up on everything since our visit to America that its only in the past few days we have had a chance to study the material properly. My wife is delighted to have such a fine record of her ancestry dating back to the 17th century. Her father Henry Cecil Osmond was one of two other sons of George Henry Osmond, Jeweler, and Ann Jarvis, of which you have no record. The other son was Ronald Osmond who died in 1947. He married Maud Mary Heath and they had a son Hubert R. G. Osmond who lives at Herne Bay, Kent, England.

My wife's father was born on 18th December 1881 or 1882 (I'll have to confirm which year with my wife's sister). He married Mary Jane Levett at the Church of St. Mark's, Brachwater Down, Sussex, England, on December 12th 1912 and they emigrated to Kaikoura, New Zealand in 1913. They had 5 children, 4 of whom are alive. My wife's twin sister Joyce was drowned in 1921 aged 3. The two eldest are also twins. Reginald Ken Osmond of Christchurch, New Zealand, married with 2 married daughters. Dorothy Margaret Osmond married to Noel Waters of Blenheim, New Zealand, 2 married daughters, and an unmarried son in Adelaide, Australia. My wife, Madge Ethel Osmond, born on 7th April 1918 and we have 2 married daughters, and the youngest Ronald Thomas Osmond of Cambridge, New Zealand, who is married and has 2 married sons and an unmarried son and daughter. When I have gathered all the relevant information I'll prepare a descendant chart for you giving birth dates etc and include the present younger generation of grand-children. My wife's father died on 28th December 1970 aged 88 or 89, and was buried at Blenheim, New Zealand. His wife, Mary Jane, was born on 23rd March 1884 at Mayfield near Tunbridge Wells, Kent, England, and died on 26th September 1972 aged 88 and was also buried in Blenheim. Would I be correct in the assumption that my wife and her brothers and sister are third cousins of George Virl Osmond, Rulon Van Noy Osmond, Ralph J. and Cora Elizabeth Osmond?

Thank you also for sending a copy of the [George Osmond Family Organization] President's newsletter and other interesting leaflets and these we are keeping on a file together with all other Osmond information we are gathering. Its only in recent years I have taken an interest in family "trees" and I had been researching the Farquhars. I was born in Scotland and was most interested in being able to trace back to my great great great grandfather in Barrhead [Glasgow, Lanarkshire] Scotland in 1776 and am certain I would have gone back further had we had more time in Salt Lake City at the excellent genealogical library.

Thank you for the nice letter from Mrs. Hunsaker and will write to her too. [Ending of letter was cut off....]

OF LATTER-DAY
SAINTS

HYDE PARK VISITORS CENTRE
64/68 Exhibition Road
London SW7 2PA
Tel. 01-584 8868

5 October 1984

David E. Gardner
LDS Genealogical Society
Church Office Building
50 East North Temple
Salt Lake City, Utah 84150

Dear Brother Gardner:

Hello from London! George and I are enjoying another mission in another part of the world now. He is the Director of the Visitor's Centre here.

Every chance I get I go upstairs to search through the microfische but I'm not having much success.

The other day I contacted a David Bethel (my cousin's husband Clayton Brough said he had found lots of names). He has found a lot of Lythgoes in Wigan, Lancashire--he said there were enough to go on indefinitely, so I got quite excited but he sent me a bill for $136 for the information enclosed and I wondered if that was expensive or not??? I just don't know.

We're trying to stay within budget and things are quite high over here so I told him to work only as I sent the money to him.

I've heard there are about 40 million names coming in soon -- an update on the microfische. Do you think the Wigan records would be on them--and perhaps I could do some of the research myself?

I really need some guidance and you are such a professional. I have more faith in you than all the rest put together.

This morning I had access to an IBM computer so I entered some information taken from the pink sheets to send in for clearance. I'm sending that along to you as well rather than sending it in directly. (I've never done that part before anyway.) Would you look them over to see if I have done them right? Then send them through the proper channels to be cleared. I'd like the names put into the Provo Temple- then my children can do the work.

I'm just "seething" with the desire to get this genealogy work done and everything moves at such a snail's pace, it makes me unhappy. What do you suggest I do? Ha!

I hope all is well with "you and yours". Please take care of yourselves.

Love,

Olive

Registered Number 763864 England

Registered Office
113 Chancery Lane London WC2A 1PL
Telephone 01-242 1222
Telegrams Interpret London Telex
Telex 261203
LDE Box No. 56

The Law Society
Services Ltd.
Records & Statistical Dept.

George V Osmond Esq
Hyde Park Visitors Centre
64-68 Exhibition Road
London
SW7 2PA

Our reference JP
Your reference
Date 24 January 1985

Dear Sir

I have received a letter dated 21 January from Mrs Olive D Osmond requesting details contained in the Society's records in respect of your ancestor George Osmond.

As explained hitherto, the Society was not required to keep records before 1907, in consequence therefore, information for the period in which you are interested are less exhaustive than one would wish.

It can only be established that George Osmond was admitted an attorney in the Queen's Bench in the Trinity term of 1829. It would appear that he practised in Bicester and died in December 1860. Regrettably, no further details are recorded. Doubtless you will know that if a birth or death certificate can be traced additional information may be gleaned, and it is possible that the Parish Registers in Bicester or the Principal Registry, Somerset House, Strand, London WC2 may be able to assist you in this regard.

In conclusion, I have conveyed Mrs Osmond's kind message to my colleague Miss E Smith, and we are gratified to learn that the information provided, albeit limited, is of some value in your long quest for information about your ancestor.

Yours faithfully

M Young (Mrs)
For Manager-Records Office

ROOTS

GEORGE OSMOND

George Osmond, father of the singing Osmonds, has traced their roots to London's East End, from where his grandfather emigrated. He talks here to Pamela Coleman

DAVID CAIRNS

George and Olive Osmond at St Matthew's Church in Bethnal Green. His grandfather was christened there in 1837 but joined the Mormons in the US

'When Olive and I married 40 years ago, right away we started tracing our roots. We knew both families came from England originally and in the last few months we've finally linked it all up. We're over here in London on a year's mission for the Mormon Church (The Church of Jesus Christ of Latter-day Saints) and have spent every spare minute searching. Now at last we've made the most exciting discovery: my grandfather was christened right here in Bethnal Green, at St Matthew's Church on 14 June, 1837. The parish registers at the Greater London Records Office prove it. It's been like doing a big jigsaw puzzle and all of a sudden the pieces start to fit.

Grandfather was the first member of the family to break away from the established church in England, and in those days it was a sin to swing into a different religion. He was more or less disowned and when he was 18 he went to the United States. It's so thrilling for me to walk around the streets he walked around and to visit the church where he was christened. It has been extensively rebuilt after bomb damage in the last war, but the shell is just the same.

I never knew my grandfather or my father. My grandfather died about seven years before I was born and my father was killed when I was six weeks old. All we had to go on in tracing our roots was grandfather's journal. We've discovered he was a great man. At the age of 14 he was a shipwright's apprentice at the Queen Victoria docks in London. He was a good scholar and did well in the classics and mathematics, according to the records. After he went to America he became a schoolteacher and then a lawyer and a judge, and he was the first stake-president of Star Valley, Wyoming. Everybody loved him and they even named a town after him—Osmond, Wyoming.

We know grandfather came to Britain on two church missions. In his journal he wrote of revisiting Brighton, the scene of his childhood and where his mother was buried. So I also have roots in Brighton but we haven't checked there at all yet.

I've found out that my great-grandfather was a solicitor who practised in London and Bicester in Oxfordshire. We've been to Bicester to trace those roots and seen his marriage certificate. We've gone back three generations there. My grandfather was born in Hackney and I feel very much at home in London. I feel English and I am really proud of my roots. During the last war I was stationed at Braintree in Essex when I was about 23, and I have fond memories of that time. I've visited eight times since but this is the first chance I've had to really explore the place. Olive's been the driving force in organising the research. Her side of the family has roots in Wales, too. There are Jenkinses, Evanses and Williamses among her relations. We think we are related to Andy Williams through them.

It was Andy's television show which gave the family group its big break in the '60s. We were with him for eight years and that show gave us the world coverage we needed. The Osmonds singing group grew from the "family nights" we had at home every Friday. We'd have dinner by candlelight and then have a floor show, and the kids would entertain. The two older ones tap-danced and then four formed a quartet, practising all week long so they had a new song every Friday night. Every one of our nine children did something and both grandmothers would come along to watch. Then we went into barber-shop harmonies and began performing at conventions and at civic clubs and church functions around the area. Eventually we performed nationwide and got a contract with Walt Disney which led to the Andy Williams Show.

Tracing your roots is a bit like doing a big jigsaw. All of a sudden the pieces start to fit

We are a very close family. Olive is a real homemaker. She used to be my secretary. We had a nice insurance and real estate business in Utah but when the family group took off we were happy to go along with the kids. We moved to California and lived out of a suitcase too—but I kept my broker's licence, just in case.

We all kept together until the late '70s when the children began to branch off. There was never any argument about who was up front. Each one seems to have their own little bit of glory. Four of the brothers dropped out of performing to become producers, Jimmy was pushed by Japan and was big in England with 'Long-Haired Lover from Liverpool', Jay our first little star, was pushed by Walt Disney, and Bob Hope took Marie under his wing. Donny is popular all over the world.

They've not been difficult to handle. We're not showbusiness people. We never pushed our children. Olive gave them the love and I gave them the discipline. She taught them music and I handled the business side. All of us have strong roots in the church, and our religion has been a great leaning post and sheltered us a bit from some aspects of showbusiness. When they toured we went with them—and often the grandmothers came too. I'm sure there must have been areas where they missed out a little through being in showbusiness, but they were compensated in lots of ways.

In California we had a big apartment house, and the married children all had their own private units, though in the evening all the grandchildren would be in our apartment. We've kept our ranch in Utah—the children won't let us sell it. I guess they feel that's where their roots are. We're a big family, we have 31 grandchildren and we really miss them, but the three boys who still sing as the Osmond Brothers (Alan, Wayne and Merrill) will be over in April for a tour.

Here in London we are working at the church's information centre and right above it is the IGI—the international genealogical index—which has 88 million names listed and has been very helpful in our own family searches. We also have a researcher working for us in the United States, who has confirmed what we have discovered here. My wife has all the information on computer and has made a disc for Donny who's pursuing his own inquiries.

Genealogy has become the number one hobby in the United States now, but it's also an important part of our church's teaching to track down our roots. At the Mormon headquarters in Salt Lake they have several million names being processed through the computers and the records are constantly being updated. There's no end to it. We just keep on digging. We believe our ancestors are very much alive and we want to find out all we can about them.'

Next week: Brian Aldiss

Published by Express Newspapers p.l.c., 121 Fleet Street, London EC4P 4JT, and printed by Eric Bemrose Ltd., Long Lane, Liverpool L9 7BG. The Sunday Express Magazine editorial, advertisement copy and production department, 11 New Fetter Lane, London EC4P 4EE (01-353 8000); management, advertisement sales and readers' advertisement queries, 121 Fleet Street, London EC4P 4JT (01-353 8000). Not to be sold separately from the Sunday Express in the UK. Newsagents may charge up to 2p for delivery.

Roots Unlimited
P.O. Box 158
Pleasant Grove, UT 84062

31 January 1991

Dear Osmond Family:

Good News! We have just received a report from our researcher and he has taken the Osmond line back about as far as it is possible to go. Lots of names have been added and he will be submitting them to the Temple soon so their work can be done.

We are in St. George right now and don't have access to our big computer, xerox machine, etc. but couldn't wait to tell you the news. We'll have copies of any of this for you when we get back (in April).

In the meantime just so you'll be excited, here is a view of what has been accomplished:

John Osmond
(abt 1575)

John Osmond
(abt 1604
Elizabeth Bery

John Osman Jr.
(c/14 Feb 1635/36)
Joane Wicks

George Osmund
C/21 Feb 1663/64)
Mary King
(abt 1670)

John Osmund
(c/29 Oct 1692)
Sarah Bly
(c/29 Oct 1688)

George Osmond
(b/25 Dec 1716
Mary Allen
(b/1721)

George Osmond
(b/15 Oct 1745)
Ann Phillips
(b/1776)

George Osmond
(b/6 Mar 1808
Nancy Ann Canham
(b12 Dec 1805)

George Osmond
(b/23 May 1836)
Christina Lovina Amelia Jacobson
(b/9 Nov 1862)

Love,

George & Olive

George

Olive

www.ingramcontent.com/pod-product-compliance
Lightning Source LLC
Chambersburg PA
CBHW081353280526
45788CB00009B/2872